THE MAN IN THE ARENA

FROM RAILWAY BRAT TO DIPLOMAT

ROGER SIMMONS

WITH A FOREWORD BY JOHN C. CROSBIE

Roger

FLANKER PRESS LIMITED
ST. JOHN'S

Library and Archives Canada Cataloguing in Publication

Simmons, Roger, author
The man in the arena : from railway brat to diplomat / Roger Simmons ; with a foreword by John C. Crosbie.

Includes bibliographical references and index.
Issued in print and electronic formats.
ISBN 978-1-77117-693-4 (softcover).--ISBN 978-1-77117-694-1 (EPUB).--
ISBN 978-1-77117-705-4 (Kindle).--ISBN 978-1-77117-706-1 (PDF)

1. Simmons, Roger. 2. Legislators--Newfoundland and Labrador--Biography. 3. Legislators--Canada--Biography. 4. Newfoundland and Labrador. House of Assembly--Biography. 5. Canada. Parliament. House of Commons--Biography. 6. Politicians--Newfoundland and Labrador--Biography. 7. Politicians--Canada--Biography. 8. Diplomats--Canada--Biography. I. Title.

FC626.S56A3 2018 971.064092 C2018-904125-0
C2018-904126-9

PRINTED IN CANADA

MIX
Paper from responsible sources
FSC® C016245

This paper has been certified to meet the environmental and social standards of the Forest Stewardship Council® (FSC®) and comes from responsibly managed forests, and verified recycled sources.

Cover Design by Graham Blair Cover photo courtesy of the Canadian Press

FLANKER PRESS LTD.
PO BOX 2522, STATION C
ST. JOHN'S, NL
CANADA

TELEPHONE: (709) 739-4477 FAX: (709) 739-4420 TOLL-FREE: 1-866-739-4420
WWW.FLANKERPRESS.COM

9 8 7 6 5 4 3 2 1

We acknowledge the [financial] support of the Government of Canada. *Nous reconnaissons l'appui [financier] du gouvernement du Canada.* We acknowledge the support of the Canada Council for the Arts, which last year invested $153 million to bring the arts to Canadians throughout the country. *Nous remercions le Conseil des arts du Canada de son soutien. L'an dernier, le Conseil a investi 153 millions de dollars pour mettre de l'art dans la vie des Canadiennes et des Canadiens de tout le pays.* We acknowledge the financial support of the Government of Newfoundland and Labrador, Department of Tourism, Culture and Recreation for our publishing activities.

IN MEMORIAM

Otto Tucker,
mentor, patriot, friend
and
Ruby Noseworthy,
Pearl Seaward,
Susie Simms,
who were there for me
with oodles of TLC

AUTHOR'S NOTES

Some of the explanatory footnotes and in-text references will strike Canadian readers as elementary and/or unnecessary. They are intended for Americans who, understandably, are less familiar with Canadian geography, history, traditions, customs, politics, and acronyms. In the same vein, a US readership is the reason I sometimes take brief historical detours to give context to certain subjects.

Award-winning author Ed Smith (1940–2017), in his great book *From the Ashes of My Dreams*, eloquently stated, "This book is intended to be futuristically productive rather than historically unkind."

I couldn't have said it better myself. My rule of thumb, in writing this volume as in life, has been: If I can't say something good about someone, I say nothing. With some exceptions, where it would have been disingenuous not to bell the cat or state the obvious, I have adhered to that guideline.

Persons who are no longer alive are identified, if the reference is complimentary or neutral; otherwise, the reference is anonymous. (Not that all the persons accorded anonymity herein are current recipients of their eternal reward.)

CONTENTS

JOHN CROSBIE

OUTSTANDING SERVICE TO NEWFOUNDLAND AND LABRADOR AND TO CANADA

- Lawyer, orator, humorist;
- Deputy Mayor, City of St. John's, NL, 1965–66;
- Member of the Newfoundland and Labrador House of Assembly (MHA) for St. John's West, 1966–76;
- Smallwood cabinet portfolios, 1966–68: Municipal Affairs and Housing, Health;
- Moores cabinet portfolios,1972–76: Finance, Treasury Board, Economic Development, Fisheries, Intergovernmental Affairs, Mines and Energy, Government House Leader;
- Member of Parliament (MP) for St. John's West, 1976–93;
- Clark cabinet portfolio, 1979–80: Finance;
- Mulroney cabinet portfolios, 1984–93: Justice and Attorney General, Transport, International Trade, Fisheries and Oceans, Atlantic Canada Opportunities Agency;
- Chancellor, Memorial University of Newfoundland, 1994–2008;
- Lieutenant-Governor of Newfoundland and Labrador, 2008–13

FOREWORD

by The Honourable John C. Crosbie, PC, OC, ONL, QC

All the world's a stage,
And all the men and women merely players;
They have their exits and their entrances,
And one man in his time plays many parts.
— William Shakespeare, *As You Like It* (Act II, Scene VII)

I was an actor on the Newfoundland and Canadian political stage through much of Roger Simmons's political career, which spanned from 1973 to 1997. Always astute and sharp-witted, he's a wily character whom I have known for many years for his commitment to public service and as an untiring and dedicated soldier of the Salvation Army and, of course, the Liberal Party.

Roger and I were political contemporaries who first met in the late 1960s, and although we were most of the time in different parties, we enjoyed a mutual respect for one another, engaging in rigorous debate as is necessary in our democratic process. Always ready with a sharp rejoinder, Roger, I recall, one time referred to me in the House of Commons as:

"the bionic mouth not attached to any known intelligent life form!"

I am honoured to have been asked by the Honourable Roger Simmons, PC, to provide this foreword to his engaging and wonderful account documenting the ups and downs of a successful and colourful Newfoundland politician. Roger consistently displayed tremendous resilience and has left an enduring impact on just about every organization that he has been associated with along the way, whether it be in the education system, Parliament, or the foreign service.

He also possesses an uncanny ability to, despite adversity, seemingly always land on his feet and move forward without missing a beat. He is widely admired in disparate circles for his tenacity and cleverness.

As the Member of Parliament for the sprawling coastal rural riding of Burin–St. George's along the south and southwest coasts of Newfoundland, Roger was a tireless advocate of constituents residing in over 150 far-flung communities. As Member of Parliament, he very ably fulfilled the role of political successor to long-serving parliamentarians Chesley Carter (1949–1965) and Donald Jamieson (1966–1979).

He has certainly enjoyed a fascinating career, and he has produced an excellent book that's well worth a read for anyone with an interest in Canadian politics and how a successful politician might operate. It is good fortune that he has decided to document in a most entertaining and interesting manner his remarkable career from how things modestly began for him, as part of a large family in Lewisporte and Bishop's Falls, to how he succeeded as an educator, administrator, entrepreneur, politician, diplomat, and consultant.

Roger Simmons has faithfully served in the political arena, and my knowledge of him as a co-combatant reminds me of the following quotation by United States President Theodore Roosevelt:

> *It is not the critic who counts; not the man who points out how the strong man stumbles, or where the doer of deeds could have done them better.*
>
> *The credit belongs to the man who is actually in the arena, whose face is marred by dust and sweat and blood; who strives valiantly;*
>
> *Who errs, who comes short again and again, because there is no effort without error and shortcoming; but who does actually strive to do the deeds;*
>
> *Who knows great enthusiasms, the great devotions; who spends himself in a worthy cause;*
>
> *Who, at the best, knows in the end the triumph of high achievement, and*
> *Who at the worst, if he fails, at least fails while daring greatly,*
> *So that his place shall never be with those cold and timid souls who neither know victory nor defeat.*[1]

I trust that you will enjoy as much as I have this well-written and engaging account of a life in progress that has been well-lived thus far.

---

1 Excerpt of a speech delivered by Theodore Roosevelt at the Sorbonne in Paris, France, on April 23, 1910

PREFACE

Remembrance of things past is not necessarily
the remembrance of things as they were.
— Marcel Proust, French novelist and critic, 1871–1922

"I am God's gift to mankind! I saved the world, all by myself!"

Are these the latest graveyard-shift tweets from the Sleepwalker-in-Chief, you ask? No, but they do belong to fake reality. Exaggerations such as those above are, too often, the unspoken premise of the memoir writer.

Publishing an autobiography is the very thing I had long vowed never to do, notwithstanding the occasional prodding of family and friends. Yes, I've been known to blow my own horn, but to do so at length and in print seemed a tad presumptuous.

My former teacher and long-time mentor, the iconic Dr. Otto Tucker[2], believed I have a story which should be told, and he encouraged, yea, cajoled me, to put pen to paper. I last spent time with Otto and his wife, Ruby, at St. Patrick's Mercy Home, a few months before his 2015 passing. His parting words to me were, "I probably won't see you again, but promise me you'll write the book." I told him I would.

I believe an autobiography worth reading should engage and entertain. And it should inform and instruct. The reader should be able to glean a few pointers, practices to emulate, pitfalls to avoid. I trust that the pages which follow will cut the mustard.

Once I had delved into this marathon project, it became quite therapeutic. The introspection and self-reflection are worth several weeks on a shrink's couch. While writing about oneself can easily degenerate into a whitewash, a pat-on-the-back routine, there are some built-in checks and

2 Salvation Army officer, education administrator, university professor, humour writer, historian

balances. Mine has been, continues to be, a very public life. Much, if not most, of what I say in these pages can be corroborated or contradicted by others.

Autobiographical musings are a long, lingering look in the mirror. If you misrepresent what you see, you may well con a whole lot of people. But you won't fool yourself. Because tomorrow morning—and every morning after—you'll be reminded of it all over again, and again, and again, as you stare into an unforgiving, brutally honest mirror.

Yet the very nature of the undertaking precludes a balanced result. And as Proust reminds us above, memory can be both partial and fallible. Within those inevitable constraints, I have attempted to represent as honest a portrayal as possible. Finally, though, this is my perspective.

As ever, I continue to forge ahead, sometimes at breakneck speed, always mindful that my every move is being watched and judged by mortals and immortals alike. Bemoaning from the sidelines has never been my default setting. Always, I have wanted be where the action is. I am the man in the arena.

INTRODUCTION

The deeper I go into myself,
the more I realize that I am my own enemy.
— Floriano Martins, Brazilian writer, 1957–

The facts of my Valentine's Day encounter with a steel bench are simple, painfully so at the time. The year was 2008, and I was at a casino in Gatineau, Quebec, minutes from downtown Ottawa, fraternizing at a pre-dinner reception with 150 law firm colleagues.[3] I spotted, in the nearby corridor, a friend I hadn't seen in four years, my former political boss, the Right Honourable Jean Chrétien[4], and his wife, the inscrutable and charming Aline. In my hasty dash to intercept them, a steel bench intercepted me, with immediate and torturous consequences.

The early diagnosis, wrong as it turned out, was "no broken bones, only torn ligaments and bruising." Believing the damage from my abortive sprint to be minimal and after popping enough little pills to make the pain go away, I stayed true to an enduring Newfie credo: Never quit a good party early, circumstances notwithstanding. I resumed my pursuit of the Chrétiens and spent a pleasant interlude sharing memories at their restaurant dinner table.

The former prime minister had lost none of his mischievous edge. I quipped, "I'm not the first guy to come to grief trying to keep pace with you!"

With that trademark smirk and drawling cadence, he responded, "You wouldn't be thinking of Paul Martin[5], would you?"

Unlike me, Martin's nemesis was not a steel bench, but himself. Like me,

3 No, I'm not a lawyer.
4 Prime minister of Canada, 1993–2003
5 Prime minister of Canada, 2003–2006

his headlong rush to stay abreast of Chrétien caused self-inflicted wounds. Mine would heal quickly. Some wounds need lifelong licking.

A LITTLE SELF-ANALYSIS

It strikes me that my little casino caper is dripping with symbolism. Recall the key elements—Valentine's Day, a roomful of lawyers, a former prime minister, a cocktail party, a casino, and a guy in a hurry—most of them a veritable array of tangents to the circle that is my life. If my matter-of-fact, working-class dad was still above ground, he'd have a few pointed questions and comments for me:

- *What the devil were you doing with a bunch of lawyers? You're not in trouble again, are you?*
- *Why were you up in Ottawa? I thought you lost that job years ago.*
- *You're not still chasing Chrétien, are you?*
- *It serves you right. You're too much like your mother, always flittin' around like a bluebottle fly!*

My late mom, too, the judgmental, raving evangelical, would weigh in with a couple of choice questions and editorials of her own:

- *What were you doing in a gambling joint? Don't you remember what the Good Lord had to say about dens of inequity?*
- *Did you really say you were at a booze party? I suppose everybody was smoking, too. And swearing. Have you forgotten everything I ever taught you? And you a former Salvation Army officer! God help us!*
- *You had it comin' to you. Just like your father, always tangled up with the wrong crowd!*

My parents' supposed questions reflect their time, their values, their biases. Other questions come to mind:

- *Have I always been a guy in a hurry, sometimes too much so for my own good?*
- *Am I blessed/cursed with a reckless spontaneity that has unpredictable consequences?*
- *Is chasing the elusive my stock in trade?*

Here I am, then, prostrate on a casino floor, the focus of a humiliating spectacle, light years removed from my earlier life. How, in the name of God, did I wind up here?

Let me try and explain. To do that, I need to double back across the years to a very different time and place, to a world ordered by taboos and imperatives totally foreign to the motley host of friends and strangers now hovering above my prone carcass, empathizing with my altered circumstance or satiating their morbid curiosity.

How I got from a small boat in the North Atlantic to a gambling joint in urban Canada is a story which, I believe, is well worth the telling.

PART 1
Moored to the Rock

'Twas here my years of innocence and youth
Accrued the native ways, of life and lore;
The salt of speech, the mood of small demand,
A sober faith, and awe of Providence.

— Dr. Herbert L. Pottle, Newfoundland politician, magistrate, and author, 1907–2002

CHAPTER 1
A GUY IN A HURRY

Unreasonable haste is the direct road to error.
— Molière

Helpless and hurting on the casino floor, I was party to an instructive incident. I had barely landed when a virtual army of earpiece-equipped security personnel appeared out of nowhere. One of their number stooped down and proclaimed to me, "We're going to lift you up now."

"No, you're not," I responded. "I'm staying right here for now."

In a matter of milliseconds, another official leaned down and intoned, "We're going to lift you up now."

"No, you're not! I'm in more pain than you'd care to know."

Soon after, but what seemed like an eternity, the rapidly enlarging circle of security personnel parted and I caught sight of a wheelchair, pushed by an attractive young lady.

"You can lift me up, now!"

Note that the two security people who had addressed me didn't say, "Are your hurt? Can I help? Just a minute, a nurse is on the way."

They had other things on their mind: This klutz is bad for business. He's making the place look untidy. Let's get him out of sight as fast as we can.

A compassionate casino! Now, there's an oxymoron.

I HAD NO SHOES, AND I COMPLAINED . . .[6]

I sat in a wheelchair in a crowded hospital emergency waiting room late on Valentine's Day. I had just been told, at ten o'clock at night, that there would be a five- to six-hour wait to see the doctor.

6 ". . . until I met a man who had no feet." — probably an old Persian proverb

Why me? How come this had to happen to me?

Wallowing in self-pity is pointless and counterproductive. Yet, for an unguarded moment, *Why me?* had become my mantra. A gruff voice shouted from behind, "Get out of the way." Which I did. As the speaker came into view, he was pulling the only other wheelchair in sight. I glanced at the male occupant. He had no legs. My troubles seemed suddenly a whole lot less serious. In time, I would get to discard my wheelchair. He may never get to abandon his.

My normal buoyancy reasserted itself, as did my well-honed skills at procrastination and compartmentalization, traits that have often brought me to misery's inner sanctum, most notably in a headline-grabbing shemozzle where my many imperfections got generously supplemented by the significant flaws of others. More about that later.

Suffice it to say that my late-night visit to the Gatineau emergency clinic was brief. I decided there was nothing wrong with my leg that couldn't wait until tomorrow. Back to the hotel I went, pigged out on Motrin, and (painfully) crawled into bed. My priority next morning was to keep a commitment to a colleague whose speech I had promised to monitor.

A BIONIC COUP

Nearly twenty-four hours after my unplanned rendezvous with a steel bench, I checked myself into an Ottawa hospital and learned I had sustained multiple fractures of the right tibial plateau, the top of the front leg bone, requiring the implantation of a titanium plate, followed by weeks of being unable to put weight on my wounded appendage.

The wait time for my surgery was mercifully short. I was told that my encounter with the surgeon's scalpel was at the top of the list, barring a more pressing emergency. Sure enough, a highway accident bumped me down a notch. Nonetheless, I was in the operating theatre just thirty hours after my condition had been diagnosed.

My son Mark came by right after I came out of intensive care, helping me to settle in and pass the time. The BlackBerry was humming nonstop with inquires from colleagues and other well-wishers. I was faced with the tedium of answering a torrent of emails. And I had to distract myself. Mind over matter is a credo I live by. Rather than respond individually to all those emails, I would take my mind off my shattered appendage by crafting a "news release" on the events of the previous couple of days and send out an all-points bulletin. It spoke of intrigue in the cause of one-upmanship while conveying the facts of my circumstance:

"Gowlings Goes Bionic: Canada's largest and, clearly, most creative law firm has assembled the latest weapon in the escalating legal services marketing war—a bionic marketer.

> In a dramatically executed coup, a seven-inch titanium plate has been implanted in the right knee of recovering politician-turned-diplomat Roger Simmons, senior policy advisor at Gowlings.
>
> North America's only bionic marketer will soon graduate from wheelchair to airplane seats and pitilessly exploit his bionic leg-up on the competition!

I soon learned that my discharge from the hospital stay hinged mainly on my mastering the ability to safely navigate on crutches. That was good news. I've had a lifetime propelling my physique on dual walking aids tucked under my armpits, thanks to several previous stunts that had also ended badly. The physical therapist at Ottawa General gave me a thumbs-up as soon as she confirmed my touted expertise on crutches.

There was one more hurdle. Since I proposed flying to BC, my surgeon had concerns about blood clotting. A little rat poison took care of that and, three days after surgery, I was on my way.

THE THERAPY OF BUSY-NESS

Back home in North Saanich, BC, I was obliged to adapt to the new reality, armed with crutches, a wheelchair, and two four-point walkers, placed near spots the wheels couldn't go. With the help of Jeff Millar, a resourceful friend and former colleague, my home office was transformed into a command centre, complete with television and bunk, since the upstairs bedroom was inaccessible to me. With two phone lines, a cellphone, a BlackBerry, and a computer as my umbilical cords, I was able to keep in touch, indeed catch up on the backlog.

Nevertheless, the wheelchair, the inevitable dependence on other people, and the limitation on my activities took their toll. Within a week or so, my wanderlust kicked in, and with son Paul as chauffeur, I hit the road, first to Vancouver, then Seattle and Bellingham, WA, for meetings and a couple of previously confirmed speeches. The next month was a blur of airplanes, hotels, and wheelchairs as I honoured commitments in Denver and Dallas, Miami and Memphis, and elsewhere.

THE VIEW FROM DOWN HERE

It was a time of altered perspectives, mine and others'. Sitting in a wheelchair, you quickly gain a heightened awareness of the special challenges faced by the wheelchair-bound. I find that the room at the SeaTac hotel labelled accessible has a bathroom threshold that cannot be crossed unless I lift the wheelchair while standing on my "good" leg—which works only because I have a "good" leg. Elevators are a special challenge. Ninety per cent of the time it's impossible, without help, to enter the lift before the door closes.

You learn all sorts of other things sitting in a wheelchair. It defines you in the eyes and minds of others. People make decisions for you. And you get used to being spoken of in the third person. It says much about the human spirit that so many persons are not defined by their disabilities but by their inner strength and achievements.

Ed Smith, my late dear friend and cousin, ranked among Canada's best humour writers and speakers. He was also quadriplegic, the result of a tragic car accident when he was fifty-eight. Time, but more significantly, Ed's incredible will, made mincemeat of his daughter, Jennifer's, prognostication that his wheelchair occupancy would be "the way he'll be defined forever."[7] Written just a couple of days after the accident, it was obviously her deep despair, not her father's never-say-die stubbornness, that pushed her pen. Less than a month later, she recorded a more upbeat and accurate appraisal: "Everything I love about my father is still intact."[8]

Mobile people and those confined to wheelchairs live in vastly different worlds. Surprisingly, the former often includes the very people whose em ployment is with the wheelchair-bound.

It was Ed Smith who recounted an unbelievable litany of faux pas and de facto insults sometimes perpetrated by front-line caregivers. His initial efforts to obtain a pass for travel on Toronto buses equipped for persons with mobility problems is a good example. He's told he must apply in person at a downtown office before he can use the service. The trouble is, the only way he can get there is on one of those buses. When he does find a way to present himself downtown and references his quadriplegia, his interlocutor, reading from her template script, persists in posing a series of dumb, tactless questions:

"How far can you walk?"

"How many steps can you walk on your own?"

"When do you expect to walk again?"[9]

Mercifully, there is a huge upside to wheelchair confinement. You find it in the many kindnesses of onlookers who open doors, hold elevators, and

---

7 *From the Ashes of My Dreams*, Ed Smith, St. John's: Flanker Press, 2002
8 Ibid
9 Ibid

otherwise proffer much-needed assistance. The occasional aggravations are easily outnumbered by the many smiling faces and gestures of kindness, not to mention the numerous empathetic stories from those who themselves have spent time in a wheelchair.

CREATIVE GENIUS, BITING WIT

Ed Smith left us in September 2017. It's agonizing to know that he's no longer with us, he who loved life so much, he who inspired untold legions of friends and strangers to live life to the nines, as he certainly did.

Ed Smith was one amazing guy. As education superintendent, I hired him as a school principal in my education jurisdiction, where he enhanced his well-deserved reputation as a progressive and caring educator. Subsequently, he headed a community college complex. But his heart was in writing, which eventually became his full-time passion and income source.

When the car accident dramatically altered his circumstances, there were those who opined that Ed's writing and speaking days were over. They didn't know Ed. Even before his rehabilitation was behind him, he was wrapping his agile mind around new endeavours: a syndicated newspaper column, speaking gigs, and several books. Prior to his wheelchair confinement, Ed had published seven books. In the following two decades, he wrote a dozen more, among them a poignant and instructive account of his life-changing ordeal and the road back. *From the Ashes of My Dreams* is a must-read. You'll need to peruse it at least twice. First, you'll find yourself racing through the pages, gripped by fate's cruel lottery, flummoxed at the mindless inflexibility of some caregivers, the empathetic grace of others, and, above all, spellbound by the indomitable spirit of Ed and the entire Smith clan. A second reading will allow you to relish the precision, succinctness, and beauty of the language, the apt imagery, the gallows humour, and the ingenious, seamless manner in which the voices of Ed, his marvel of a wife, Marion, and daughter, Jennifer, spell off each other, giving the reader a fast-paced, lucid portrayal.

Marion Smith is no mean wit herself. She told me of being in a restaurant with Ed. Once Marion had made her menu choice, the waitress tucked the menu under her arm, signalling the end of the ordering routine. A furious Marion, in a shaking voice saturated in sarcasm and disgust, scolded, "He eats, too!" The waitress had seen the inanimate wheelchair but missed the obvious. In the chair sat a real live human being.

TWO PEAS IN A POD

My self-inflicted immobility gave me a fuller appreciation of the mettle of those whose movements depend on wheelchairs and/or the assistance of caregivers. Long-time wheelchair users are amazingly adept at being masters of the conveyance rather than its prisoner. For an upcoming visit to Seattle by Rick Hansen[10], I was tasked with finding a US champion for his fundraising initiatives. A friend suggested John Kucher, who, like Hansen, had a life-changing accident as a teenager. I tracked Kucher down, only to find he and his late wife, Linda, resided in my neighbourhood.

I love to watch John make his lightning-fast transition from his collapsible wheelchair to the driver's seat of his Saab convertible. In a near-simultaneous series of moves, his arms catapult him off the wheelchair; while he's in mid-air, his hands collapse the chair behind his back; his left hand throws it behind the seat as, with his right hand, he jabs the ignition key into position and the engine roars into life.

Hansen and Kucher are two peas in a pod. The similarity of their physical situations seemed incidental to the bond they quickly forged. Their agile bodies brook no barriers. Their focus and love of life, their humour and humanity are what define them. After Rick's Seattle Rotary speech, we all debriefed over Kentucky Fried Chicken at John and Linda's place. The rapport between John and Rick was a symphony. Hansen's insatiable curiosity and attention to detail and John's aw-shucks demeanour made for a memorable afternoon.

Seattle, 2002, with Rick Hansen
(Author photo)

LIFE IN THE FAST LANE

John Kucher is the proud owner of a sailboat. Most every Tuesday, he competes in the craziest of all water sports, Seattle's Duck Dodge Race[11], listed in Fodor's as one of the "Top 100 things to do in North America." With as many as 250 craft entered in a race to the finish, tracking a zigzag course across the harbour in every conceivable direction, the experience is not for the faint of heart. I'm always game to try anything once, though, not being suicidal, bungee jumping is my one no-no. So, when John suggested I go along for the ride, I did just that.

The two-hour, heart-stopping event was a bigger adrenalin rush than I

10 Canadian Paralympian and a crusader for persons with spinal cord injuries
11 See www.duckdodge.org

had thought possible. Harrowing, yes, but thrilling! We survived with nary a nick on gunwale or crew. Some other daredevil was the victor, but we finished the course, and respectably so, doing justice to John's more modest objective—*"No DL, no dead last."* While I busied myself with heartfelt paeans of thanksgiving, John calmly secured the sailboat till next week's race. A standing invitation, recently renewed, will shortly see me back on the water with John, hanging on for dear life and gratefully admiring his impressive sailing skills.

CHAPTER 2
CHIP OFF THE OLD BLOCK

The apple doesn't fall far from the tree.
— ANONYMOUS

June 3, 1939: Hitler was putting the finishing touches on his diabolical plan to ravage Europe. FDR was halfway through his historic twelve-year stint in the White House, and Winston Churchill was in political limbo, his best days still ahead. The Oscar-winning *Gone with the Wind* was in theatres. And I was about to make my first move. I was born in Lewisporte, Newfoundland. Well, nearly. My mom, with lots of practice delivering God's little soldiers, opted to sever my umbilical lifeline aboard a small boat in Notre Dame Bay, minutes before we tied up to the wharf, on the very eastern edge of the North American continent, just 1,800 miles west of Ireland.

US Supreme Court Justice Stephen Breyer, addressing an American Bar Association luncheon in Washington, DC, in August 2007, unwittingly gave me the ultimate trivia question to stump even the most finicky US history buff. The question: Despite the stipulation in the US Constitution that *no person except a natural born citizen . . . shall be eligible to the Office of President*, which US president probably didn't meet the test?

Mr. Justice Breyer told us that a future US president may have been born in Canada, at Stanbridge East, Quebec. The parents, patriots certainly, but maybe also clairvoyants, had the good sense to whisk the newborn, belly button still damp, across an international border so he could claim citizenship in the land of his parents, not the land of his birth. Chester Arthur[12] may have had the credentials to be the world's first dual citizen, though he never did apply for a Canadian passport. His loss! Like Arthur, I was hatched on the way to somewhere else.

12 Twenty-first US president (1881–85)

I wasn't born a Canadian. Rather, I got my start in life in a fiercely independent dominion of 300,000 souls clinging to a remote island in the North Atlantic, Newfoundland, 1,000 miles northeast of New York.

THE SIMMONS CLAN

There were fifteen of us in the Simmons litter. I'm number eight. Dead centre. Halfway. My dad, Willis, chatting up a girlfriend I was trying to impress, put it this way: "When he was hatched, I took one look and decided to keep going!" Dad was right to keep going. Arrival number fifteen is my youngest sister, Cavell. She has made the family proud by her thirty-five years' service to Canada as a military nurse.[13] Ten of the brood hung around to experience the joys of adulthood. Six of us are still above ground, strewn until recently from a perch on Vancouver Island to bustling St. John's, Canada's oldest city.

Left: Bishop's Falls, Newfoundland and Labrador, 1952. At the age of thirteen, I bought my first wheels for ten bucks. (Author photo)
Right: Bishop's Falls, 1953. My brother Howard, right, and I donned our Sunday best for the itinerant photographer. (Author photo)

My brother Noel left us much too soon at forty-eight. His joie de vivre, ingenious schemes, madcap adventures, and fierce loyalties captivate, enrich and inspire us still. Howard, my protective big brother during the formative years, died in 2015. His easygoing demeanour masked a quick, creative

13 Cavell has been named to Team Canada for the Australian Invictus Games in October 2018.

mind; his generosity, love of nature, wacky wit, and fix-the-unfixable ingenuity knew no bounds.

Calgary, 1996. Embracing my four sisters. L-R: Rose, Cavell, Yvonne, and Bonnie. (Author photo)

Pasadena, circa 1989. With four of my brothers. L-R: me, Scott, Howard, Dale, and Dave. Noel (inset) died at age forty-eight in 1984. (Author photo)

The near-sudden passing in February 2018 of my fabulous sister, Yvonne left a gaping void. Kindness and a calming disposition were her defining hallmarks. The family's mother hen, she provided safe haven and nurturing for many, a role model for all.

Scott, my oldest brother, served as a volunteer member of the 9/11 cleanup team in New York. His doing so underscored both his trademark outreach and his lifelong quest for new challenges. Sadly, he passed away in May 2018, leaving a marvellous legacy of business acumen, caring, and humanity.

GO FORTH AND MULTIPLY

Religious beliefs were a driving force behind the large families of yesteryear.[14] The biblical injunction to "be fruitful and multiply"[15] was the eleventh of the Ten Commandments and, like the others, was to be obeyed without question. And obeyed it was.

Both sides of my family tree heeded the scriptural edict. My mother had eight siblings, my father, seven. Of these, two died in infancy, and only my maternal Aunt Emma remained single, serving for over forty years as a Salvation Army officer. So, I had twenty-five aunts and uncles, most of whom produced large families, giving me armies of cousins. The Simmons-Williams-Simms-Cobb gene pool has sent hundreds out across Newfoundland, Canada, and the world, some in prominent roles as a missionary, diplomat, legislative Speaker, author, corporate director, business tycoon, Hollywood film actress, and university president.

A STRONG WORK ETHIC

Dad's immediate forebears were from England's West Country. Like tens of thousands of other people from Devon, Dorset, and Somerset, they came as indentured servants of fishing interests. My mother's ancestry was Welsh and English. Her clan, too, had come to Newfoundland for similar reasons.

Willis Simmons and Ida Williams were both born into families with a strong work ethic. Grandfather Sam Simmons, boat builder and construction contractor, was a dour martinet who expected all to pull their weight. His three sons were conscripted into the workforce well before puberty, as were most of the daughters.

Herbert Williams, Ida's father, and her mother, Maud Simms, were the offspring of fishing families. The father and his five sons took up the family trade as youngsters. One went on to become a prominent entrepreneur in building supplies and transportation, another in retail, and a third served as

14 Of course, a comprehensive analysis of then-and-now family size would need to canvass the impact of other factors, such as economics, evolving values, and the advent of the pill.
15 Genesis 1:22, KJV

a merchant mariner during the Second World War and survived to tell the tale. The Williams girls, too, got an early start in bringing home the bacon. My parents, Willis and Ida, spared no opportunity to drill into us that same work ethic. The unkindest epithet Dad could hurl at you was, "You're worse than a hangashore"—someone regarded as too lazy to fish; a worthless fellow, a sluggard; a rascal.[16]

That term certainly didn't apply to my dad. By day, he was a carpenter with the railway. He spent most of his evenings in his backyard workshop fabricating various items for sale in the local community. His signature creation was the four-seater garden swing. His product line also included clock shelves and pincushions (for sewing needles and thread spools), both of which were emblazoned with one of three assertions: *God is love, Jesus saves, Christ died for our sins.* Employing these inscriptions had less to do with evangelical grandstanding than marketing! Another of his for-sale items, a flower stand, proclaimed no gospel message at all. It obviously targeted the agnostic niche market! Peddling Dad's output was accomplished by his very own door-to-door sales force, my siblings and me.

SLIDING INTO HOME PLATE

Dad could see humour in all things. The neighbour's very obese wife was in a St. John's hospital, 300 miles distant. For Joe, the doting husband, the nearest phone was at the railway station, just beyond our house. As he returned from his weekly phone call to the hospital, my dad asked, "Joe, how's the missus comin' along?" Obviously not familiar with the term "up and around," Joe responded, "She's up and hoppin' around."

The dramatic imagery of this obese woman's newly acquired agility fired my dad's imagination: "At that rate, Joe, she'll be here by sundown—on foot!"

THE CHROMOSOMES MADE ME DO IT

Herbie Dart acquired his nickname for his agility and energy. As a youth, he and his friends would arrange ten puncheons[17] in a row. The challenge was to leapfrog from one barrel into the next. Only he could reach the final barrel. Herbie Dart was my maternal grandfather. His daughter, Ida, definitely had his genes. My mother was intense and focused, had energy to burn, well-honed social animal instincts, and a fast, lethal, hinged-in-the-middle tongue. She could work a room better than Bill Clinton or Paul Martin, Sr[18].

16 *Newfoundland Dictionary of English*, 2nd ed, 1999, University of Toronto Press

17 Large wooden barrel of varying capacity, but usually eighty gallons (304 litres)

18 The father of former prime minister Paul Martin served Canada with distinction as a Member of Parliament, cabinet minister, and High Commissioner to the UK.

A multi-tasker, though not a workaholic, she knew how to change gears, to relax, to have fun.

Like my father, I'm *sawed off*[19]. I'm saddled with his ducktail rear end, his warped sense of humour, his eschewing of confrontation. He was a very egalitarian and tolerant person who was at ease with all he met.

In sum, I'm a Simmons chassis that laughs, seeks compromise, and has no choice but to look up to almost everyone I meet. And I'm a Williams engine that propels, often at breakneck speed, and belches, always for a reason, laudable or otherwise.

IRRECONCILABLE DIFFERENCES

Mom routinely drove my dad round the bend with her scathing denunciations, her non-stop energy, her impatience to launch the latest household improvement or community project. Gamblers, boozers, partygoers, adulterers. They topped the list of my mother's prime candidates to be Lucifer's eternal charges: "Hell is too good for that clique, that band of rogues."

As fast as I put pictures of Doris Day or Kim Novak on my bedroom wall, using little dabs of a homemade flour-based adhesive, my crusading mother would tear them down in the continuing challenge of saving her boy from Satan's clutches. Any female photo showing bare flesh below the chin or above the knee she deemed evil pornography. My mother had very definite ideas about many things. Her world was pitch-black and lily-white.

Dad saw a grey universe and functioned accordingly. Skipper, as the offspring often referred to him, saw people as individuals, not as exhibits to be categorized and labelled.

A "DOCTOR" DOES DOUBLE DUTY

In my early years, Mom was bedridden during the cold-weather season because of a rare disease, phlebitis. For an agonizingly long time, her condition had been misdiagnosed and, consequently, mistreated by a quack. The "doctor" whose patient she had been was in Lewisporte on a very different assignment. A few hours before a German U-boat sank the SS *Caribou* in the Gulf of St. Lawrence in October 1942, sending 137 passengers and crew to their deaths, he wired a telegram which read "Don't sail on the *Caribou*" and promptly disappeared. Spies make themselves scarce once their cover is blown.

When the Simmons clan relocated to Bishop's Falls, Dr. Davey Tulk quickly recognized Mom's symptoms because his wife, Dr. Helen Tulk, suffered from the same rare condition. Davey Tulk recommended hot water

19 i.e. short of stature, for those lacking a proper Newfoundland vocabulary

bottles. The Lewisporte impostor had prescribed ice packs! In no time, Mom had a whole new lease on life, and in her later years, a new drug eased her situation even further.

Small wonder, then, that Mom named the next male member of the litter Davey Grenfell, the latter to honour Sir Wilfred Grenfell, the legendary English-born medical missionary to the Labrador and northern Newfoundland coasts. Ida Williams Simmons was a prolific reader, and this reflected in her choice of baby names. No Mary, Ann, Jim, or John for her. Almost all of my fourteen siblings were given less-common monikers. For example, my three surviving sisters were christened Primrose, Bonnette, and Cavell, evoking the memory of Edith Cavell, the British nurse executed by Germany during World War I.

THE CASE OF THE LIVING DEAD

My dad was the go-to coffin maker in Bishop's Falls at a time when store-bought caskets were not an option for a couple of reasons—lack of availability and exorbitant cost. When the much-disliked George Cobb, the railway's local head honcho, escaped the mortal coil, the whole town turned out to watch the funeral cortège go by, not to pay last respects, but to get a look at "the most expensive wooden overcoat ever seen in these parts," as Dad put it.

My father's coffin-making was his version of moonlighting, and a familiar ritual unfolded every time there was a new demand on his services: A knock on the door would announce the passing of a local resident and request that Billy Simmons, as he was known in the community, "make a box" for the newly departed. There was no time to lose. Tradition dictated that the body be waked in its bed the first two nights, placed in the coffin late on the third evening, and interred the next day.

Billy sprang into action. His regular job at the railway occupied him during the day, so he had just two or three evenings to complete the task. One of my most enduring memories is of my father bursting into the house late in the final evening and announcing, "She's done!" That was his way of inviting us to his workshop, behind the house, to critique the finished product, an irregular hexagon covered in fabric, purple for the very old, grey for other adults, and white, pink, or pale blue for a child.

Dad, though largely introverted, could be a showman when circumstances warranted it. The family coffin inspection was such an occasion. My dad would, with a theatrical flourish, climb into the casket, adopt the pose of a laid-out corpse, and, addressing the soon-to-be occupant by name, would intone with mock solemnity, "Sam, boy, I sure hope you have a smooth ride over Jordan in this one!"

Carpentry and inspection ritual complete, one of the sons would be enlisted to "grab the end of the box," and with Dad at the other end, they would carry the coffin to the home of the deceased, sometimes a mile or more away. Soon after, body and box got together for eternity.

Claude Andrews had died, we had been told, and it was my turn to grab one end of his newly finished coffin. Arriving at the Andrews home, Dad paused a moment near the still body and then joined the wake in the kitchen, leaving ten-year-old me sitting in the doorway of the master bedroom with a good view of the wakers just off to my left and of the comatose form directly in front of me.

Mr. Andrews sat up! He stared at me, clearly puzzled that I was there. After all, no one told him he had died! Claude, we soon learned, had "died" twice before. Each time, a deep coma had been mistaken for death. He lived another seven months before dying for good. Just to be sure, he was waked for five days before the burial—in, of course, a custom-tailored wooden overcoat stitched together by Billy Simmons.

Forty years later, while attending a Port aux Basques house party, I had launched into the above story which, on many previous recitals, unfailingly evoked an awkward, skeptical silence, if not outright dismissal. This time, as my hostess sensed where my story was leading, she interrupted me, summoning a guest in the adjoining room, and said, "Calvin, get in here. Roger is talking about your grandfather!"

Calvin Andrews, the local newspaper editor, had been getting the same less-than-convinced stares as I had whenever he tried to tell friends of his forebear's miraculous return to life and of the ten-year-old boy who was there to witness it. At last, Calvin and I had found someone who had good reason to believe our tall tale. My good friend is himself very much alive these days as Pastor Calvin Andrews, retired General Superintendent of the Pentecostal Assemblies of Newfoundland and Labrador.

CHAPTER 3
ONE RASCAL AMONG MANY

I went through the usual stages:
imp, rascal, scalawag, whippersnapper.
— George Carlin, American comedian,
social critic, and actor, 1937–2008

Bishop's Falls was a frontier town, hewn out of the forest at the turn of the twentieth century to accommodate a railway terminus and, soon after, a logging and pulp mill enterprise. It had grown to 3,000 people during my time there at mid-century.

This new industrial centre in the interior of the island was a magnet for underemployed fishermen from coastal communities. Outport[20] Newfoundland had been settled, de facto, largely along religious lines. Whole stretches of settlements along one bay were Catholic, along another, Protestant (Methodist, Anglican). Notre Dame Bay, on the northeast coast, was predominantly Protestant but with a smattering of Catholic villages. It was from there that many of Bishop's Falls burgeoning population migrated, bringing with them their legendary work ethic, their marketable skill sets, *and* their fierce religious loyalties. And so, unwittingly, the town became a field experiment in multi-denominational cohabitation.

The community's industrial character also attracted an infusion of other influences as management personnel, trained specialists, and educators from across the island and abroad flocked in to run the railway, operate the mill, and staff the schools. The result was a diverse mix, more cosmopolitan than most other Newfoundland communities, save for urban enclaves such as St. John's.

20 An outport is a small isolated coastal community in Newfoundland and Labrador.

MAKING A LASTING FIRST IMPRESSION

September 5, 1944: It was my first day in kindergarten. Six-year-old Ivan lived on my street not far from my house, but we hadn't met. That would soon change in a manner he would not forget, as he often reminds me.

As one of the large Simmons clan, I had learned early the first law of the jungle. Survive. Protect yourself. Defend your territory. Ivan, with just one sibling and a doting parent who had obviously digested Emily Post's *Etiquette in Society*, came to school that first day determined to be true to his mother's dictates: "Make friends. Walk up to the first boy you see and say 'Hello, my name is Ivan.'"

He did just that. I was the boy he approached, and I wasted no time responding to his gesture of friendship. I landed him a lightning right hook to the chin. You can't blame a guy for defending his space, especially when there are mouthy, suspicious strangers on the loose. Lawmakers in Florida call it standing your ground. Our own once trusty Mounties now get their man by practising a whole new mantra: Taser first, ask questions later. It's a devastating commentary that the knee-jerk reaction of a kindergartener has become, for some, the template for modern law enforcement.

Ironically, the bizarre impact of that first encounter with Ivan Seaward sprouted a cherished friendship which thrives more than seventy years later. I like to think that, on my very first day of formal education, I learned an important lesson. There's no need to get nasty when responding to the innocent behaviour of others. Unless you don't know any better. Which could mean you're a trigger-happy police officer.

Ten Toronto pedestrians died and fourteen others were injured in late April 2018, when a crazed van driver mowed them down. Constable Ken Lam of the Toronto Police Service arrested the murderer without firing a shot. The takedown was a courageous, by-the-book, faith-restoring sequence that was uplifting to watch. Let's hope the video footage becomes required viewing wherever law enforcement personnel carry weapons.

THE THREE Rs

Formal education had its ups and downs for me. In high school, one of the subjects, civics, I especially liked, thanks to the teacher/principal, Dr. Hubert Kitchen, later to be Newfoundland's Education minister and a long-time friend. Classmate Art Thomas and I became engrossed in journalist Harold Horwood's "Political Notebook," a daily newspaper column, and we mailed a question to the well-read scribe:

> Would long-term civil defence preparations have adverse psychological effects on the mass of the population?

The year was 1954. The Cold War was upon us. Bomb shelters were all the talk. Horwood took three columns to respond to the "two learned gentlemen." Art and I had just begun the tenth grade! I credit/blame Kitchen and Horwood for my lifelong addiction to politics. Kitchen also has the distinction of being the last, though not the only, teacher to motivate me with a strap.

TWO SOLITUDES

Initially, the Catholic-Protestant togetherness idea in Bishop's Falls was a non-starter. The Micks, as we Protestants called them, kept to themselves, as did we. Catholics were not to be trusted, Mom decreed for the umpteenth time. Usually, her husband suffered in silence during her self-righteous rants. Not this time. "Ida, my dear, they don't have horns!" He had reason to know. At the railway car shop, he spent his working days with the Hannons, Glavines, O'Reillys, and other good Irish Catholics and counted them among his friends.

Religious prejudice was rampant in eighteenth- and nineteenth-century Newfoundland and can be traced back to the British Isles whence came the island's early settlers, bringing their long-festering biases with them. Fortunately, the more macabre manifestations of that feuding, then a daily occurrence in Ireland, were not replicated on this side of the Atlantic, for the most part.

There were several tragic exceptions. In 1835, the good Catholic inhabitants of Carbonear and Harbour Grace took exception to the writings of Henry Winton, editor of a Protestant newspaper, ambushed him at Saddle Hill, the rise of land separating the two towns, and relieved him of his ears. Even more tragically, five Harbour Grace men were killed in 1883 when Orangemen clashed with Catholics. In more recent times, manifestations of religious bigotry were less tragic, though far from absent.

Because of the pattern of original settlement and the island's small population, it is often easy, on hearing a person's surname, to deduce his/her ancestral community and religious affiliation. I sat next to Austin Lake at a St. Lawrence seniors' luncheon. "Austin, Lake is a Fortune name. How did the Lakes wind up in St. Lawrence?" He told me that, two generations earlier, three Lake brothers from Fortune went annually to Labrador to fish. One year, only two of them returned home and reported that John had drowned. Their widowed mother, a devout Protestant, went to her grave twenty years later, still mourning her son's untimely death. The truth is that John didn't drown. Rather, he met, fell in love with, and married a young lady from St. Lawrence. It was easier to tell Mother that John was dead than to let her know he had married a Catholic. "That's how the Lakes wound up in St. Lawrence. John was my grandfather!"

MANY HANDS MAKE LIGHT WORK

Life in Bishop's Falls was a daily smorgasbord of school and chores, pranks and pastimes. In a large family, chores were an inescapable given. During the school week, we took our turn washing dishes, sweeping and scrubbing floors, cleaving wood junks and keeping the woodbox behind the kitchen stove replenished, weeding the vegetable garden, toting drinking and washing water from the nearby well, feeding the hens and collecting the eggs, hanging out the laundry. We were an equal opportunity family!

Saturday evenings, shoes had to be polished, Sunday clothes pressed, and vegetables peeled. The approaching Sabbath precluded all forms of activity that could be done beforehand. In the summer, berry picking was a must. Blueberries, raspberries, and partridgeberries were jammed and bottled for later consumption.

During the winter, I went with Dad and my older brothers to get firewood, using four or five dogs and a sled. That's where we were headed on February 6, 1952. While grabbing a mug of tea and a thick slice of bread—homemade, of course—generously smothered in molasses, we switched on the radio sharp at six o'clock, the beginning of the broadcast day. Fully expecting the standard sign-on music, the familiar strains of the "Ode to Newfoundland"[21] with which the local CBC affiliate began the day's programming, we heard instead strains of a solemn dirge, probably Mozart's *Requiem in D minor*, interrupted soon after by the announcer:

> The King is dead! Long live the Queen!
> The King is dead! Long live the Queen!

King George VI had died in his sleep. His twenty-five-year-old daughter, travelling in Kenya, was the new monarch. In a radio address to the Commonwealth four years earlier, the then princess had pledged, "My whole life whether it be long or short shall be devoted to your service . . ." Seven decades later, Queen Elizabeth II continues to do justice to that commitment. Long live the Queen!

21 When Newfoundland was an independent country, the "Ode" was its national anthem. It is still a frequent feature of public events, analogous to the regular use of "America the Beautiful" as an unofficial anthem in the US.

MISCHIEF IS MY MIDDLE NAME

Growing up in Bishop's Falls, there was no shortage of ways for a risk-taker to get into mischief, a circumstance in which I was not wanting. In those days, it seems, the whole town was crawling with daredevils and pranksters. Some of the stunts we pulled would probably land us in court nowadays.

Canadian troops were camped on the riverbank a few hundred yards from our house, guarding against wartime sabotage. The trestle spanning the Exploits River provided a vital link in the trans-island railway, critical to the movement of troops and fuel to Gander Airport and the Botwood seaplane base. I recall the blackouts. Homeowners and motor vehicle operators were required to cover windows and headlights, respectively, to minimize enemy detection of potential targets.

For conniving rascals, the presence of the soldiers served a more immediate purpose. Though scarcely more than a toddler at the time, I soon became as adept as older kids at removing clothespins from the camp's outdoor laundry lines and being rewarded with cookies for returning the "lost" pins.

One of our more deadly summer pastimes was almost unique. It capitalized on the presence of an eighteen-inch-diameter, underground wooden pipe that stretched nine miles, from the town's pulp mill to the Grand Falls paper mill, and transported warm pulp under pressure. The pipe, with its shallow earth cover, was easily located. Any sharp object—a pick, a crowbar—quickly punctured the pipe, sending its contents fifty feet into the air, an instant beige-coloured fountain.

The novelty of simply watching the spewing pulp had long since worn off. Like boys in snowy climes, we built snow forts and had snowball fights all winter long. Unlike these guys, we had pulp forts and pulp-ball fights all summer long. There's a brutal difference. The former is a bit of harmless fun, the other is assault with a deadly weapon and, in today's climate, probably an indictable offence. Snowballs disintegrate on impact. Pulp-balls, especially leftovers from yesterday's fight, are like rocks and can do real damage on impact. Hurling these deadly projectiles provided daily confirmation of the law of impenetrability: Two bodies cannot occupy the same space at the same time. If the intended target failed to duck in time, he ran the risk of having a part of his anatomy displaced. Scarcely a summer went by without one or more of us being carted off to the hospital or emergency clinic with a cracked skull or a somewhat rearranged face.

Bonfire Night was a bit of English tradition that we observed to the hilt. Celebrated on November 5 to mark Guy Fawkes's 1605 doomed attempt to torch the parliament buildings at Westminster, our annual event was also incendiary, though lacking any political motive, other than to settle a few scores with local merchants, neighbours, and bullies.

Preparations began in late September when four to six of us would band together to amass the necessary materials for the bonfire. The aim was to have the biggest show in town, and we often succeeded. A heavily wooded forest stood within easy walking distance. We made almost daily excursions there to harvest boughs, which we stored in backyard sheds. We also had our sights on other inflammable items—pork barrels, molasses puncheons, wooden crates, and oily waste[22]. The problem was these items were the private property of others, the local merchant and the railway. But that was a temporary situation.

Barrels, puncheons, and crates were easy to get. All you needed was a well-crafted strategy, three guys to execute the plan, and darkness. One person scaled the high fence surrounding the merchant's precious containers and, in a tricky manoeuvre rife with the potential for disaster, jumped onto the doghouse roof while simultaneously shutting and latching the doghouse door, thus immobilizing the ever-present, vicious guard dog. Split-second timing was called for.

Alerted by the yelping animal, the owner would appear in the doorway of his abode. But our plan included immobilizing him as well. The guy on the doghouse roof had a second assignment, namely to blind the owner with a bright flashlight beam. Not knowing whether the guard dog was loose and unable to see the intruders, the owner stayed put. The remaining two members of Operation Molasses Barrel moved into action, one passing the barrels and crates over the fence, the other taking possession on the far side.

Our annual oily waste capers followed a similar game plan. The railway used the material to lubricate the carriages (wheels) of rolling stock. Our three-man team, again under cover of darkness, arrived at a rail siding equipped with a wheelbarrow, a pitchfork, and, you got it, a flashlight. One of us forked the contents of the wheel boxes into the wheelbarrow, which a second had positioned. The third provided light for the illicit activity and, most importantly, kept an ear open for an approaching watchman, in which case our lighting specialist shone the flashlight backwards as we skedaddled, not to take a last fond look at where we'd been, but to blind our pursuer from seeing who we were or where he (and we) were going. It was a clean getaway, most of the time.

The bonfire itself was a full-fledged neighbourhood festival. Entire families showed up to roast potatoes, make molasses taffy, and watch the tow-

22 A shredded, oil-drenched fabric used to lubricate railcar wheels

ering inferno. Every few minutes, one of us would throw a blassy bough[23], an old rubber tire, or a wad of oily waste on the blaze, creating a momentary fireworks effect as flankers[24] leapt into the sky, eliciting oohs and aahs from the appreciative crowd.

Nowadays, the bonfire is a much less frequent occurrence. Its near-total demise is a factor of changing times—increased urbanization, stringent fire regulations, the demise of insular, self-contained communities, and the emergence of other leisure-time options, including television, the Internet, and electronic games.

There was no shortage of the more commonplace pastimes. In winter, we frequented the local hillsides, skiing on suitably re-engineered pork-barrel staves and sliding on a piece of floor canvas, a doormat, or, in the case of the more affluent, a coaster. We skated and played football (soccer) on the river. There was almost daily pickup hockey using a three-quarter-inch-thick puck cut from a birch tree. The long winter evenings often found us around the kitchen table working on a giant jigsaw puzzle. We didn't miss television—we didn't know it existed.

Summer fun included trouting, boating, and swimming, both in the river and the Lily Pond, just across the rail trestle. Summer also meant it was time for the annual pilgrimage to Lewisporte for an extended stay with my paternal grandparents, Sam and Sarah (Cobb) Simmons. That was a mixed blessing, since the grandfather was a miserable character and did his daily best to ensure that everyone around him was equally miserable. He was a martinet of the first order. I recall having to sit silently for hours on a chair in the kitchen along with my siblings and cousins. His reasons were clear and non-negotiable. It was Sunday, not an occasion for frivolity, and children must he seen and not heard unless an exchange was initiated by an adult. The upside of the Lewisporte sojourn was the grandmother. She was as nice as her bedmate was nasty.

A coastal town, Lewisporte was a pleasant contrast to the bustle of Bishop's Falls and offered a whole new range of opportunities for mischief and fun. Favourite pastimes included jigging for codfish from a rowboat and catching conners on the public wharf, using snails that clung to the stanchions for bait.

Lewisporte also provided a seasonal employment opportunity for boys eager to make a few bucks. The local fish merchant owned a derelict ship, the

23 A dry, red branch of a fir tree (*Newfoundland Dictionary of English*, 2nd ed, 1999, University of Toronto Press)

24 Live spark from a wood fire (*Newfoundland Dictionary of English*, 2nd ed, 1999, University of Toronto Press)

HMS *Briton* (formerly the British corvette HMS *Calypso*[25]), moored a few hundred feet from shore, where he kept a supply of salt for curing codfish. The salt had to be shovelled from the ship's hold into containers and brought to shore in a smaller boat. The labour-intensive shovelling was tailor-made for preteen boys, and several of us would get hired for the job. It was a win-win. The fish processor got cheap labour. We got pocket money.

There were a couple of other less common diversions. During spring break-up on the Exploits River, we went copying, leaping from one piece of floating ice to another as the participants followed or copied the leader[26], a bit of sport much frowned upon by parents and certain to afford you your first (involuntary) swim of the season.

In the summer, on those few days when the weather was just too hot for comfort, we retired to the ice house, a pre–refrigeration era shed owned by the railway to store huge cubes of ice cut from frozen lakes the previous winter, and insulated in sawdust until it was needed to service passenger trains. Here we had our very own jungle gym as we did chin-ups and otherwise took full advantage of the elevated horizontal steel bars which supported the structure. Needless to say, we were regularly chased out of there for hygienic reasons.

It is the misfortune of some to be born on the wrong side of the tracks. Others are hatched on the right side. And then there's me and my clan. We were born or, rather, lived between the tracks.

The main trans-island line of the Newfoundland Railway[27] ran within 500 feet of our front door. A second railway[28] was just 400 feet from our back door. This convenient proximity afforded me frequent and free commuter service to the key towns impacting my diverse interests, whether sports (participant and spectator), movies, or dating.

The free transportation had nothing to do with railway generosity. Rather, like every other young fellow in Bishop's Falls, I was skilled at riding the rails, open-air style. You simply positioned yourself near a bend in the railbed, and as the train slowed to navigate the curve, you grabbed a rung on the boxcar's ladder and held on for dear life.

---

25 *More Fighting Newfoundlanders*, G. W. L. Nicholson, Government of Newfoundland & Labrador, 1969, p. 448

26 *Newfoundland Dictionary of English*, 2nd ed, 1999, University of Toronto Press

27 As of 1949, Canadian National Railways

28 The Anglo-Newfoundland Development Company (AND) railway's total trackage was less than a hundred miles and carried ore products from the mines at Buchans and paper from the Grand Falls paper mill to the port at Botwood for shipment to US and European markets.

HE SHOOTS! HE SCORES!

The radio was our link to the world. Every evening, we gathered around the battery-powered radio to hear Winston Churchill talk of "blood, sweat, and tears," and England's "finest hour," and to share Vera Lynn's[29] optimism that "There'll be bluebirds over the white cliffs of Dover," as war raged in Europe and the Pacific. Radio dramas transported us to worlds of intrigue, cataclysm, and romance. A favourite was *Amos 'n' Andy.*

None of the above, though, could quite deliver the thrill, the excitement, of Saturday-night hockey. "Hello Canada and hockey fans in the United States and Newfoundland!" Foster Hewitt and NHL hockey were on the air, live from Chicago or Montreal, Boston or Detroit. For the next two or three hours, Hewitt's screaming, lightning-speed falsetto would bring to our home the historic rivalry between the Toronto Maple Leafs and the New York Rangers or another of the six teams which comprised the NHL in those days, compared to today's thirty-one teams. The famed play-by-play announcer's trademark "He shoots! He scores!" set off more standing ovations in our kitchen than Carnegie Hall has ever seen.

The brilliant Newfoundland playwright Ted Russell, in his radio drama series, *The Chronicles of Uncles Mose*, immortalized the impact of sports radio on Newfoundland with his hilarious portrayal of a world hockey championship game between Canada and Russia. Like everyone else who could get near a radio, the fictitious Grandpa Walcott listened to the play-by-play. He was especially impressed by one of the players, "a fella with a strange Roosh-an name. Was it Boboff?" asked Uncle Mose. "Or Pushemoff? Or Shovemoff?"

Then, Grandpa remembers: "A spry fella he was. One minute he'd be in one end, the next in the other, and before you could blink, there'd be this fella smack in the middle!—Faceoff, yes! Faceoff, that was his name!" It is clear that neither hockey nor Russian surnames was Grandpa's speciality.

Contriving bizarre episodes and spinning tall tales were author Russell's vehicles for making social comment. In this episode, Grandpa had come to a very definite conclusion which he was not about to change nor reluctant to share, his dearth of knowledge of the subject notwithstanding. Bill O'Reilly[30], take note.

Amateur hockey games were all the rage and one of the few sources of organized entertainment. Grand Falls, nine miles up the road, had an artificial ice

29 English singer and songwriter whose morale-boosting performances during World War II were very popular

30 O'Reilly is a conservative commentator on American TV. In his many rants about Canada, the former Fox News host has never let the facts get in the way, or as Britain's Harold Macmillan noted, "I have never found, in long experience of politics, that criticism is ever inhibited by ignorance."

arena and a competitive senior hockey squad, made all the more so by the presence of five brothers from Bishop's Falls's storied hockey family, the Faulkners. Three of the brothers, George, Alec, and Jack, later played professional hockey. Alec was the first Newfoundlander to play in the National Hockey League[31]. George was the top scorer on Canada's national team that won the bronze medal in the 1966 world hockey championship in Yugoslavia.[32]

Grand Falls and teams from other centres across the island were each permitted to include in their rosters two or three paid "imports" or professional players. That's how we came to see the home team's Clobie Collins in action, nicknamed "Speedy" for a reason. His rink-length goal-scoring streaks, a fixture of nearly every game, dazzled us. Every boy wanted to skate and score just like Speedy. He was the first person of colour I had ever seen. And that's when I formed a positive impression about black people, and I've had it reinforced many times.

Two of the most delightful persons whom I came to know during my years in politics were Jean Augustine[33], a Jamaican-Canadian Liberal MP from Mississauga, and Linc Alexander[34], a Tory MP of West Indian ancestry born in Toronto, both of whom served in a federal cabinet. Among my fondest memories of the five years I lived in Seattle, until 2003, are the many wonderful hours I passed with African-American friends. Pastor Pat Wright. King County Executive Ron Simms. NAACP President Karl Mack and his wife, Jamiyo.

31 Alec Faulkner played just one game with the Toronto Maple Leafs during the 1961–62 season before being traded to the Detroit Red Wings, where he spent two seasons, scoring key goals in both regular season play and in the Stanley Cup playoffs.

32 *Faulkner: A Hockey History*, Tom Rossiter, St. John's, NL: Breakwater Books, 2011

33 Grenadan-Canadian educator, first black MP and cabinet minister

34 Lincoln Alexander was Canada's first black viceregal appointee, serving with great distinction and flair as Ontario's lieutenant-governor from 1985 to 1991.

CHAPTER 4
ENTREPRENEUR WITH ACNE

Opportunity is missed by most people
because it is dressed in overalls and looks like work.
— Thomas Edison, American inventor and businessman, 1847–1931

As I completed the ninth grade, the home front was in turmoil. My parents would separate, for good, a year or so later. I decided to skip town. I made a clean getaway, sleeping that first night on the lam curled up on a concrete dock, the lights of my hometown reflecting across the water.

SCREAMS IN THE NIGHT; HANGOVER IN THE MORNING

I was awakened by an early-morning freight train headed east. As it slowed to navigate the turn near the dock, I hopped aboard and clung precariously to a boxcar ladder until we came upon a horrible train wreck I'd learned about just before skipping town. Hiding in the bushes and under the cover of pre-dawn, I watched as rescuers tried to extricate from the wreckage a man in excruciating agony. His blood-curdling screams I shall never forget. I was to hear that same scream, from that same man, five years later in very different circumstances.

My father was among the rescuers. Whenever there was a train wreck, and there were several each year, Billy Simmons was seconded from his regular job as a carpenter to cook for the crew.

Morbid curiosity satisfied, I caught the morning passenger train west, first to Corner Brook, where I landed a three-day fencing job, and then on to North Sydney, Nova Scotia, after an unforgettable ordeal at the Port aux Basques ferry terminal. The town, in later years one of my favourite haunts for quite different reasons, can be bleak, foggy, and cold, even in June month. This night, the town lived up to its billing!

Lousy weather was, however, just a small part of my nightmare. On the train from Corner Brook, I had hooked up with six guys in their late teens, all headed to Toronto[35] to make their fortunes, and one, to my fifteen-year-old eyes, stunningly beautiful female in her mid-twenties, returning to her job in Ontario after a trip home to reconnect with family.

The eight of us bonded over poker, and I had my first serious introduction to booze. On arriving in Port aux Basques, the woman proposed we all go to a local bar, which we did, in the process missing the boat to Nova Scotia and spending twenty-four hours waiting for the next one.

Now, as I reflect on those days, a couplet from the World War I ditty "Hinky-dinky parlez-Vous" comes to mind:

You didn't have to know her long,
To know the reason men go wrong!

With apologies to Dickens, *it* was the best of times, it was the worst of times. I was finally hanging out with the guys—and a gorgeous chick. All too soon, though, I had other preoccupations. The booze kicked in. Boy, did it kick in. When I regained some semblance of sobriety and rational thinking, I chewed myself out royally. And I made myself a promise: I would never, ever again surrender my thinking capacity to a bottle of booze.

IDYLLIC INTERLUDE

As I leaned against the rail of the passenger ferry SS *Cabot Strait* on its approach to North Sydney, I chatted with two teenaged girls, identical twins coming home from a Newfoundland holiday. When asked where I was going, I wasn't about to admit to my latest heartthrobs that I was vagabonding. Instead, I responded, "Sydney. 148 Vulcan Avenue." I knew there was such an address, having seen it umpteen times on the fat envelopes my older brother received almost daily from Ruth, an old flame who wouldn't let go. "Our house is right across the street. We'll give you a ride," gushed a twin. With that exchange, I killed not one, not two, but three birds. I solved my immediate accommodation problem. I got free transportation to my destination. And my embryonic love life had just hit the jackpot. Two at-

35 Even before Newfoundland's confederation with Canada, many thousands of young Newfoundlanders, mainly males, trekked off to Toronto each year to find employment, many never to return except for periodic junkets back to see family, gorge on Newfie cuisine, and revisit pastimes of days gone by, fishing, hunting, camping, partying, and swapping stories with friends and strangers alike.

tractive females would be my groupies, guides, and, if I played my cards right, girlfriends!

The good folks at 148 Vulcan Avenue treated me as the returning prodigal son, although I was a complete stranger to the parents. My foot in the door was Ruth, who jumped at this chance to vicariously connect with the guy back in Bishop's Falls who wasn't answering her letters.

I spent my days that summer mowing lawns, washing cars, anything that eased my tight cash flow situation. Ruth and I had a weekly routine. She, my senior by seven years, liked to frequent the local bars and clubs. I, as her surrogate, underaged date, tagged along, thanks to doorkeepers who turned a blind eye or couldn't see well. Ruth became my first and only dance instructor, trying with minimal success to teach me the finer points of waltzing. The only tangible results were my bruised ego and her bruised feet as the floor evaded my clumsy missteps. Perhaps I was preoccupied pondering what my mother's scathing assessment would be if she knew her saintly son had surrendered to the Devil's wiles, dancing being at that time a Salvation Army taboo.

Most evenings, though, I spent with the twins. They took turns being my date, going to movies, biking, walking. At least, I was told they were taking turns. I couldn't tell them apart, so I nicknamed them Tweedle-dee and Tweedle-dum. They got their kicks out of confusing me on the subject. At fifteen, I was madly in love with a girl. But which one? Or was it both?

After two months largely freeloading off Ruth's family, it was time to move on. I bid a teary farewell to my summer flings, T-dee and T-dum, and was back in Bishop's Falls in good time for the start of the new school year.

PREMATURE GRADUATION

A daily newspaper route had been my main source of income since I was eleven. I got to wondering how it could be cost-effective for the St. John's publisher to ship my newspapers by rail right past my front yard to a circulation guy in the next town and then pay him to drive twenty miles a day to deliver them to me. If the newspaper's owners had money for a middleman, I set out to become that middleman. Having pumped the paper's sales from thirty to over 200 during my tenure, I put in writing the case for a separate circulation manager in my town, namely me. The ploy worked, and at fourteen years old I had seven of my buddies each peddling thirty papers under my paid supervision. The administrative load was not onerous: Count out seven piles of papers each day, collect from my carriers each week, and remit the proceeds by postal money order to St. John's.

Meanwhile, my school attendance, particularly at French class, became increasingly more erratic, earning me a summons to the principal's office. Ray Wight, with the entire teaching staff looking on, threw down the gauntlet: Take French or quit school! For a brash, know-it-all fifteen-year-old, the choice was crystal clear. Without a word, I headed for the door, regretting my move before my hand grasped the doorknob, but not about to show weakness in front of judge and jury. So, with one month in the tenth grade behind me, I was free to pursue my burgeoning business ventures full-time.

DOOR-TO-DOOR MARKETING

With my newspaper delivery business on a secure franchise footing and my formal education apparently behind me, I soon discovered the potential of moonlighting, both as a way to kill time and as a supplementary income source. My Uncle Roger, a travelling salesman, frequently passed through town, often staying a few days with us while he worked the immediate territory. I became his door-to-door surrogate, hawking cosmetics and ladies' dresses.

Norris Arm North was a tiny village fifteen miles down the railway tracks from my hometown plus a short boat ride. The ladies of this isolated outpost depended exclusively on Eaton's and Simpson's mail order empires for the latest fashions. But today, standing right outside on their doorstep was a fast-talking teenager with a whole suitcase full of the prettiest dresses imaginable, and in all sizes.

Sales were brisk. I was fast running out of product. The latest delirious customer had just taken off my hands an ill-fitting number with an outrageous floral pattern and was strutting about her kitchen modelling her new prized possession for me and her brood, all the while assuring us but mainly herself that, once she "took it in" here and there, it would "fit like a glove." I blanched at the thought of how much "taking in" she would have to do but kept my mouth shut, opening it only later to ask her advice. You see, I had a problem. I had just one dress left, extra, extra large, and ugly as sin. Who, I asked her, might be interested in this exquisite garment? Pointing through the window, she said, "See that big purple house with the chimney? That's my aunt's. She'll love it. Just her size, too."

And so I made my final sale. But I wasn't quite out of the woods yet. The word had gone 'round the harbour that my dress selling was in full swing, and it seemed every last female was determined to contribute to my bottom line. As I headed for the boat ride and home turf, I had to run a gauntlet of crestfallen would-be customers who had emerged from their houses to extract a promise I would return with more dresses.

The promise was made, but never kept, partly because I had soon moved on to other get-rich-quick ventures and, just maybe, also partly because of an oft-recurring thought: Once my buyers, so titillated that day, had to endure their husbands' scathing appraisals of the new wardrobes, should I risk life and limb by returning to the scene of the crime? Discretion and love of life won the day.

EARLY-MORNING RETAILING

I had another well-paying gig. Because of it, my business day started early and finished late, seven days a week. It began at 5:15 a.m. That's when the westbound trans-island passenger train, affectionately dubbed the "Newfie Bullet"[36], rolled into the railway station near my house. I was already at the station, my custom-built, bike-mounted larder stuffed with egg sandwiches, chocolate bars, chewing gum, and soft drinks, eager to slake the thirst and feed the sweet tooth of my captive clientele, at premium prices, of course. The routine was repeated at ten twenty each night when the eastbound train came through.

TYCOON WITH ITCHY FEET

At the ripe old age of fifteen, I was sitting pretty, economically speaking. Three regular jobs, one in management, two in sales, all turning a tidy profit. But the days were long and lonely. All the guys my age were in school. I needed a new challenge. So, I signed on as a logger. This was clearly my big break! No more hawking women's apparel and sachet powder. My ship had come in!

Chainsaws and tree harvesters had not made their debut. So, I had to settle for a bucksaw and an axe, both company issue. And I had to pile the logs. The work was back-breaking and solitary.

My career as a professional logger lasted four days. Math being one of my better subjects, it took no time at all to compute that the value of the logs I'd cut minus what I owed the employer for food and equipment left a difference of $27, in whose favour I can't recall. The one thing I know for certain is that there couldn't have been any income tax implications, a matter that would trip me up later in life.

Fortunately, my core enterprises were going concerns. Newspapering, door-to-door marketing, and confectionery sales were each making a buck. Family-wise, things were not quite that rosy. The impending parental breakup was in its final stages, so I decided to take a sabbatical from my well-oiled entrepreneurial operations and hit the road. For the second time in less than a year, I became a vagabond, my true calling.

36 The Newfoundland Railway, after 1949 Canadian National Railways (CNR), ran its trains at a snail's pace because of the antiquated, narrow-gauge tracks.

CHAPTER 5
DISTRACTED SCHOLAR

If you think education is expensive, try ignorance.
— Derek Bok, president of Harvard University, 1930–

St. John's, July 1955. I was living the dream. I had conned my way into a cushy job at Fort Pepperrell[37] Air Force Base. The US military installation was one of several in Newfoundland and Labrador, the result of the 1941 Lend-Lease deal between the Americans and the British. I arrived in St. John's on my sixteenth birthday and, that afternoon, convinced the base's hiring officer that I was eighteen and promptly landed a position as busboy in the officers' mess.

Living quarters were my next preoccupation. An until-then futile search eventually took me to Brazil Square in the seedy part of town and to Chatfield House, a nondescript three-storey walk-up. I told the boarding mistress I wanted a private room. She smiled grimly and said, "Come with me." After a hurried climb up two flights of steep, rickety, creaking, narrow stairs, we entered a room with four beds.

"Four guys in one room?" I muttered, incredulous.

"Eight," she shot back. "Counting you, eight."

The boarding house lady suggested adding a single cot. I agreed, having run out of options. Soon after, the empty spot in the fourth double bed was filled. For the next month, nine of us, I being by far the youngest, bunked in that room.

The $35-a-week paycheque was just a fraction of my Fort Pepperrell income. Senior, well-paid officers, enamoured by a gabby teen who loved to talk pol-

37 Sir William Pepperrell was an Anglo-American soldier who led American colonists in the capture of the fortress of Louisbourg, Nova Scotia, from the French in 1745.

itics, ask questions, and tell stories, tipped me handsomely, sometimes as much as $150 a week.

The job was a blast. Regular hours. Lots of friendly people to talk to. And I was flush with cash, more money than I knew what to do with. So, I bought a car, used but nice-looking and reliable. The horn worked but was superfluous; the roar of the faulty muffler alerted the endangered. Too young to qualify for a driver's licence, I had one of my suddenly large circle of friends do the driving.[38] At sixteen, I had my own chauffeur! Clearly, I had arrived!

PLOTTING A NEW COURSE

It was then, on a sunny July day, that I met a Salvation Army officer in downtown St. John's, an encounter that dramatically changed my life. Major Charlie Woodland approached me or, more accurately, accosted me: "You're Roger Simmons. I've heard all about you, how you got kicked out of school, how you're throwing everything away."

The Major invited me to his nearby home for lunch, and it was there I met his wife, Major Sarah Woodland, a beautiful, spirited woman who would be my mentor and friend until the day she died nearly fifty years later. Her husband pursued his mission: "My son, you gotta get back in school. The train leaves at five this evening. Be on it. Go to Windsor. There's a welfare officer there, Julia Morgan. She used to be a teacher, a good one. She can help you play catch-up in grade ten math and English."

As the well-meaning Major droned on, I mentally dismissed his every word: *You idiot! Don't you know how good I got it? A job, lots of money, a car. No parents around to hassle me. And besides, I plan to go to night school.* Even if Major Woodland could have heard my thoughts, I doubt they would have swayed him. Indeed, the more I mulled over the specifics of his proposal, the less sure I was of my own argument. By five o'clock, I had quit my busboy job, picked up my paycheque, sold my beloved car, bid a hasty adieu to my palatial boarding house digs, and was sitting aboard the westbound passenger express, headed for home, for Windsor and for an entirely new twist in my already circuitous pilgrimage.

At nine the next morning, I found myself at the Windsor welfare office. As I approached reception, a voice off to my left pronounced, "You must be Roger Simmons. Come in." Half-lenses perched on her nose, Dr. Morgan exuded a no-nonsense yet amiable aura. She drew my attention to eight scribblers[39] on her desk, then pushed four of them, labelled Algebra, Geometry,

38 Most of the time, it was my late friend, Harry White, a fellow bandsman at the Salvation Army's Duckworth Street Corps, who later distinguished himself as bandmaster of Army bands in the Toronto area.

39 Newfanese for exercise books

English, French, toward me. "You'll see I've put some assignments in them. Do what I wrote. Come back next Tuesday at two o'clock. I'll take a look at what you did, and I'll have another load of work for you in these." She nodded toward the other four scribblers.

Dr. Morgan arranged for me to meet with the principal of the newly constructed all-grade Salvation Army School just up the street from her office. Captain Otto Tucker got quickly to the point: "I'll take you into grade eleven—for a month. If you can handle it, you can stay."

During the next eight weeks, I morphed into a hermit, leaving our house on Tuesdays only, hustling night and day to keep abreast of the merciless mounds of equations and theorems, essays and conjugations which Dr. Morgan kept dishing out, covering, she said, the entire grade ten course requirements in the four subjects. Fortunately, my early fascination for history and geography meant they wouldn't trip me up in the year ahead.

MENTOR PAR EXCELLENCE

I enrolled in grade eleven. Daily, for the entire school year, I hitchhiked the ten miles from my Bishop's Falls home to the school at Windsor. While there was a teaching staff of a dozen or more, large by rural Newfoundland standards at the time, the senior classes were sparsely populated. The previous school building had burned down, obliging the dispersal to other schools of secondary students, most of whom elected to remain there for their final year or two. There were so few students in grades nine to eleven that we were all corralled in one classroom. There were just two of us in grade eleven, Ray Brooks and me.

The good Captain was a teacher-principal. He ran the school and taught some of the courses. A brilliant communicator, he married a devastating sense of humour with a gentle humanity to motivate even the most apathetic scholar. Two or three weeks into the term, Tucker decreed that Ray and I would spend most of our school day in the unstaffed library. We were ecstatic because we had the place all to ourselves. Tucker told us he trusted our good sense to spend our time productively. The trust was misplaced. His grade eleven twosome quickly found creative, though not Board of Education–approved, pastimes, often smirking at the Captain's presumed naivety and our ability to fool him. It didn't take long, however, to realize the joke was on us. It dawned on us that we had two choices: fritter away the year or do whatever we could to graduate. We asked Tucker for specific assignments. He let go one of his trademark raucous laughs: "You boys are smarter than I figured. I was going to give you another week or two."

There had been a method to his madness and an early glimpse into the creative mind of a top-notch educator who employed trust as a teaching tool. He recognized that leadership sometimes means simply getting out of the way, yet staying close enough to inspire, course-correct, and adjudicate. In dispatching us to the library, Tucker's unspoken purpose was to get us to self-motivate and assume some responsibility for our education. It worked. For the balance of the school term, Captain Tucker functioned as the resource person to two inquiring minds, not a talking head who dispensed pearls of wisdom in fifty-minute monologues.

As the school year was winding down, the principal gave Ray and me info on the government's student-teacher indenture program aimed at enticing high school graduates into a career in education. I was silently dismissive of the notion that I should become a lowly teacher. I had a grander scheme in mind.

It didn't take long to figure out that the realization of my dream would come with a hefty price tag. I soon concluded that my only ticket to university was the indenture program. There was no choice but to fill in the application and drop it in the mail. Though the paperwork for enrolment at Memorial University was in place, there remained one big obstacle: money. The bursary would cover my tuition, but there would also be textbooks and living expenses.

CHASING THE ALMIGHTY BUCK

Soon after writing the final school exams, off to Ontario I went to seek my fortune, as untold thousands of Newfoundland guys and gals had done before me. My travel companion, John Pelley, had relatives in Oshawa, so we made a beeline for Canada's auto manufacturing nerve centre. Within hours of stepping off the train, I joined Oshawa's workforce, first as a carpenter's helper, and three days later as a confidential clerk in General Motors' truck plant.

The latter job was a boondoggle, at least, for me. The job title messaged my assignment as an indispensible insider, the custodian of the closely guarded paint codes which, it was asserted, gave GM an edge on the competition. Whenever assembly line workers needed paint, they came to me, holed up alone among endless shelves of oversized paint cans. Hours, sometimes days, would pass without a single customer, facilitating marathon literary pursuits and, on occasion, a welcome nap. Alas, my utopia was short-lived. The plant routinely shut down in August for staff holidays, which didn't include me, a short-term, non-unionized worker.

With family and friends in Toronto, I decided to try my luck there and became a mailroom clerk at Colgate Palmolive. My routine included twice-daily tours of the building's six storeys, delivering mail and emptying "out" baskets. The manufacturing floors I dreaded. Gagging lye fumes hung heavily in the air. I became adept at exiting the stairwell at a sprinter's pace, delivering the goods, snatching the outgoing mail, and disappearing into the stairs, all the while holding my breath.

Company policy allowed us a free hand in soaps and toothpaste. We regularly subsidized, ever so slightly, our meagre paycheques by swapping our freebees for chewing gum with Wrigley's workers across the street.

Early September 1956, my best buddy since childhood, Ivan Seaward, and I took the train east to North Sydney, Nova Scotia, then the ferry to Port aux Basques and the legendary "Bullet" train to Bishop's Falls. A few days later, we were off to St. John's and university.

First-year college was a coming-out for me. I was soon knee deep in campus politics, a stringer for the student newspaper, a gofer member of the debating society, and an officer-cadet in the Canadian Officer Training Corps (COTC), an army reserve unit.

St. John's, 1956. The *Muse* (student newspaper) office, Memorial University. L-R: Garf Fizzard, Harry Stamp, Dave White, Dave Pike, and me. (Author photo)

BOOT CAMP

As a COTC cadet, I participated in a mid-week drill and a rifle practice on Saturday. I was assigned to the provost corps and spent the summer of 1957 at Camp Shilo, near Brandon, Manitoba. Sweltering temperatures and the endless sand justified the base's nickname, Little Sahara. During a field exercise, cocooned in full battledress, I succumbed to the heat and was carted off to the hospital.

The cadets were a motley host and hailed from pretty well every province and territory: three Newfs, my buddy Ivan, Ralph Dale, later a member of my teaching staff, and me. Feldman, an insufferable elitist from Quebec. David Searle, a pleasant fellow from Northwest Territories, now a retired lawyer, having been Speaker of the NWT legislature and a UBC professor. Our drill sergeant, surnamed May, nicknamed Maysie, did justice to the stereotype. Brutal, loud, abusive, vulgar, merciless. I've met a few obnoxious types but none who took such pleasure from being mean and nasty.

Shilo, MB, 1957. Officer Cadet Roger Simmons, COTC. (Author photo)

Weekends, I played tenor trombone in the Brandon Salvation Army Band. I was often seconded to another, the Ellice Avenue Band in Winnipeg. With that group, I toured around Manitoba on weekends, doing concerts in Riding Mountain National Park, the International Peace Garden at the US border, and other venues.

I had signed up for a parachute course at the end of the summer camp, but it got cancelled. My early departure meant that I had to forgo a much-anticipated outing. The new prime minister, John Diefenbaker, was coming to town for a fishing trip with the local MP and cabinet minister, Walt Dinsdale, who had invited me to join them. Dinsdale was my bandmaster at Brandon Citadel.

A few months earlier, I had seen the mercurial Diefenbaker at an election rally in St. John's. At the old CLB[40] Armoury, the Conservative leader wowed an overflow crowd as he invoked the name of a Liberal warhorse:

"Jack Pickersgill[41] says he has a sixth sense, the political sense. Ladies and gentlemen, what a fine man he'd be if he had the other five senses!"

I never did get to meet Diefenbaker. He was still an MP when he passed away in August 1979, three months before my election to the House of Commons.

40 Established in Newfoundland in 1892, the Church Lads' Brigade is an Anglican youth organization.
41 Newfoundland's representative in the federal cabinet

CASH FLOW

Personal financial realities made my first university stint a short one. With just a year under my belt, I had to forsake the joys of college life and find a source of income, becoming a teacher in a remote outport. Over the next five years, I alternated between teaching and studying, completing the second-year university requirements in summer sessions, and graduating from the Salvation Army College for Officers.

My return to Memorial full-time was by a roundabout route. Although accepted for the 1962–63 academic year, an unexpected family circumstance gutted my savings and necessitated a hasty change of plans. I found myself in Wabush, then an embryonic mining town in western Labrador, as a junior high school teacher. The principal was my long-time friend, Dom Howse, a gentle soul and highly competent administrator. Two weeks into the school term, a doctor diagnosed a condition which threatened to get more complicated, and he advised me to immediately relocate closer to adequate medical facilities, there being no hospital in Labrador West at the time.

Back in St. John's, it was time to reactivate Plan A, if possible. With the fall semester already started, was I too late to enrol? I called on the university registrar. H. T. Renouf found a way. I was basically back to square one. However, the reason I had wound up in Wabush rather than in a college lecture theatre was still very much in play. I needed money, and fast.

My one Wabush paycheque gave me a little working capital, which I promptly invested. A classified ad in a St. John's daily announced my availability as a tutor in high school French and math. Responses to the ad flooded in. Almost overnight, I had more students than I could handle alone. I had tapped into a niche market where there was real demand, and not just in my advertised specialties. How about English, the callers asked, or Latin, or history?

I responded by incorporating, well, just about. The St. John's Tutorial Service was born, sizable print ads proclaimed *tutors available in all subjects*, and, to respond to the ever-increasing demand, I contracted twenty-five fellow Faculty of Education students, all experienced teachers upgrading their qualifications. I hired a secretary to track the tutoring requests and assignments, bill clients, and pay tutors.

EXPANDING MY PORTFOLIO

My French tutoring spawned two other lucrative spinoffs. The Department of National Defence (DND) signed me up to conduct oral French classes for its officer personnel at Fort Pepperrell.

My high school tutoring ritual included leaving with the student a one-page summary of the concepts covered during a session. These notes came to the attention of several teachers, who requested copies. And that's how I stumbled onto the idea of formalizing, expanding, and publishing the notes. *All About* (French) *Verbs* was the result. To ensure a quality product and to give some legitimacy to my presumptuous undertaking, I sought out the reigning expert on the teaching of high school French, school principal Clifford Andrews. He generously agreed to edit the work and provide a preface, and he became an indispensable mentor and cherished friend. For more than half a century until his 2013 death, I never ventured anywhere near St. John's without seeing Cliff and his bride, Joan. We enjoyed great get-togethers puzzling over the present, crystal-balling the future, and telling lies about the past.

All About Verbs shortly became an ancillary text for the teaching of high school French and received the provincial Department of Education's approval as such. Demand for the slim volume was brisk, with considerable impact on my bottom line.

Soon, I was gearing up for another publishing endeavour. The province's school boards, numbering nearly 300 at the time, depended largely on St. John's and Corner Brook[42] dailies to advertise available teaching vacancies. This left the more remote boards and would-be applicants at a disadvantage. The choice jobs were snapped up by those who first got their hands on the newspapers, namely teachers in urban areas. An up-to-the-minute listing of available teaching and administrative openings, regularly available to all the province's educators, would help mitigate the problem. Voila! *Educators' Gazette* was hatched! The publisher? You guessed it: me. The new service was an immediate hit and continued biweekly publication for eight years, until the consolidation of school boards to fewer than twenty rendered the *Gazette* a much less viable enterprise.

By early 1963, I had two popular publications, a tutorial business that was humming nicely along, a small DND teaching contract, several tutorial students, and twenty-seven part-time employees, including a staffer to handle the minutiae generated by the *Gazette*. And, oh yes, I was also a full-time university student.

Throughout the next two and a half years, the hectic pace of my sundry pursuits continued. Multi-tasking was the watchword; a growing bank balance, the social life of a Buddhist monk, and sleep deprivation, the consequences. My faculty advisor in my senior years[43] was Dr. Phil Warren, later minister of Education in a Wells[44] cabinet. As I awaited Dr. Warren's arrival, his office partner, Dr. Ray Barrett, spoke up.

42 A city on Newfoundland's west coast

43 I graduated at Memorial University in 1964 with a Bachelor of Arts (education) and in 1965 with a B.A. (French).

44 Clyde Wells was premier of Newfoundland from 1989 to 1996.

"We've been talking about you. If you didn't have so many irons in the fire, you could graduate with a first-class degree."

Dr. Barrett recalled many years later that my reply at the time was, "Who wants a first-class degree when I can have all the fun I'm having and get a second-class degree?"

The two profs had read my situation perfectly. Less-than-optimal time management, coupled with a little old-fashioned greed and overreaching, had me juggling university obligations with more tutoring assignments than I should have accepted.

SPEAKING FOR THE AFFIRMATIVE

Those latter three years at Memorial weren't all business and study. I chaired the Students' Representatives Council and headed the campus branch of the Newfoundland Teachers' Association. I was increasingly active in the debating society. Fellow Lewisporte native Gordon Moyles and I were the university champions.

A debating partner and I got to represent our alma mater at inter-varsity debating events in other provinces, with mixed results. Our low point was at St. Dunstan's, now UPEI, in Charlottetown. Two of the judges, one of the opposing debaters and the chairman, were all surnamed McDonald. Unaware of the proliferation of the McDonald clan in PEI, we were sure the cards had been stacked heavily against us. Our suspicions robbed us of our usual aplomb, focus, and good humour. A distracted, lacklustre performance cost us the debate. It was a self-inflicted wound—and a valuable lesson. *Do not distress yourself with dark imaginings.*[45]

The Methodist College Literary Institute (MCLI) had been a catalyst and venue for debating showdowns in St. John's since 1866. It was my privilege only once to debate under its auspices and on its historic turf. My team was challenged to a debate on public education versus church-operated schools. The challengers were the legendary Albert Perlin, editor of the St. John's *Daily News* and a journalistic icon, and Memorial's president, Dr. Raymond Gushue. My debating partner and I acquitted ourselves well and were declared the winners.

Notwithstanding my many extracurricular preoccupations and the need to maintain focus as a student with graduation aspirations, my involvement in student activities earned me the President's Gold Merit Award, *for outstanding contribution to student affairs*. I could never quite decide wheth-

45 "Desiderata," a 1927 prose poem by American writer Max Ehrmann, 1872–1945

er I was deserving of the commendation or if Dr. Gushue was affirming he bore no grudge for the MCLI debate outcome.

My tutoring enterprise had quickly become a thriving business that continued to prosper, until I folded it two years later to accept a rural school principalship. Career-wise, that was a defining move, away from education as a business to educational administration. It was also a lifestyle change, a conscious values decision to trade my rapidly improving financial circumstances for a less opulent but, hopefully, more satisfying challenge in an arena I knew and loved, rural Newfoundland and, specifically, Springdale, a coastal community of 2,000 population, where I had earlier spent two rewarding years as a clergy-teacher-principal.

AMERICA BECKONS

In the days when Newfoundland was still independent, several American universities enrolled a sizable number of graduate students from the Rock. Even after we cast our lot with Canada, the practice continued. In May 1964, just days after my first Memorial University convocation, I joined the pilgrimage to American academe. My objective was a master's degree in educational administration. This time, money, that is to say, the lack of it, was not an obstacle. My myriad business ventures of the previous two years had secured a sound financial footing for me.

Which is undoubtedly why I was able to quickly immerse myself into the course of study at Boston University (BU). Without the time demands of my many extracurricular schemes, the master's program had my undivided attention. Well, almost. One diversion was hard to resist. The storied Fenway Park and the fabled Red Sox were just a stone's throw away across Commonwealth Avenue, and many an exciting afternoon I spent there.

I got my undergraduate degrees at Memorial. I got an education at BU. That's not an aspersion against Memorial, rather a comment on my mindset, increased maturity, and focus by the time I arrived at BU. The much smaller graduate classes also helped, as did their composition. My fellow Newfoundlander and good friend Ern Cluett and I were usually the youngest students in the room and, unlike most of the rest, without any administrative track record. Many of the others were seasoned educational managers at mid-career. The pressure was on Ern and me to measure up. Anonymity also played a role. Without the baggage of prior association, we were seen for who we were, just two more students determined to complete the program.

The presence of Ern and, surprisingly, three dozen other Newfoundlanders, made the adjustment to a foreign campus quite manageable ?

indeed, enjoyable. Eric Abbott, who would later become a valued member of my teaching staff, was completing his doctorate, as were Salvation Army officers Wil and Val England. A future Newfoundland minister of Education, Wallace House, and dozens of other school administrators from the Rock, were also there.

COMFORT FOOD

The rooftop of the Englands' accommodations was a welcome spot to cope with Boston heat and humidity and, especially, to gorge on Newfoundland cuisine.

Speaking of comfort food, Nestle's Pure Thick (canned) Cream was always a popular condiment among BU's Newfie mafia. On my second trip to Boston, the car trunk contained two cases of Nestle's. The US agent at the Calais, Maine, border crossing didn't buy my story, suspecting the cans concealed something far less innocent, maybe diamonds or drugs. With his bayonet, he pried open one can, then another, but found nothing to confirm his suspicions. As he stood there looking ridiculous, his hands dripping my precious cream, I tried a little humour: "If I were you, I'd lick 'em!"

He was not amused. His sticky right hand fled to his gun holster; he glared at me and walked away. All but two of the ninety-six cans of cream made it to the appreciative palates of Newfoundlanders in exile. Had the border agent taken my advice and licked his fingers, I might've had to surrender the whole stash!

Over the years, I have made literally hundreds of trips to the US, regularly interfacing with law enforcement personnel at border crossings, airports, and highway checkpoints. I'm sure that, in their off-duty hours, they're no different than the overwhelming majority of Americans whom I know—personable, generous, and inclusive. But here's the rub: When those same people don a uniform, wear a badge, or tote a gun, too many of them become stark raving maniacs, confrontational, humourless, and stone deaf. In a nod to Clint Eastwood, I call such types the *Make my day* posse. Rodney King[46] would have known exactly what I mean, as would Katie McCrary, the homeless woman in Decator, GA, beaten by police in July 2017 for begging in public.

---

erican construction worker beaten by Los Angeles police officers in 1991

CHAPTER 6
SON OF THE REGIMENT

While women weep, as they do now, I'll fight;
While little children go hungry, as they do now, I'll fight;
While men go to prison, . . . as they do now, I'll fight!
— William Booth, co-founder of the Salvation Army and its first General, 1829–1912

If we are to better the future, we must disturb the present.
— Catherine Booth, co-founder of the Salvation Army, 1829–1890

The Salvation Army's roots are in the east end of nineteenth-century London, England. Its founders, William and Catherine Booth, were moved by the need to minister to the unchurched and to mitigate poverty, alcohol abuse, and loneliness. The Booths' fiery brand of evangelism, with its humanitarian message and promise of redemption, found a ready following in Newfoundland and Labrador. A century and a half after the Army's 1865 founding, forty per cent of Canada's Salvationists live in the province.

DYED IN THE WOOL

My mother was a Sally Ann on steroids, a religious zealot. Decked out in the requisite navy blue serge uniform and the trademark Army bonnet of the day, weapons at the ready (a tambourine and a King James Bible rivalling in size a Canadian Tire auto parts catalogue) and a face-exploding smile showcasing her pearly whites, she conjured up a latter-day Ulysses Grant about to make his sixth and successful assault on the Mississippi.

The Skipper had a decidedly dim view of organized religion. Born into Methodism, Dad married Mom and the Army at the same time. His reasons for both, certainly the latter, seem to have been practical, rather than spiritual.

I was born in the Army. I am a son of the regiment. At eight years of age, I played in the junior brass band. At ten, I joined the senior band as second trombonist.

PROMOTION TO GLORY

The corps (church) brass band is sometimes pressed into service at Army funerals. As a boy wrestling with a man-sized trombone, I was intrigued by a song (hymn) often used on such occasions: "Rejoice for a comrade deceased!" For me, a preteen bandsman, the incongruity of a widow and her now-orphaned offspring standing before the husband's coffin singing about rejoicing while sobbing their hearts out seemed far-fetched. My fertile mind conjured up a deliciously mischievous paraphrase: "Thank God, the old fool is dead!"

The Salvation Army theology implicit in that sentiment—*Rejoice for a comrade deceased*—was lost on my young mind. Promotion to Glory, a blissful eternity in the afterlife, was not a concept I had internalized. Many years later, I sat near the saintly Janet Wiseman at the funeral of her husband, General Clarence Wiseman[47]. The beatific serenity which lit up her face as she gazed into the open coffin bespoke the absolute certainty of her faith that his passing was but a temporary parting until, in the words of another Army staple, "we meet at Jesus's feet."

My irreverent rewrite of the funeral hymn sounds like a copycat adaptation of "Ding-dong, the witch is dead." Not so. Though Dorothy and the Munchkins hit the big screen the year I was born, I was blissfully unaware of *The Wizard of Oz* or any other film since moviegoing ranked among the Army's comprehensive list of deadly sins. The first movie I saw was *Singin' in the Rain*. Well, I saw part of it. Within minutes of falling madly in love with Debbie Reynolds, my fantasy was rudely interrupted by the theatre manager with a summons from my dad, but really from my mother, who had dispatched him to order me home, rescued yet again from Satan's persistent clutches!

By the age of twelve, I knew precisely what my future would be. The Army's Canadian weekly fired my imagination with stirring accounts of its overseas onslaught on poverty, disease, and godlessness, and I pictured myself at the centre of the action. I would be a medical missionary in Africa! In pursuit of that dream, I would later enrol as an officer cadet at the College for Officer Training in St. John's. By then, two years in close quarters and cut off from

47 The Salvation Army's tenth international leader (1974–1977)

the larger world at St. Anthony had prepared me well for the monastic routine at the training college. Importantly, the year in officer training gave me a solid grounding in theology, sharpened my moral focus, and schooled me in the imperatives of social service.

Hospital visitation was an integral part of our training college routine. One such occasion I still vividly recall. As my fellow cadet Wilbur Seabright and I made our way along a corridor of the old St. John's General Hospital, we were startled by piercing shrieks. I froze in my tracks. "I know that voice. I've heard it before. That has to be Skiffington!" It was. Years earlier, I had watched from the shadows as my father and his crew extricated a badly scalded man from a train wreck. Now, five years after the derailment, he was enduring yet the latest of excruciating skin-grafting procedures which, coupled with a low pain threshold, would have accounted for his screaming.

At twenty-one, I was ordained as a clergyman. Medicine and overseas service continued to be my game plan. In what must have been one of my first press interviews, I told a reporter, "I've had my eyes set on Africa since grade six."[48] Subsequent career choices, as you will see, took me well away from a missionary trajectory.

Meanwhile, I was dispatched to Springdale as principal of the Army's all-grade school. In addition to my education responsibilities, I wore a second hat as assistant corps officer (pastor). It was my job to pinch-hit for the senior clergy when they were indisposed or out of town. Such an occasion was a cemetery committal for an infant. As I approached the grieving family's home, the father, tiny coffin under one arm, a shovel in hand, emerged and got into my car.

My preparation for the committal rite had presumed an audience of more than one. Yet here I was at the open grave with just a distraught father, a miniature casket, and a shovel. For his sake, I felt I had to go through at least an abbreviated version of my carefully planned order of service, in the process racking up a dubious achievement, just one of many to follow. It marked the first and, I promise, the only time I got to render a tenor solo, heartfelt, though not especially melodic.

> "Gentle Jesus, meek and mild, look upon a little child . . .
> In the kingdom of Thy grace, give a little child a place."

My audience didn't join in, being consumed with his loss. At the appropriate moment in the ritual, he put the shovel to use. The sight of a par-

48 *Evening Telegram*, St. John's, July 28, 1960 ("Teacher-Preacher Has Busy School Days")

ent burying his own child was too much for me. I grabbed the shovel. "Alf, go, sit in the car!" I finished the job. Reflecting later, I realized it had been a learning moment. Basing your plans/actions on incomplete information or false premises can result in unexpected, unpleasant, even bizarre outcomes.

BITING THE BULLET

I've always balked at rules, especially those which seem to serve no logical purpose. Even when they do, the one-size-fits-all template can create more havoc than solutions. That's one of the reasons I turned in my commission as a Salvation Army officer fewer than three years after ordination. That was one tough decision. I love the Army. Its ingenious formula for outreach has stood the test of time for over a century and a half. A book published in 2001 declared the Army to be "the most effective organization in the United States." Its track record in 127 other countries is equally impressive. According to the late Peter Drucker, American management consultant and author, "No one even comes close to [the Salvation Army] in respect to clarity of mission, ability to innovate, measurable results, dedication, and putting money to maximum use."

Since many of the Army's services are volunteer-delivered and its full-time personnel receive rock-bottom salaries, the organization invests in its programs more than ninety cents of every dollar raised. This is in sharp contrast to other charitable organizations. For example, out of every dollar the United Way receives, about fifty-one cents goes to related charity causes. In the case of the American Red Cross, it's thirty-nine cents.[49]

The genesis of my departure from officer ranks can be traced to the family situation referenced earlier. Suddenly confronted with a severe financial dilemma not of my making, my plan to return to university was no longer possible. The one person I needed to turn to was back home in England on holiday. Army protocol required that any change in my plans needed the okay of the vacationing Provincial Commander. Only he could assign me to an alternate posting. In his absence, I bit the bullet and took a teaching position in Labrador for the express purpose of mitigating my severe financial conundrum.

On his return, the Colonel was not amused, as I had fully expected. What surprised me, though, was the hard line he adopted which, from my perspective, rode roughshod over my predicament. His inflexible, oft-repeated mantra was "Rules are rules." Society and institutions have rules for good reason. But a robotic application of them, irrespective of circumstances, is cockamamie and, more to the point, counterproductive.

I was determined to hang in, to put our disagreement behind us, but in

---

49 www.snopes.com/politics/business/charities.asp

several meetings with my superior officer, the Colonel didn't budge, leaving me with few options. After six months of this stalemate, I threw in the towel. I reluctantly resigned my officership and went to ground, ignoring repeated attempts by the Colonel, my officer girlfriend, and other friends to contact me. The die was cast. It was my Rubicon.

The whole experience cemented my abhorrence of rules for rules' sake. Happily, it did not sour my passion for or my commitment to the Army. The organization's value set and goals continue to be my standard, a litmus test of principle in my decisions. I was a proud member of its advisory board on Vancouver Island for thirteen years and was involved in a similar capacity in Seattle. During my Ottawa days, I served on the Army's national Commission on Moral and Social Issues.

"WITH HEART TO GOD AND HAND TO MAN"[50]

In 1990, I was in Nairobi, Kenya, for the Commonwealth Parliamentary Association AGM. As is my habit when travelling abroad, I phoned the Salvation Army's headquarters: "Is there anybody here from Canada?"

The receptionist, a Brit, picked up on my accent: "I can do better than that. There's two Newfies here, Majors Wil and Val England!" I couldn't believe my luck. Dr. Wil and Dr. Val were old friends from my Boston days. Wil asked what I'd like to do. "I'd love to go to Thika," I said, trading on my boyhood fascination with the Army's work among the disadvantaged. Thika, thirty miles from Nairobi, is an amazing operation. Close to 1,000 visually impaired children and adults are in residence, attending either school or job-training programs. It's a labour of love that the Army has been carrying on for nearly a century.

Major Wil and I spent an unforgettable, exhilarating day at Thika. An indelible memory are the happy faces of several hundred children singing a succession of inspirational songs. Though the lyrics were in Swahili, the familiar tunes were the same ones I had so often played as an Army bandsman in Bishop's Falls and St. John's, Springdale and St. Anthony, Cambridge, MA, Oshawa, and Ottawa.

TWO-PRONGED ARMY

The Army's dual role as a social agency and an evangelical religious organization and its long-standing outreach in 175 languages around the world are a reality that many people in urban North America do not comprehend. I recall a conversation in the fall of 1981 with the minister responsible for

50 An early Salvation Army slogan popularized by the Army's founder, William Booth. Of late, political correctness discourages its use.

Canada Post, André Ouellet, an erudite Montrealer. The Salvation Army's request for a postage stamp to mark the organization's centenary in Canada the following year had been denied. As the lone Salvationist in Parliament, I had agreed to see if the decision could be reversed. After André and I got past the pleasantries, it soon became clear that he knew zilch about the Army, including any cognizance of its humanitarian focus. Once up to speed, Ouellet kindly recommended to the Stamp Advisory Committee that a stamp be issued. It was my pleasure, on behalf of the Government of Canada, to launch the new stamp in the presence of the Army's leader, General Jarl Wahlstrom, Manitoba Premier Howard Pawley, my good friend Lloyd Axworthy[51], and 3,000 appreciative Sally Anns attending the organization's national congress in Winnipeg.

A former federal caucus colleague and House of Commons Speaker displayed his ignorance of the Salvation Army at a most awkward time for me. General Bramwell Tillsley, the Army's fourteenth international leader and the third Canadian[52] to hold that office, had come to Ottawa for a meet-and-greet with parliamentarians. I approached the Speaker with a request, that the General's presence in the House gallery be acknowledged from the Chair, standard practice for international office-holders, but also for provincial ministers and celebrities. The Speaker turned thumbs down on the request. I was not amused.

"What if he was the Pope?"

"Absolutely! It would be an honour to welcome His Holiness."

"I agree. What about the moderator of the United Church of Canada?"

"Yes, it would be my pleasure to do so."

"Tell me, what's different about my guy?"

"Your guy is not the head of a significant organization."

The Speaker did agree to receive the General and his entourage in private, but it was clear that gesture had more to do with extending a courtesy to a fellow MP than showing respect for an international church leader and humanitarian.

Not "a significant organization"? Tell that to the legions of homeless persons who get to sleep in the Army's 25,000 hostel beds worldwide. Tell that to the 16,000,000 destitute people in more than 100 countries who were served by Army caregivers in 2017. Every fifteen seconds, someone in Can-

---

51 Manitoba MLA, MP, minister, university president

52 The Army's first Canadian to head the organization was a Newfoundlander, Clarence Wiseman; the second was Arnold Brown. A fourth Canadian and the third woman, Linda Bond, led the Army from 2011 to 2013. Brian Peddle's 2018 election as General made him the second Newfoundlander and fifth Canadian chosen by the Army's High Council. One American, Paul Rader, has held the position (1994–99).

ada is served a meal by the Salvation Army. Significance, like beauty, is in the eye of the beholder. Speaker Peter Milliken handled a similar request from me with aplomb and class. The Army's leaders for Canada and Bermuda, Commissioners Bill and Marilyn Francis, and its provincial leaders in Ontario and Quebec were hosted at lunch by Speaker Milliken and later welcomed to the House as guests in the Speaker's gallery.

I played in Salvation Army bands for more than fifty years. During my Ottawa days, I welcomed the regular respite from the machinations and prima donnas of Parliament Hill by participating in the weekly band rehearsal at Ottawa Citadel. In 1992, the band toured the Netherlands. We were humbled, again and again, by the Dutch response to the Salvation Army and to Canada, both of which had figured so helpfully during their World War II ordeal and their 1945 liberation.

Glenwood, NL, 1954. On a weekend road trip with the Bishop's Falls Salvation Army Band. L-R back row: Bandmaster Allen Deering, Billy Kennedy, Steve Deering, Billy Vokey, Don Thorne, Jack Stanley, Harold Pelley, Ray Reid, Jack Deering, Ray Wight, Captain Frank Jennings. Middle row: Bill Randell, Carl Budgell, Herb Mitchell, Roger Simmons, Jack Pretty. Front row: Howard Thorne, Lloyd Earle. (Author photo)

The Canadian war grave at Groesbeck is close to the bridge in the 1977 movie *A Bridge Too Far*. On behalf of the Parliament of Canada, I laid a wreath at the cemetery, the final resting place of more than 2,000 Canadian soldiers. As band members paused before individual markers, noting the ages of the fallen, our flugel horn player put into words what others around her were thinking: "They were younger than I am!" Nineteen-year-old Debbie van der Horden had internalized war's mad butchery.

St. John's, 1957. The Salvation Army Citadel trombone section. L-R: Doug Osmond, Fred Garland, Roger Simmons, Dave Dawe, Rance Crocker, Lloyd Abbott. (Author photo)

Left: St. John's, 1959. Cadet Roger Simmons, the Salvation Army. (Author photo) Right: Groesbeek, Netherlands, 1992. While on tour with the Ottawa Citadel Salvation Army Band, I laid a wreath at the Canadian War Cemetery on behalf of the Government of Canada. (Author photo)

Ottawa, 1994. With Salvation Army maestri. L-R: Colonel Robert Redhead, Bandmaster, International Staff Band; Doug Burden, B/M, Ottawa Citadel Band; Brian Burditt, B/M, Canadian Staff Band. (Author photo)

Vancouver, 2003. General John Larsson and Commissioner Freda Larsson were my guests of honour at a reception I hosted during the Salvation Army's congress. (Major John Murray photo)

Victoria, BC, circa 2015. Majors (later Lt-Cols) John and Brenda Murray, me, Marcella and (later Bandmaster) Dave Osmond. (Author photo)

CHAPTER 7
MENTOR ON THE MOVE

The mind is not a vessel to be filled, but a fire to be kindled.
— Plutarch, Greek-Roman biographer and philosopher, 40–120 AD

Before the advent of roads ended the isolation of most of outport Newfoundland and Labrador, the SS *Northern Ranger* and several sister ships serviced outlying communities, bringing mail, foodstuffs, building supplies, and people to remote settlements. As the storied *Ranger* entered St. Anthony harbour on Labour Day, 1957, I got my first glimpse of the town that would be my workplace for the next two years. And what a spectacular sight it was! My initial reaction was relief. Ever since I had learned the location of my first teaching assignment, everyone felt compelled to prepare me for the worst.

"You won't last till Christmas in that godforsaken place," they predicted.

"You'll freeze," they warned.

"How will you pass the time? There's no hockey rink, no place to swim, no road connection to the highway system."

As the *Ranger* glided up the harbour, the stunning vista unfolding before me was an animated, odourized, audio postcard. The occasional motorboat chugged across our heading while others danced at their moorings as our wake invaded their calm. Colourfully painted dwellings clung to the shoreline and the hillsides. Dozens of quaint-looking fishing stages teetered precariously above the landwash. Men could be seen on the stageheads, probably mending fishing nets or splitting cod after a day on the water. A woman retrieved laundry from a clothesline. Two other women and a child were busy on a fish flake[53]. The occasional vehicle navigated the gravel road which traced the harbour's contour.

53 A flake is a raised horizontal lattice of small lungers (poles), usually covered with spruce boughs and supported by upright poles, allowing the air to circulate underneath. Codfish, having been salt-cured, are spread out on the flakes to dry in the sun.

The shock treatment doled out by my well-intentioned friends back home was doing its therapeutic job. Abysmally low expectations gave way to exhilaration as I rapidly revised my prospects for surviving, thriving even, in this surprising, pleasant place. I pressed against the rail on the ship's port side. A clutch of institutional-looking buildings caught my attention. One of the structures proclaimed in billboard-sized words: *Faith, hope, love . . . and the greatest of these is love.*

LIFE IS A FIELD OF HONOUR[54]

I soon learned that the signage was the work of Dr., later Sir, Wilfred Grenfell. The young English doctor had a desire to provide medical service in a far-flung corner of the world, the selfsame dream that had long been my obsession. He was dispatched to Newfoundland to investigate the conditions in the Labrador fishery, arriving in St. John's the day after the Great Fire of 1892. It was the start of Dr. Grenfell's lifelong work among northern people. Within a year, he built a hospital at Battle Harbour, Labrador. An ever-expanding network of nursing stations sprang up across northern Newfoundland and on the Labrador coast. Grenfell tapped into the wanderlust and conscience of young doctors and nurses in the US and Europe, recruiting a team that transformed St. Anthony into a culturally diverse enclave.

Grenfell's marriage to a wealthy Chicago socialite launched a whole new phase in his legendary career. Now, with a ready pipeline to the monied aristocrats of corporate America, coupled with his already well-cultivated access to England's deep pockets and Canadian philanthropy, he was able to dream big, and dream he did. By 1927, a new state-of-the-art medical facility replaced the original St. Anthony hospital built in 1900.

First and foremost, Sir Wilfred was a social reformer, as evidenced by his initiatives to mitigate poverty and his outreach to orphans. He was also a prolific writer and authored more than a dozen books. *Adrift on an Ice-Pan* chronicles his close call with mortality on Easter Sunday, 1908, when his dogsled went through the ice. He survived the night on an ice pan and "avoided freezing to death by sacrificing three dogs for their skins. The next day he . . . was rescued by local fishermen."[55]

By my standards, St. Anthony was a remote outpost. My world, heretofore, had taken for granted hydroelectricity, paved streets, indoor plumbing, and artificial ice arenas. Movies, train travel, and year-round road transportation were the norm for me. Some homes in St. Anthony had electricity, but only intermittently. The reliable Delco engine in the shed behind the house

54 The inscription on Dr. Wilfred Grenfell's burial plaque in St. Anthony
55 http://www.biographi.ca/en/bio/grenfell_wilfred_thomason

was coaxed into life at dusk and switched off at bedtime, allowing its owner and a lucky neighbour or two a brief respite from the ever-present kerosene mantle lamp. The generator was a welcome source of light for reading and listening to the radio. Powered refrigeration was the luxury of the few who could afford to run their Delcos round the clock. TV was all but unknown, certainly unavailable.

The town of my childhood, Bishop's Falls, though in the same latitude as Seattle and Paris, is no stranger to cold winter temperatures and snow. Compared to St. Anthony, however, Bishop's, as the locals call it, is a tropical paradise. My detractors had been right on one count. A guy could freeze to death in this place!

Situated at the northern tip of Newfoundland, St. Anthony faces the brooding, unforgiving North Atlantic. The winter weather can be brutal. It wasn't uncommon, following a winter night's sleep, to wake up to the sight of frost buildup on the wooden ceiling and snow on the bed, as much a comment on the house insulation as on the storm raging outside. In an age before duct tape and silicone sealant, I minimized the indoor snowdrift by stuffing my socks into the small openings between wall and window.

Not that the weather was always miserable. Picture-perfect, sun-drenched winter days with not a cloud to be seen were frequent. The spectacular moonlit nights and the kaleidoscopic aurora borealis displays were surreal, captivating panoramas. Your encounter with adrenalin is incomplete until you've hustled through a game of hockey on the frozen harbour in sub-zero temperatures. A guy's youth is less magic if he doesn't get to chauffeur his favourite girl in a rowboat under the floodlight that is the northern moon.

ALL IN A DAY'S WORK

Yes, sailing into St. Anthony harbour on Labour Day was an exhilarating moment. The following morning, not so much. I stepped into the classroom of the two-room all-grade school, of which I was the teacher-principal with direct responsibility for students in grades six to eleven, at that time the final year of high school. Reality, plus a good dose of nostalgia, kicked in.

I surveyed my uninspiring surroundings, essentially four dingy walls and a ceiling that had once been white. Years of smoke from a pot-bellied stove in the middle of the classroom had transformed both ceiling and walls into a drab, depressing grey. I sized up my thirty-two new charges, ranging in age from eleven to seventeen, garbed in homespun sweaters and pants, skirts and white blouses, most of which, I later learned, were hand-me-downs from older siblings, bought at the Grenfell Mission's annual clothing sale or newly arrived from Eaton's or Simpson's. I was the oldest person in the room, but only by a year. Second-guessing why I had signed up for this kamikaze venture and seized with the enormity of the task ahead, I mentally editorialized on the prospects at hand: *There's not much here!*

The following few days, I somehow fumbled through. Evening hours were spent planning enough activities to keep five grades occupied, ideally in a productive way, while I attempted to teach math or English to the remaining grade, all the while doing my best to rein in the restlessness and chattiness of two dozen or so preteens and teenagers. The heat source was that pot-bellied stove. Parents supplied the firewood, and male students took turns lighting the fire an hour or so before class time. On bitterly cold days, the desks were rearranged in a tight circle around the stove, and I involved the entire class, all six grades, in a single exercise, which worked especially well for literature, history, and geography.

One Sunday evening at the Salvation Army Citadel, I surveyed the worshippers, including many of my students, as they joined in a heartfelt rendering of "Abide With Me." I wondered how many of them understood what they were saying in song. Monday morning, I began the school day by writing a line from the hymn on the blackboard: "*Swift to its close ebbs out life's little day.*" I asked the students to paraphrase. None could. Only after I reconfigured the sentence, prodded them to substitute synonyms for *swift*, and canvassed the ebbing imagery did they realize what the author[56] was saying: Life is short.

Unfamiliar literary and cultural references can trip up a student. The province-wide exam in grade ten art that year called for the design of a restaurant placemat. The question was worth a third of the total mark. My students, indeed rural scholars as a whole, were at a distinct disadvantage. There were no restaurants in St. Anthony. Placemats were a foreign concept. I was so incensed with the urban bias of the question that I protested to the provincial exam authority, which agreed to eliminate the placemat item from the scoring process.

As circumstances, but especially my attitude, got better, I began to address some matters requiring immediate resolution. First among these was the urgent need to make the classroom a hygienically fit place in which to teach and learn.

56 Henry Francis Lyte (1793–1847), an Anglican vicar in Brixham, England, was a published poet and accomplished hymnist who also penned "Jesus, I My Cross Have Taken" and "Praise, My Soul, the King of Heaven."

Having decided that a little soap and water could do no harm, I commandeered the entire class to join me on a Saturday morning, buckets, mops, and scrub cloths in tow. We applied lots of elbow grease to the walls and ceiling, with mixed results. When we threw in the towel several hours later, the surfaces we had tackled were as depressingly grey as ever. However, the session proved to be a highly effective bonding exercise.

It was time for a cover-up. So, off to the general store I went. I asked proprietor Ben Fennimore if he had a few gallons of paint that wasn't selling, probably because of its ghastly colour. And he did. The school had its first corporate sponsor as Ben donated the ugliest dark green paint imaginable. That, and a can or two of white, did the trick. Soon after, I had hand-brushed the classroom wainscotting a dark green. The upper walls and ceiling became a soothing pastel green, thanks to the white paint. Not quite like the upper reaches of the Sistine Chapel, but, like it, my paint job served its intended purpose.

Next, I tackled classroom management. One of the challenges of a multi-grade class is trying to instruct one grade without unduly distracting the others. I sought to minimize the problem by having three of the grades face the blackboard-equipped front wall while the other grades faced a side wall. That called for a second blackboard. When the specialty paint I had ordered from St. John's arrived, it was, alas, not black. The new green blackboard cemented the notion already rampant around town that the new teacher was a bona fide nutso! Everyone knew that blackboards are black, other than city paint suppliers.

Now that I was irretrievably immersed in my dual passions of broadening minds and reprising Michelangelo, my dismissive assessment of the students and their environs, muttered to myself on that unnerving first day of school, badly needed a rewrite. As I found my feet and upped my game, I discovered my comfort level with the class and began bonding with individual students.

And I soon realized that a real gem of a young woman was right under my nose. Glorina, one of two grade eleven students, sat in the front row. All the pedagogy textbooks and professors warned of the folly of getting too friendly with students. "Incubate them; don't date them. Coddle them but don't cuddle them." Ahem! Let's just say that, once the winsome blonde over by the window caught my attention, a whole new chapter in pupil-teacher relationships blossomed as we rowed across the harbour in the family punt, hung out with friends, and oohed and aahed at the magic of the northern lights.

Once high school was behind her, it was time for Glorina to pursue her dream of becoming a nurse. On a January night, she boarded the SS *North-*

ern Ranger, a full two months before her Grace Hospital training began. The early departure for St. John's was dictated by the impending ice blockade, an annual occurrence in St. Anthony's harbour and other northern ports. As dockhands freed the ship's lines, I bid my bosom pal a fond farewell. The ship sounded a long blast, signalling its departure and Glorina's. It would not be the last I saw of either, the weather-beaten old ship[57] or the vivacious young woman.

St. Anthony was a friendly, inclusive place. There were frequent invites to supper with students' families and the scattered chance to attend a Grenfell social event. Fraternizing with a medic from London, befriending a nurse from Edinburgh, and snowshoeing with a Manhattan lab aide were among my new pastimes. My detractors back in Bishop's would not get the last laugh after all.

There was courting, St. Anthony style, on the hilltop overlooking the endless, turbulent North Atlantic, the moon dancing on the breakers below, the endless lament of the lighthouse foghorn moaning nearby. And on Saturdays, there was brook trout fishing. If you're going to make inroads with the girlfriend's folks, what better way than tagging along with her father on his weekly trouting excursion and ending the day with a scoff of trout and tatties, rustled up by her mother?

St. Anthony, NL, 1958. Glorina Simms, Roger Simmons. (Author photo)

57 The SS *Northern Ranger* was launched in Scotland in 1936 and operated by the Newfoundland Railway/Canadian National Railways for thirty years.

CLOSE CALLS

My first sojourn in St. Anthony was, except for one brief excursion, a long one, lasting from early September to July 10. That's the day the long-awaited first passenger boat of the season was able to punch its way through pack ice in the harbour.

St.Anthony, NL, 1958. Headed for a bash in high society. (Glorina Simms photo)

The one respite was during the Christmas school break. Having arranged to hook a ride on the twice-weekly mail plane, I was excited at the prospect of getting home for the holidays. But the weather didn't play ball. Six days of watching the sky and checking the barometer crawled by before bush pilot Bill Bennett and I finally lifted off the harbour ice on Boxing Day. I rode shotgun and was given a vital task. The window beside me had a gaping hole, remedied by having me hold a mailbag against it. The two-hour trip promised to be cold but otherwise uneventful. Cold, it certainly was. And Mother Nature threw us a scary curveball.

Visual flying conditions were marginal, so we followed the coastline south. The weather abruptly closed in, leaving us without a point of reference. Instantaneously, Bill spiralled upward. With mountains to the west, he stood the aircraft virtually on its end and sped toward a safe altitude, as we frantically peered into the driving snow, searching for a patch of sky. I spotted a sheer rock face straight ahead and yelled, "There!"

Bill hauled the Cessna 172 sharply upwards and to the left, snatched a glance at the instrument panel, and headed out to sea. Gingerly, he inched the plane downwards, and eventually we spotted the ocean 600 feet below. The harrowing and freezing ride ended an hour or so later without further incident as we bounced onto the runway at Gander. A short train ride put me in Bishop's by sundown.

More than twenty years later, I would have another, eerily similar brush with mortality, this time with my wife, Miriam, and three-year-old Paul aboard the aircraft. Following an election campaign event in Burgeo, we were flying west to Port aux Basques in a Cessna 180 float plane. It was late on a November evening, and the weather was threatening but flyable. Well into the flight, though, we found ourselves in a snowstorm. The pilot made a split-second U-turn and found a hole in the sky. Still, with nightfall approaching, we had lost valuable time. The pilot decided we couldn't make it back to Burgeo before dark, so he headed westward once more, flying just above the waves and taking his bearings from the coastline. After a couple more hairy encounters with the blinding, swirling snow, we put down safely in Harbour le Cou[58] well after dusk and covered the final thirty miles to our destination by car.

IN THE RINK AND ON THE MOUND

The wireless operators at St. Anthony, Wils Calloway and Ed Collis, had, like me, spent their earlier lives in less rural environments and were itching for some action. Ours was the age-old choice: Do we sit around and grumble about the problem or tackle it? We decided an outdoor ice rink would fit the bill and set about to make it happen. Identifying a piece of level land and receiving generous donations of plywood from local merchants kick-started the project. Needing a little seed money, we concocted the St. Anthony Athletic Association and peddled membership cards at fifty cents a head.

Our next institutional creation was the St. Anthony Amateur Hockey League. In no time, I was suiting up as left-winger and playing coach of the Eastside Ramblers. In later years, the town graduated to an artificial ice surface, and hockey continues to thrive there.

My moment in the sports spotlight, professionally speaking, would have to wait another forty years or so. When it finally came, it lasted a full ten seconds. I was drafted by the Seattle Mariners organization—to throw the first pitch at a Toronto Blue Jays game. With a dazzling windup and a Herculean toss, the ball hurtled toward home plate. My friends were certain I had just made baseball history, combining a splitter, a curveball, and a knuckler in a single pitch. Alas, major league scouts must have been looking the other way. Or, just maybe, they were not that impressed with where the ball landed. Midway between the catcher and me. Details!

MOVING ON

The two years in St. Anthony were an unforgettable experience and a transformative period for me. The marvellous humanity of the locals, their solid work ethic, and upbeat demeanour were infectious. I felt very much a part of the community. All too soon, it was time to move on, first to a summer ses-

58 Burgeo, Port aux Basques, and Harbour le Cou are communities on Newfoundland's southwest coast.

sion at Memorial University, then to the Salvation Army College for Officer Training in St. John's.

Graduation from the College meant I had become an ordained clergyman with the rank of Probationary Lieutenant. As well, I held provincial accreditation as a teacher. The Army brass appointed[59] me as an assistant clergy and teacher-principal of its five-room school at Springdale. My teaching responsibility involved grades eight to eleven, then the last year of high school and the prerequisite for university enrolment.

A PROGRESSIVE TOWN

One of the most idyllic places you'll find anywhere, Springdale hugs the western coastline of beautiful Hall's Bay, a long, sheltered finger of Green Bay, on Newfoundland's northeast coast. First inhabited by the aboriginal Beothuk and Mi'kmaq peoples, European settlers arrived in the area in the late nineteenth century, drawn by its huge stands of harvestable timber and a freshwater spring. Sawmilling thrived and, in 1878, a massive copper discovery earned nearby Little Bay the title of the El Dorado of Newfoundland. Other discoveries followed, and mining employed hundreds until 1972, when slumping world copper prices forced the shutdown of all three local mines. When I took up residence there, the mines were in their heyday, employing more than 1,000 workers.

Springdale, like St. Anthony three years earlier, would become an epiphany for me. It was there I came into my own as an educator and community activist, there that my approaches to leadership and teamwork were shaped, there that I was impacted by countless manifestations of generosity and compassion without limits.

MEASURING UP TO THE CHALLENGE

The Salvation Army Academy to which I had been assigned, though a brand new building, was a bare-bones facility—five classrooms, an auditorium, a staff room, and an office. The library was a wall of shelves in the staff room. There were no sports facilities. The Army also operated a two-room, all-grade school in Springdale's west end.

It takes a whole lot of ingenuity and dedication to provide a well-rounded education in such straightened circumstances. My four teacher colleagues were very much up to the task, and together we improvised on the fly. My

59 Unlike the accepted practice in other churches, Salvation Army officers did not have much say, if any, in which community they would minister. Rather, they were assigned to their posts at the behest of the organization's regional leaders. Nowadays, appointees are canvassed to determine their preferences before assignments are finalized.

inherited carpentry skills were brought into play to construct a couple of Ping-Pong tables, in the process introducing the game not only to the school but to the community as well. Years later, the town would boast a provincial table tennis champion, Cathy Wells.

Next to the school, we built the community's first outdoor ice rink, drawing on my St. Anthony apprenticeship. Our humble achievement was shortly mimicked elsewhere in town. In jig time, the community had two good ice surfaces, subject only to the vagaries of weather and volunteer upkeep. People of all ages flocked to the rinks for skating parties and pickup hockey games.

MIXED MESSAGES

A sombre atmosphere hung over the Monday morning school assembly. Two days earlier, Byron, a kindergarten student, was sledding when his coaster collided with a passing car, killing him instantly. In one of life's tough coincidences, I had previously arranged for an RCMP officer to talk to the student body about safety. On this heartbreaking occasion, the constable had no trouble commanding the attention of even the most fidgety child as he stressed the wisdom of walking on the left side of the street facing traffic, reinforcing his message by engaging students:

"On the street, where should you walk?"

"On the left!" shouted the students as one.

The next item on the assembly's agenda was a choral recital by the primary grades, including Byron's classmates. The teacher/conductor had chosen a medley of Salvation Army ditties, including one which drew on biblical imagery of life as a highway. Thirty or so five-to-eight-year-olds lustily contradicted the constable's admonition as they broke into song:

"Little children, if you want to go to Heaven when you die,
Walk in the middle of the road."

Even a good metaphor has its limitations. How could I explain to an audience so young that treading life's one-directional highway can be even more treacherous than dodging two-way traffic and entails very different choices?

EDUCATION MAKEOVER

In addition to the two Salvation Army schools and the United Church School, Springdale had a fourth, operated by the Pentecostal Assemblies. All four taught kindergarten to grade eleven. The duplication of school facilities was robbing the town of 2,000 souls of any chance to offer an adequate education to its children and youth. Yet factions within the community clung steadfastly to the status quo. Fortunately, wiser minds eventually prevailed. All three school boards decided to integrate their high school students in a single institution. At the eleventh hour, provincial Pentecostal authorities overruled its local board. The remaining two sects forged ahead, and in short order, Springdale's amalgamated high school graduated from idea to construction project.

Meanwhile, after two eventful and satisfying years at Springdale, I had reluctantly pulled up stakes to head back to university. By the time the new amalgamated regime was gearing up, I had been away from the town nearly three years, though I had kept a close eye on what was happening there. As I was completing my studies at Memorial University, I got a call from the secretary of the amalgamated school board, offering me the principalship of the new high school. Flattered though I was, and in the market for just such a position, I nevertheless declined the offer. I said I would apply for the position only if it was publicly advertised. The prospect of that job excited me, but having it handed to me on a silver platter could spell trouble down the road.

When the ad ran, I responded. Once again, the position was offered to me. I accepted, once I got clarification from the board concerning a specific issue. I needed the freedom to assemble my own team of professionals. This ran counter to existing practice across the province. School board staffing committees did the hiring of teachers, almost always on the basis of written applications and, usually, without interviewing prospective teachers. This method was, in my view, a recipe for disaster. The board agreed and gave me authority to engage the required personnel in consultation, of course, with the board's staffing committee. The result was a cohesive team of professional educators and support staff who proved key to successfully kick-starting the new school.

Premier Joey Smallwood was on hand to officially open the school and to announce its name: Grant Collegiate. It paid tribute to a very special man. Harvey Grant was Springdale's first mayor, a position he held for twenty years, and a wily community leader whose ingenuity earned him the nickname "The Fox." My senior by nearly half a century, Grant and I became good friends. I learned much about humility and courage from him, and it was on my recommendation that the school board named the new facility to honour this man whose exemplary community activism, feistiness, and integrity set the bar very high for those who came after.

The premier's presence turned the official opening into a media event. CBC's legendary Harry Brown did a one-on-one with the new school's namesake:

"Mr. Grant, this place is state-of art. Science lab, French lab, lecture theatre, gymnasium. Quite a change since you went to school."

A priceless moment is captured on film. A split-screen composite amplifies the interviewer's deer-in-the-headlights reaction to Grant's laid-back demeanour and matter-of-fact response: "I never went to school."

The teaching team was top-notch—professional, well-educated, and caring. We rolled up our sleeves. In short order, Grant Collegiate established itself as a progressive learning institution and was soon holding its own provincially, winning awards in music and sports. Academic excellence was reflected in student success in the mandatory province-wide exams. As my four years as principal wound down, a national study team cited Grant as one of Canada's top ten high schools.

TRAGEDY STRIKES

On a December morning, I was in the Grant Collegiate staff lounge striving, as principal, to manage a heart-rending crisis as my fellow educators, Brian Peckford included, tried to come to grips with the previous night's shocker. The school secretary, Peggy Fair, and her banker husband, Bob, drowned when their car missed a curve and plunged into a frozen lake while returning home from a dinner party that included the entire school staff.

The double tragedy was not only the talk of the town but was all over the regional airwaves. Initial radio news flashes identified the victims as a Grant Collegiate staffer and a bank manager. I fielded the non-stop barrage of phone calls from parents, friends, and the press. Larry Peckford was an early caller. Aware of his brother's friendship with Bob Fair, Larry expected, indeed assumed, the worst. As I mouthed a muted hello into the phone, he bellowed hysterically, "Roge, where's Brian?"

"He's here with me."

"No, he's not! He's in that car!"

As I indicated that Brian was coming to the phone, Larry, convinced I was playing a cruel joke, continued to verbalize his despair: "No, no! He's in that car! He's gone!" You can imagine Larry's relief and joy when he heard his brother's voice!

Perhaps the most unforgettable moment occurred a few hours after the tragedy. Our library assistant, Joan Spencer, had driven to the party venue with the Fairs. In what turned out to be a fateful move, she switched to Maurice Budgell's car for the ride home. It was Maurice and Joan who were the first on the accident scene, arriving moments after the fatal event and knowing the identity of the occupants in the car which had preceded them out of the party venue's parking area.

Later, having been told by police that nothing could be done till morning, we commiserated and consoled each other. I noticed that Joan was absent and learned that Maurice had dropped her off at her house. Convinced that the tragedy had reduced her to a basket case, I felt she shouldn't be left alone with her inconsolable grief. I phoned her number. It was 2:00 a.m. Her mother's sleepy, annoyed response told me volumes.

"Joan's in bed."

"It's important I speak to her."

The mother put her eighteen-year-old daughter on the phone, and I said just one word, "Joan." Her response was blood-curdling. "It's true, isn't it!" she screamed. This was the same teenager who had, a few short hours earlier, stood at lakeside, saw the hole in the ice and the headlights of the car below, pondered the monumental significance for herself, and gasped, "I was supposed to be in that car!"

Joan had gone home and eaten a bedtime snack as she enthusiastically dazzled her mother with details of a wonderful dinner party. She made no reference to the double drowning, showed no signs that anything was amiss, and, soon in bed, fell fast asleep. In the blink of an eye, the sound of my voice had intrusively reasserted the catastrophic reality. The phenomenal ability of the human mind to shield us from the unthinkable is truly amazing.

BETWEEN A ROCK AND A HARD PLACE

A member of the Grant teaching staff poked his nose into my office doorway with the school troublemaker in tow and tossed me an ultimatum: "Either he goes, or I go!" The student was a frequent visitor to my office as teacher after teacher tried to cope with his insolence. Staff meetings regularly contemplated his fate. The consensus was that all our woes would vanish if we kicked the nuisance out of school. I had a problem with that. The student was me a few years earlier, collateral damage from a marriage gone south. I knew his family circumstance, two addicted partiers for parents who were scarcely aware of his existence. I also saw the potential of this bright, extroverted kid who needed a leg-up and was making a serial plea for attention, but really for help. More than a culprit, he was a victim. Giving him the boot would certainly have solved our problem. It would have aggravated his, probably sentencing him to a lifetime of trouble or worse.

US president John F. Kennedy observed, "When written in Chinese, the word 'crisis' is composed of two characters. One represents danger and the other represents opportunity." With that quote in mind, I saw an opening in the teacher's ultimatum. In another capacity, I needed to fill a job vacancy, a position that appeared to be a good fit for him. The pay was competitive, and the job's diversity and flexible hours would be right up his alley.

My erstwhile teacher took to the new job like a duck to water, provided effective leadership, stability, and focus to an embryonic enterprise, and in time became a successful entrepreneur. It was my pleasure a couple of years ago to spend an evening with him. I asked how, after all the intervening years, he felt about his career switch away from teaching. "It was the best thing that could have happened to me." Had he remained as a teacher, his future may well have been far less happy and fulfilling.

SWITCHING JOBS

The province's 1969 Schools Act gave impetus to a consolidation and restructuring of primary and secondary education services. In my area, for example, dozens of community boards were rolled into one, the Green Bay Integrated School Board, and I became its superintendent of education.

My successor as principal of Grant Collegiate was Lorne Wheeler, an appointment I was delighted to make. An outstanding educator and a marvellous friend, he would go on to key leadership roles in province wide education, including chair of Memorial University's Board of Regents, deputy minister of Education, and head of the panel which oversaw the merger under a single board of all English schools in the province. Lorne also served as senior policy advisor to Newfoundland and Labrador's federal cabinet representative, Fisheries and Oceans Minister Loyola Hearn.

LEADING BY LISTENING

During my four-year tenure as superintendent of education, an ambitious school construction program and a dramatic improvement in teacher qualifications were the high points. There were also a few low points. Each of three small coastal communities, separated from each other by a mile or two, operated all-grade schools with as few as one or two students per grade. The school board accepted my recommendation that the three buildings be combined as one elementary school with bus transportation; the high school students bused fifteen miles to the nearest high school.

A board member and I were dispatched to the affected communities to outline our plan for improving educational opportunity. Many of the parents who attended our meeting saw things quite differently and said so, in words and in action, but especially the latter. We managed to get from the meeting hall to our car unscathed, but we couldn't go any farther with four flat tires.

The French have a great phrase, *l'esprit d'escalier*, literally, staircase wit, the kinds of things you tell yourself, after the fact, that you should have done or said. The botched outcome of our abortive attempt to improve the students' lot had me scratching my head. What did I do wrong? In hindsight, that wasn't hard to figure out. I had told the parents there was a problem but failed to tell them what the problem was. Then I told them my solution. I didn't give them the opportunity to examine the problem or canvass the options for themselves.

A week or so later, I was back in the communities. This time, I remembered that God gave me two ears and only one mouth for a reason. Initially, the parents pushed their one preferred option, the status quo. Until I explained, for the first time, what the problem was. Declining school enrolments would soon force the closure of one of the schools and, shortly after, a second school. By then the parents were asking me what the choices were. The sensible thing, I said, would be to close all three schools and bus everyone fifteen miles down the road. Whereupon a parent, maybe the one who let the air out of my tires the previous week, suggested another option: "Why don't we combine the three schools into one and put a bus on for the students? That would be the sensible thing to do!" Now, didn't I hear that idea somewhere before? The room exploded in prolonged applause and verbal concurrence. "Right on!" "Hear, hear!" "That's the way to do it!" When the handclapping and the whistling subsided, I humbly announced we would be pleased to implement the wishes of the parents.

Several lessons learned: Avoid issuing decrees, no matter how well-intended. Consult beforehand those who will be affected by your decisions. Mould consensus wherever possible. And the lesson I've never forgotten: A know-it-all demeanour can cause flat tires. Or worse.

A CON ARTIST PAYS HIS DUES

Overseeing a school construction project can quickly spiral into a migraine. Two challenges in particular keep you on your toes, the creative builder and the unscrupulous contractor. The first can be managed by saying no to his non-stop schemes to *enhance the quality of the facility*. Decoded, that means *put more money in my pocket*. If you're not that good at saying no, you'll need an unlimited contingency provision built into your capital budget. However, it's the con artist you have to be one step ahead of. He thinks he's smarter than you, and all too often that turns out to be the case.

It was eight o'clock Saturday morning as I geared down for the long holiday weekend. The ringing phone summoned me. It was my school board representative in the town of Triton, where I had been the day before, at the contractor's insistence, monitoring progress on the construction of a new high school. The caller, my Uncle Roger, whose sales apprentice I had been as a thirteen-year-old, advised, "You'd better get down here fast. Something is going on at the new school."

The builder's unvarying routine had been to shut down the job sharp at five o'clock Friday so workers could travel home for the weekend. But not this time, though they would have appreciated the extra day with their families, Monday being a statutory holiday. Instead, the boss had decreed the work would continue through the weekend and, according to my informant, had hired two extra shifts to keep the job going 'round the clock. Something was indeed going on.

Off to Triton I went. To the complete and, clearly, unwelcome surprise of the builder, there I was, standing in the middle of a tiled gym floor, a complete contrast to the plywood underlay I had seen less than twenty-four hours earlier. A quick tour revealed that several classrooms had also benefited from some overnight miracle. I not only smelled a rat. I knew exactly where to find it. To a worker, I said, "Pull up a tile."

The contractor, now quite agitated, protested.

"You can't do that. I'll have to redo the whole floor."

"You could be absolutely right, if I find what I think is under that tile."

We were both right. Beneath that tile, and every other floor tile in the building, was a cheap particleboard, not the more expensive plywood called for in the specs. Sheer greed had driven his decision to pull a fast one. His reasoning must have seemed watertight: *Simmons was here yesterday. I saw to that. So, I don't have to worry about him showing up. And he's single. He'll be too busy chasing women all weekend to even know we exist.*

I couldn't argue with that. But what he obviously didn't know was that a small town is no place to abruptly change your routine. People notice. Word gets around. The wily contractor lost his shirt on the job. Tiling the same floors twice can do that to you. It was his contingency fund, not mine, that was depleted. His reputation didn't do that well either. Smart people sometimes do dumb things. Especially when they think they're smarter than they really are.

FLYING HIGH

Brian Peckford, an energetic and well-liked member of the Grant Collegiate teaching staff, and I, both single, would sometimes get away to

Florida for some sun and fun. Live performances were a special treat—Louis Armstrong belting out *What a Wonderful World* and *Hello, Dolly*, Connie Francis purring "Evening shadows make me blue," the comedic zaniness of Myron Cohen, and the musical magic of Ray Anthony and his band.

On one such junket, we got fast-talked by a slick salesman with an offer we couldn't refuse. Off we flew, much too early on New Year's morning to have recovered from the previous evening's merrymaking, to inspect some *prime real estate* that turned out to be a swamp on the edge of the Everglades. Both of us became landowners before the day was done.

Brian was catching a few winks in the back seat. I sat up front in the single-engine four-seater Cessna 180, its dual controls an irresistible invitation to brag about my flying expertise. The pilot took the hint and told me to take over. My less-than-gentle touch sent the aircraft into a steep climb, and I heard a high-pitched outburst from behind. I snatched a glimpse over my shoulder. Brian was far too busy making peace with his Maker to appreciate my aeronautic finesse!

When I heard that Peckford had been declared the local Progressive Conservative candidate in the impending election, I knew what his first order of business would be, and it involved me. He showed up at my office early next morning, seeking leave of absence from his teaching responsibilities. I was quick to oblige, too quick it seemed for the freshly minted candidate. I summoned my stenographer, the incredible Bev (Ivany) Wells, to take down the leave letter. Peckford, convinced I was out to give him a hard time, exploded.

"I didn't come here for you to make a fool of me. All I want is a three-week leave."

"That's exactly what I'm going to give you."

"You can't do that. Don't you have to call the board chairman or have a meeting?"

True, as superintendent of education, I took my orders from a school board. But Brian's leave request was a no-brainer. So, I gave him what may well have been his first Politics 101 tutorial, to wit:

"If you and I were of the same party stripe, I'd have to get formal board authorization for your leave. In this case, though, I can do no wrong. All the Tory board members will decide I had no choice; the Liberal members will grudgingly applaud my magnanimity."

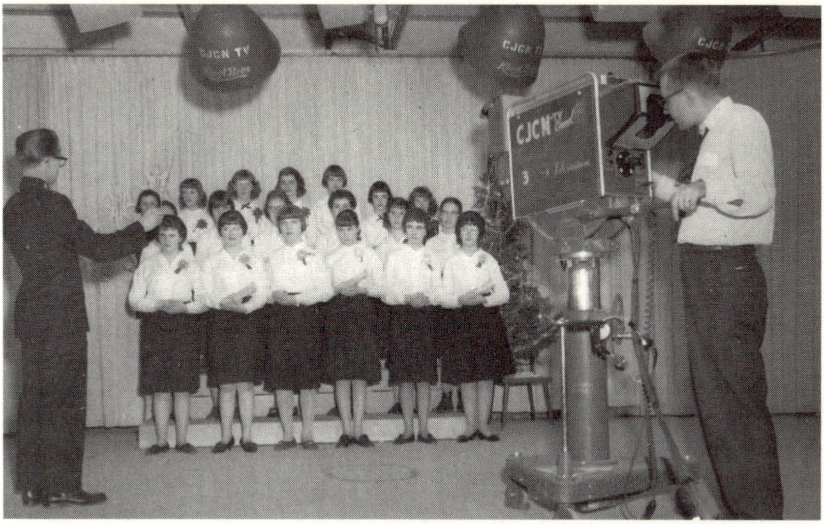

Grand Falls, NL, 1961. The Springdale Salvation Army Academy glee club's rendition of the French Christmas carol "Il est né, le divin Enfant" (He Is Born, the Divine Child) and other seasonal songs was televised. (Author photo)

Miami Beach, FL, circa 1968. Brian Peckford and Roger Simmons. (Author photo)

As a firm believer in the unfettered right to seek public office, and, especially, as Peckford's close friend, I was proud and pleased to sign the leave authorization which would facilitate his successful bid for election to the House of Assembly. What would make me less happy later on would be the milestone significance of that morning's encounter. His demeanour and body language telegraphed an impersonal formality which was foreign to our relationship heretofore. I dismissed it as a manifestation of nervous energy and his impatience to get on with the job at hand. Sadly, I would come to realize that his nomination as a political candidate foreshadowed the estrangement of a camaraderie that was flourishing twenty-four hours earlier.

CHAPTER 8
COMMUNITY ACTIVIST

It's been a theory of mine that the only thing in which you can take an interest is something you are part of.
— Ted Russell, Newfoundland playwright, teacher, and politician, 1904–77

Springdale was an eclectic, vibrant cluster of humanity when I first showed up there in July 1960 and remains so to this day. Sure, it had some of the trappings and drawbacks of a small town. But it had something else far more edifying—a clear vision of what could be and an undaunted determination to make it happen.

During my first stint there, I dabbled in community affairs, organizing debates and speak-offs, making a few tentative stabs at ecumenism and facilitating the rink projects mentioned earlier.

When I returned to Springdale as principal of Grant Collegiate in 1965, I once again became engaged in the community at large. Green Bay's then-thriving mining sector and Springdale's business interests were largely in the hands of a cadre of young progressives, men, and a handful of women, who weren't intimidated by change. Importantly, they controlled the levers that would mobilize a thorough makeover in educational, social, economic, and transportation infrastructure and services, resulting in significant quality-of-life improvement.

The imperative was to overhaul the town's inefficient school system, the crying need for better medical and seniors' care, the provision of recreational facilities, highway improvements, establishing a community newspaper, diversifying the economy, and taking steps to reduce unemployment. It was a formidable to-do list for a modest-sized town. Every item formed part of an urgent community agenda, and the movers and shakers never let up until the job was done.

Springdale became, and remains, the envy of towns its size and larger. Social scientists and community planners flocked to the town, hoping to understand what was happening, scrutinizing the local chemistry to determine its potential for replication elsewhere. One such interloper was Anthony Cohen, a British social anthropologist, who skilfully dissected the town's decision-making mysteries in his authoritative literary work, entitled *The Management of Myths: The Politics of Legitimation in a Newfoundland Community*. Dr. Cohen decided that I, still in my twenties, was one of four men who *run the town*, asserting I was regularly consulted by the mayor, the magistrate, and the leading businessmen, and was *the instigator of locally based initiatives*. Notwithstanding, Cohen perceived that,

> [Simmons] . . . suffered from three disadvantages . . . he was clever, smart (a label which is a liability in Springdale) . . . he was young (and seen as) aggressively ambitious with a pernicious self-interest . . . Third, he could not talk in the local idiom.

It was an exciting, demanding, transformative time. And I was smack in the middle of it all. As a founding member and officer of the local chamber of commerce, I helped make the case (successful) for a paved road link to the island's highway network.

When a town delegation was dispatched to lobby Premier Smallwood, I was one of the four who made the pitch (successful) for the establishment at Springdale of a vocational school/community college.

When the municipal council tasked a volunteer commission with raising capital for a hockey and curling facility, I was part of that initiative (successful). The need for a swimming pool was identified. I got involved in the effort and had the honour of emceeing the ribbon-cutting to launch the new facility.

The local education district sought provincial funding to enlarge and refurbish the town's regional high school. Of course, as the school board's administrator, my fingerprints were all over that undertaking. And yes, success!

When the founding editor of the local newspaper moved away, I bought it, upgraded to commercial typesetting and offset printing, hired a staff, and published the paper for a few months, until I sold out to my employee and former student Francis Hull. The newspaper continues to this day and is now one of thirty-five weeklies and dailies owned by Halifax-based SaltWire Network.

TACKLING UNEMPLOYMENT

For five years as president of the economic development organization, I helped catalyze a successful drive to bring industry to the town and region after the collapse of the local mining sector, a victim of falling world copper prices. First, though, I had to deal with a more immediate problem. The retired judge who was executive director of the development agency treated the job as a sinecure. The critical times the community was facing needed a proactive go-getter with ideas and energy to burn, someone with a results-oriented drive and a healthy work ethic. And I had just the right person in mind, Maurice Budgell, a teacher colleague.

Maurice took on the job. He and I became an inseparable team as we helped to spearhead the economic revitalization of a community devastated by mine closings. A jewellery manufacturing enterprise based on locally quarried virginite[60], an assay lab which services the province's mining industry, a dramatically expanded farming sector[61], and a highway beautification project were among the success stories. Regionally, we helped kick-start several ventures, among them a fish processing plant at Triton and a cottage industry in craft production. A tangible reminder of our efforts survives to this day, nearly a half-century later. Motorists on the Trans-Canada Highway approaching the Springdale area from east or west drive through one of two masonry walls bearing the words *Welcome to scenic Green Bay*, part of a make-work stonecutting initiative.

An inspiring sidebar to the highway beautification project relates to the stonecutter. After combing the province for a qualified candidate, we found the guy with the required skill set right under our nose, living in a community close by. In his late fifties, he had been unemployed for so long that he had given up all hope of ever finding a job. He and his family scraped by on welfare. Local stereotyping pigeonholed him.

"He's too lazy to drag himself out of bed, let alone do a day's work."

We hired him anyway. Not only was he a whiz of a stonecutter, he taught others his trade, and together they quarried and cut stones, built the ornamental walls, and installed a masonry facade on our new office building.

For the stonecutter, it was a new lease on life as he went on to other jobs. For those of us who saw him in action, it was an instructive reality check. Too often, the easy judgment is to conclude that unemployed people are lazy. The truth is that, like the stonecutter, most jobless people will jump at the chance to work again.

60 A decorative facing stone resembling Connemara marble in appearance

61 Memorial University produced a video on our farming project. Go to http://greenbayfeed.com/green-bay-economic-development-association-1975

Ottawa, 1970. L-R: Maurice Budgell, executive secretary, Green Bay Economic Development Association (GBEDA); Hon. Jean Marchand, minister of Regional Economic Expansion; Hon. Don Jamieson, minister of Transport; Roger Simmons, President of GBEDA. (Author photo)

I was juggling a lot of balls. The education superintendency, my day job, had its own set of demands and priorities. Extensive travel, mostly over winding dirt roads, was a given. The more isolated communities were a three-hour drive from my Springdale office. Three schools were accessible by boat only. There was always a construction project to monitor, a speech to deliver, a small personnel problem to resolve before it became a big one.

CALCULATING FRIEND

All told, I lived in Springdale for eleven years. Overall, my time there was immensely rewarding and enjoyable. Notwithstanding, I do recall a couple of incidents where snobbery and prejudice got the upper hand.

My teacher friend and I were headed out of town for Christmas. I decided to make a quick stop at a festive house party to which I had been invited and persuaded him to join me. The host, a prominent businessman, met us at the door. As my friend mingled with the other guests, most of whom he knew as parents of his students, the host took me to task: "Roger, you're always welcome in our home, but please don't bring your second-class friends around here."

A few short years later, the businessman had a change of heart. The fact that my friend had in the meantime become the premier of Newfoundland and Labrador was, undeniably, just a happy coincidence! Even second-class creatures sometimes get a second chance.

CHAPTER 9
MAN OF THE HOUSE

Family is the most important thing in the world.
— Princess Diana, 1961–97

I've fallen head over heels in love with many women. Miriam Torgerson and I met in a hotel bedroom in Halifax. That's not as scandalous as it sounds when I tell you the room was doing double duty as an interview venue, the hotel having muffed my boardroom reservation. An elementary school teacher and reading specialist, Miriam was among the dozens of out-of-province professionals I recruited each year, in my capacity as education superintendent, to mitigate the severe shortage of teachers in my rural school district. Miriam and I tied the knot in Quesnel, her BC hometown, and parted company civilly after seventeen years as husband and wife, most of them happy. With no desire to make lawyers richer and ourselves poorer, we sorted out a separation agreement over coffee and lunches at a neighbourhood Burger King. The day we separated and the weeks and months that followed were the most miserable days of my life.

Lady Diana's diagnosis, "There were *three* of us in this *marriage*, so it was a bit crowded," certainly did not apply to our situation. The marital breakdown, more my fault than Miriam's, was the result of irreconcilable differences. Divorce, frowned on by Salvation Army teachings, was a tough pill for me. My reticence and the possibility of a reconciliation, though slim, delayed the actual divorce for several years.

Miriam was, is, a wonderful human being and a caring mother of our two sons. I have been blessed with a continuing strong bond with Paul and Mark largely because she distinguished between our fractured relationship and our parental roles. Until the boys were of age, I continued to participate in family celebrations—birthdays, graduations, Christmas Day festivities including early-morning gift opening and dinner. I admire her resilience, and I'm proud of the life she has built for herself and grateful for the years we spent together.

Among the most wrenching aspects of marital separation are the ramifications for the children of the marriage and the implications for an ongoing relationship with them. If you are, as I was, the parent who's physically leaving the home, these issues can be quite traumatic, as they certainly were for me. You ask yourself: Does my departure from the household mean that my relationship with my kids will deteriorate? How often will I get to spend time with them? Here again, it was Miriam's attitude that came to my rescue. Not once did she try to limit my access to the boys or play them off to score a point at my expense.

DIFFERENT STROKES

Our older son, Paul, was born at the Grace Hospital in St. John's. I have many cherished memories of his early years. As a toddler, strapped into his bike seat behind mine, he loved to ride from our Patrick Street home to the St. John's waterfront, where we checked out the harbour activity and admired the latest port arrivals. It was there that Paul got his first glimpse into the larger world as we noted the diverse ports of registry emblazoned on the ships' bows.

Our early, Saturday morning biking jaunts, intended to give his mamma a little extra shut-eye, inevitably included a lingering visit to the model train supplies store just off New Gower Street. There was always a need for yet another piece of rolling stock or a trestle to add to the miniature railway back at the house.

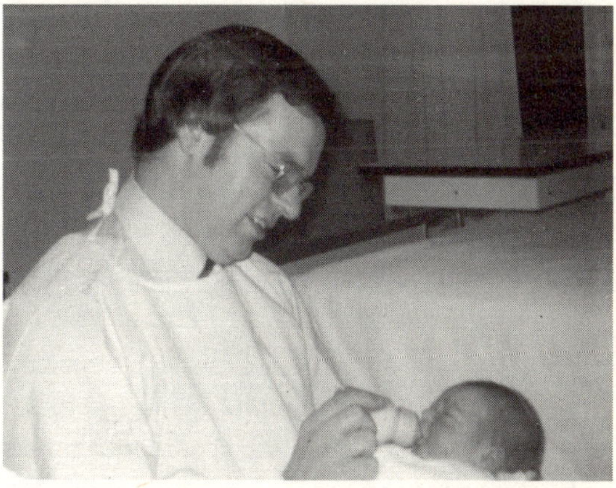

St. John's, 1976. With my first child, Paul, three days old. (Author photo)

Paul's pride and joy was the oversized sandbox which I built in the backyard. The perimeter of the box was topped with a street, complete with lane markings. An elevated launch area and a ramp to the street below gave him the option of racing his dinky cars, a fascination that he often indulged. Paul lived in Newfoundland

(St. John's and Kona Beach) for three extended periods, most recently as a graduate student in oceanography at Memorial University. All of which copper-fastened his status as an incurable Newf.

Mark, the younger of the two boys, spent just four of his childhood years in Newfoundland, so, understandably, he has less emotional attachment to the Rock, certainly fewer memories of the place. Hatched in Ottawa, urban living has been his lot and, in time, his choice, whether Ottawa, Berlin, Toronto, his present domicile, or Karlskrona, a city in southern Sweden, where he obtained his master's degree in industrial design.

Deer Lake, NL, 1984. Paul, left, and Mark with my dad and me. (Author photo)

The boys are close-knit, yet very different passions and pastimes propel each. Paul is most at home standing knee deep in his favourite salmon stream, hoping to reconnect with that big one that got away last time, or shaping a piece of Douglas fir in his fully-equipped, tightly organized workshop. Especially, he has a keen interest in antique carpentry tools, researching their origins and restoring them. His enthusiasm for the outdoor life and his skill at woodworking authenticate his Simmons credentials.

Though not a workaholic, Mark interacts with a laptop during most of his waking day, since his job is all about manipulating digital data. As well, he has an online business, marketing items he conceived and designed. His interests include art, woodworking, and cycling. He loves to travel, dine out, and otherwise spend time with friends.

Mark gets pigeonholed as the city slicker in the family. He does thrive in the heart of the city but has no time for suburbia. He loves being at an ocean beach. Hiking in the mountains and exploring the deep woods also get his juices flowing.

IF LOOKS COULD KILL . . .

Awaiting the arrival of two come-from-away guests, renowned Newfoundland artist David Blackwood kept an eye on his latest creation, *Cape Spear, Newfoundland, 1983*, a painting of the old lighthouse in which we were standing. Canada's minister for national parks, John Roberts, was there. Indeed, dignitaries from all over had sandwiched into the cramped space. The guests of honour were expected at any minute. Blackwood's exquisite piece of art would be the memento of their visit.

Roaches Line, NL, 1988. Mark, left, and Paul with Joey Smallwood at his home. (Author photo)

Miriam, Paul, and I were keeping an eye on Mark. The three-year-old's fidget level was up on max, and the tripod supporting the masterpiece was precariously close. You guessed it! Mark toppled the tripod. Instinctively, I switched to multi-tasking mode, using my left hand to grab Mark by the shirt collar, and with my right palm I cupped the corner of the framed painting a nanosecond before it could impact the stone floor.

Tripod and painting were repositioned. Mere moments later, our guests made their entrance. Minister Roberts presented the painting. Graciously accepting it were the intended recipients, Prince Charles and Princess Diana! The date was June 24, 1983.

Mark had missed his shot at infamy, but just barely!

The aforementioned model railway survived the family's move to Ottawa, underwent several upgrades, and engaged both boys frequently. As well, at Mark's request, I built a treehouse in the back garden, and he spent many happy hours there with his friends.

As a family, we travelled a fair bit. Mark was heavy into Legos, so, as part of their first trip to western Europe, Miriam and I took our boys to the Legoland resort in Billund, Denmark, which draws 2,000,000 visitors annually. London was also on our itinerary. There, the highlight for the guys was the famous London Trocadero, an entertainment complex on Coventry Street until its closure in 2014. For Paul and Mark, the changing of the guard at Buckingham Palace was no match for the gigantic video arcade at the Troc.

Cavendish, PEI, 1983. L-R: Paul, Doug (my nephew), my younger son, Mark, and Greg (my nephew). Author photo.

AND, HERE HE IS, WILLIS THE CHARMER!

Paul's better half, Tiffany, is a beautiful daughter of the Ottawa valley. Her spare-time passions are biking and sewing, at which she is quite accomplished. Her day job and Paul's are with the same BC government agency in Kamloops. Tiffany extended the family line in 2016 by giving birth to their son, Willis, my father's namesake.

So, yeah! I'm a doting grandpa! Willis was twenty-six months old when I last got to hold and play peekaboo with him. He's nearly three now, and via Skype, I look on as he exhibits growing comprehension, perfects his mischief-making skills, and flashes his knock-'em-dead smile. Willis began verbalizing a long while ago, though what he's saying sometimes makes no sense, indisputable proof that he has my genes!

Willis (Tiffany Simmons photo)

CHAPTER 10
FELLA FROM THE ROCK

You can take the man out of the bay,
but you can't take the bay out of the man.[62]
— Translation by Newfoundland playwright Ted Russell

The straitjacket of political correctness has foisted upon us a barrage of unwieldy or, at least, lengthy mouthfuls. No stewardesses, but airline attendants. Blacks in the US have become African-Americans, though I continue to meet many who prefer to be called blacks.

The term Newfie has been deemed politically incorrect by the purists. The irony is that the term probably had a neutral, if not salutary, origin. Its kick-start may have been as innocent as that of the term Yankee, believed to have come from Dutch immigrants to America in the 1600s who referred to the English colonials as "Jan Kees" (John Cheese), which became Yankee, approximating the Dutch pronunciation. "Yanks" is simply a shortened version. Or consider the word Aussie, defined in dictionaries as short for Australian. The folks down under invoke it with pride and gusto, chanting, *Aussie Aussie Aussie, oi oi oi,* at Australian sport events.

PROUD NEWFIES

The usual explanation for the word Newfie is that Allied military personnel posted during World War II in a then-independent[63] Newfoundland found

62 "Caelum non animum mutant qui trans mare currunt." — Epistles by Horace, 20 BC

63 Actually, the Dominion of Newfoundland's democratically elected government was, at the request of its legislature, suspended in 1934 and supplanted by a Commission of Government appointed by Britain, this development having been largely triggered by fiscal mismanagement and government scandals galore. The *coup de grâce* was the Great Depression's disastrous impact on Newfoundland's public accounts.

the four-syllable "Newfoundlander" cumbersome, so they shortened it to Newfie or Newf. However, there is some evidence that the term may have been adopted long before the Second World War and first used by Newfies themselves, a delicious twist for those Newfoundlanders who maintain the sobriquet is a put-down. Consider these lines from the highly successful British war song "Mademoiselle from Armentières":

Mademoiselle from Armentières, Parlez-vous?
Mademoiselle from Armentières,
She hasn't been kissed in forty years! Hinky-dinky, parlez-vous!

The popular song was often adapted. Here's the reworded version popularized by Newfoundland infantry on the European battlefields:

The Yankees thought they won the war, Parley voo!
The Yankees thought they won the war,
The Newfies won it the day before! Hinky-dinky, parley-voo!

The time frame may have been World War I. That's when the song's authentic version and its many knock-offs were at the height of their popularity. The Newfie takeoff was still in vogue in the early 1950s. It was one of the ditties I sang as a child. But whether it was during the first or the second global conflict that the lads from the Rock were spoofing the Americans with their tongue-in-cheek lyrics, one thing is obvious: Newfoundlanders themselves were invoking the Newfie label and in a context that was clearly positive.

It stands to reason that people whose home was the Rock and who had frequent occasion to reference fellow islanders would have long since opted for the term Newfie or Newf rather than repeated use of the multi-syllabic mouthful, Newfoundlander. We do the same thing a zillion times in talking to or about persons whose names are lengthy. The four-syllable Isabella becomes Belle. Alexander gets shortened to Alex or Al. Are we to expect that these truncated monikers will soon be deemed put-downs, now that I have planted the notion with the purists?

Politically incorrect the term Newfie may have become, though I don't know why. I like it anyway, indeed, wear it proudly. To be a Newfie is to love life, work hard, play harder, revel in the company of others, swap stories, laugh often, love much.

STUPID NEWFIES?

In 1989, Prime Minister Brian Mulroney's Environment minister, Lucien Bouchard, and I sat immediately opposite each other in the House of Commons. Just to my right sat a caucus colleague and, I thought, a friend. In a previous Parliament, he and I had been members of the same Commons committee, so we had a familiar and ongoing relationship. As we waited for the daily Question Period to get under way, Bouchard and I were bantering back and forth in English when I said something to which my colleague apparently took offence, though Bouchard was all smiles. My confrère shouted across to Bouchard:

"Pretez aucune attention, car il est seulement un terre-neuvien stupide!"

Translation: "Don't mind him. He's only a stupid Newfoundlander!"

My colleague obviously didn't know that, while I can massacre spoken French with the best, I have less difficulty understanding it. More to the point, he revealed a bigotry that surprised me and an assessment of Newfoundland intelligence that did him no credit, though, I'm sad to say, there are those who regularly trade on that stereotype. Indeed, as recently as August 2017, American TV's Penn Jillette, as a guest on HBO's *Real Time with Bill Maher*, characterized Newfoundland as "just a euphemism for stupid." His utterance went viral, and he spent the next few days dispensing remorseful retractions and abject apologies. His granddaddy, born on the Rock, would not have been impressed.

SMART NEWFIES

To return to my Liberal colleague's news flash to Bouchard, I don't doubt there may be a few stupid Newfoundlanders at large. But if I were you, I wouldn't count on it. Indeed, let me warn you, there's actually some of our breed out there somewhere with whom you wouldn't want to tangle.

Dr. Bruce Aylward, a senior director at the World Health Organization's Geneva headquarters, spearheaded its highly successful polio eradication project and was recently seconded to the United Nations Office for the Coordination of Humanitarian Affairs. How's that for stupid!

Lawyer George Furey is Speaker of the Canadian Senate. His son is orthopaedic surgeon Andrew Furey. In the heart-rending aftermath of the 2010 Haiti earthquake, Dr. Furey, working with his wife, pediatric emergency room doctor Allison Furey, and Dr. Will Moores, orthopaedic surgeon, founded Team Broken Earth.[64] It's a group of volunteer Canadian physicians, nurses, and therapists who provide aid in the impoverished country.

Malcolm Rowe sits on Canada's Supreme Court, the first Newfoundlander to do so. General Rick Hillier as Chief of the Defence Staff reinvented the Canadian military as a worthy calling.

64 http://andrewfurey.ca

General Brian Peddle is the international leader of the Salvation Army, based in London, England. For several years, Commissioner Max Feener spearheaded the Army's operations in the southern US and was a candidate for General.

Mi'kmaq Chief Mi'sel Joe devotes his smarts, energy, and integrity to creating economic opportunity for his people while preserving and promoting their proud traditions. David Strong, a former president of the University of Victoria, founded University Canada West in 2005.

Retired Navy admiral Harry Steele is an entrepreneur extraordinaire, as is former Newfoundland and Labrador Premier Danny Williams.

In men's curling, Brad Gushue and his team captured Olympic gold in 2006 and the world championship in 2017. At the age of twenty-one, Tom Power began hosting a national CBC radio show, and now, ten years later, he anchors the network's daily flagship national music program.

And that's just a few examples of the Newfoundland male species.

Newfoundland women are also making their mark, both locally and abroad. Twenty-two-year-old figure skater Kaetlyn Osmond is the 2018 ladies' singles world champion and earned medals at two Olympics, including gold in 2018.

Theatrical director Donna Butt, with her creative genius and magic touch, is in a class by herself. Actresses Cathy Jones and Mary Walsh treat national TV audiences to non-stop servings of madcap comedy. Bernice Morgan is a highly rated short story writer and novelist.

Springdale's Karen Huxter founded and directs Hands Across the Sea, a non-profit organization and registered Canadian charity serving needy children and families in Haiti with a children's home, a school, and community development initiatives.

Moya Greene was the CEO of Canada Post for five years. Since 2010, she has been running the Royal Mail, the first non-Briton and first woman to hold the post, the highest-paid UK civil service position. The BBC has voted her the twelfth most powerful woman in the United Kingdom.

Catherine Courage is a senior vice-president at Google. In 2013, she made *Forbes'* list of "Top 10 Rising Stars at the World's Most Innovative Companies." Jane Rowe, Moya Cahill, and Bernadette MacPherson are movers and shakers among Toronto's corporate elite.

Elaine Dobbin has long been a driving force behind fundraising campaigns for several health causes in Newfoundland and Labrador, including autism, cancer treatment, and the Janeway Children's Hospital. In the United States, Elaine and her late husband, Craig, established a professorship for advanced lung disease at the University of Pennsylvania.[65]

Entrepreneur and philanthropist Zita Cobb turned her back on urban office towers to give back to the community that cradled her. Her visionary, gutsy approach is catalyzing a dramatic makeover on Fogo Island and drawing the curious and the coddled from all over.

Educator Marilyn Luscombe has provided innovative community college leadership in Newfoundland and Labrador, British Columbia, and New Brunswick.

For three decades, Iris Petten has provided dynamic leadership in the seafood industry. And she is the Chair of Memorial University's Board of Regents.

My good friend Dr. Edna Turpin is recognized internationally as an educational leader and strategic planner.[66] Dr. Linda Inkpen, registrar of the province's Council of College of Physicians and Surgeons, is a Member of the Order of Canada.

Heidi Bonnell is the vice-president of Federal Government Affairs at Rogers Communications. She's also "the founder of Hope Live, an annual fundraising effort to make fertility preservation services accessible to young cancer patients."[67]

Gail Penney heads one of Newfoundland and Labrador's largest business enterprises and is a community activist and generous philanthropist.

Appropriately on International Women's Day 2018, Ella (Crowley) Goss was appointed CEO of Alaska's largest hospital, the first female to hold the position in forty-two years.[68] She grew up in Holyrood, Newfoundland and Labrador, and is a St. Clare's nursing graduate.

And then there's the uplifting story of Dr./Major Dawn Howse, who at twenty-one became one of Memorial University's youngest medical graduates ever. That was in 1978. Just over three decades later, in 2010, she had come full circle, standing once again on her alma mater's convocation stage to receive another degree, this time an honorary doctor of laws in recognition of her humanitarian work, having spent twenty years in Zimbabwe practising medicine. University orator Dr. Donald McKay noted that, along the way, the soft-spoken Salvation Army officer had "plunged [bungee jumped] 110 metres from the bridge at Victoria Falls, zip-lined over the Zambezi River gorge, and flew in a hot-air balloon."

65 theextraordinarywomen.com
66 zoominfo.com
67 2015.leadershipcanada.ca
68 alaska.providence.org-alaska-medical-center

NEWFOUNDLAND ICON, NATIONAL TREASURE

Fellow Newfoundlander and Rhodes scholar Rex Murphy is an unlikely folk hero. With a lexicographer's arsenal of multi-syllabic, obscure words, the memory of an elephant, and the scathing indignation of a crocodile, his regular rants on TV and in print cut close to the bone. Yet his take-no-prisoners approach commands a wide and loyal following, not that everything he says is fully comprehended by the masses.

The top echelon of US and Canadian security had gathered in Vancouver soon after 9/11, and it was Murphy's task to provide a change of pace at the requisite dinner. He did not disappoint.

Rex had been my speech writer, and I was asked to introduce him. My challenge was to say something that the Canadians present didn't already know about him. I was obliged to resort to an old crutch: If you don't know what to say, wing it. So I did, as follows: "A recent CBC poll reveals that eighty-seven per cent of viewers agree with what Rex Murphy says. Nine per cent disagree. Four per cent understand!"

Stupid is not a characterization that comes to mind when I think of Rex Murphy. Or Jane and John Crosbie. Or Zita Cobb. Or any of the other bona fide Newfoundlanders mentioned elsewhere in this volume. Are these the "stupid Newfies" who fuelled my fellow MP's blinding insight that day in the Commons? A mind that brilliant is rare. Thank God!

A LOYAL CLAN

Newfoundlanders can be clannish when it matters. How else to explain what happened in Ottawa a few years back? Don Jamieson, Newfoundland's representative in the federal Liberal cabinet, and Bill Doody, the Newfoundland provincial Tory Transport minister, squared off over a federal-provincial transportation funding agreement. With the negotiation all but complete and Minister Doody signalling that the latest federal offer was acceptable to the province, Jamieson, to the bewilderment of all present, launched into a tirade, ending with a call for an unscheduled recess. The federal Liberal took the provincial Tory aside and quietly whispered, "Bill, you're leaving $30 million on the table!"

Once reconvened, the meeting soon ended with the Newfoundland treasury $30 million richer. Partisans, yes, but Newfies first!

As Liberal MP for the town of Channel-Port aux Basques, I had a similar experience with federal Tory cabinet minister John Crosbie. The town needed a $6 million infusion of funds to address a water-system-related health issue. Crosbie got the approval to flow the money. Once again, when it mattered, partisan politics had to play second fiddle. Newfoundlanders stood together!

NUMBSKULLS ON THE LOOSE

An apparently uncontrollable urge seizes countless numbers of mainlanders[69] whenever they encounter a fella or a gal from the Rock. They just must regale him/her with a "new, real Newfie joke," and proceed to do so whether the listener wants to hear it or not. The story, inevitably, is neither new nor Newfie. It's been told about Italians, Poles, and Ukrainians ever since humankind began applying ethnic labels and fabricating stereotypes.

Nor is there anything funny about the story. Demeaning, insulting, yes. But not funny. Why, then, is the storyteller laughing so hard? Well, that's where reality raises its head. The only real aspect to the entire incident is that the teller is a bigot, whether s/he knows it or not. If s/he told that story about females or black people, s/he'd rightly be labelled a sexist or racist. S/He seems to think, though, that it's all right to talk about us Newfies that way. That's not just bigotry. It's also certifiable stupidity.

Our legendary forbearance, coupled with an innate pity for bereft, insufferable wretches, usually allows the awkward moment to pass, but from time to time, when some interloper from upalong gets too big for his britches, we indulge the pure joy of unloading a real Newfie joke, such as this one:

Question: Why do Newfies talk so fast?

Response: To keep up with our brains!

WANDERLUST

Newfoundlanders have always gone where the jobs are. They can be found ministering to the ailing in a Texas hospital, crewing Great Lakes ships, and populating the workforce of Fort McMurray. You may have seen one of them on the big screen (Natasha Henstridge, my cousin).

Newfoundlanders have often been at the centre of historic events. Captain Bob Bartlett accompanied Robert Peary on three separate attempts to reach the North Pole. Colonel Cluny MacPherson invented the gas mask while serving with the Newfoundland Regiment at Gallipoli. Desmond Jones and Vincent Wakeham were awarded bravery medals for their role in the evacuation of Dunkirk. Wallace Cake was a crew member on the HMS *Prince of Wales* during Churchill's historic 1941 rendezvous with FDR in Placentia Bay. Hundreds of Newfoundlanders served in heavy equipment units that stormed the Normandy beaches on D-Day. Prisoner of war John Ford[70] survived the Nagasaki bomb attack.

---

69 Newfs use the term to refer to other Canadians, just as Hawaiians do to refer to Americans in the lower forty-eight states and Alaska.

70 A Royal Air Force aero-mechanic and a native of Port aux Basques in my federal constituency, I spent many a pleasant moment with him. He died in September 2013.

Lloyd Seaward of Bishop's Falls, my childhood hometown, spent three and a half years in a Japanese PoW camp after his Royal Navy ship, the HMS *Exeter*, a York-class heavy cruiser, was sunk during the second Battle of the Java Sea in 1942. Now a vigorous centenarian, he is one of three remaining survivors. He regularly regales his nephew, Ivan Seaward, and me with graphic and poignant word-pictures of his long-ago exploits. In March, 2018, Lloyd travelled to England to participate in a commemorative event at Exeter Cathedral.

Newfoundlander Marie O'Flaherty, a communications specialist at the Canadian embassy in Tehran, helped plot the escape of six American diplomats who had evaded capture during the 1979 Iran hostage crisis. Regrettably, her effort and Canadian Ambassador Ken Taylor's historic role were no match for Ben Affleck's obsession with fiction over fact in his 2012 film *Argo*.

"MY BROTHER'S KEEPER"[71]

It's a well-documented fact that, in any society, there is a direct correlation between economic misery and suicide: the higher the unemployment rate, the higher the suicide rate. Yet Newfoundland and Labrador[72] has had, ever since it became a part of Canada, the highest joblessness rate in the nation. And the lowest suicide rate! In Newfanese, "Sure, I can't get any work, but 'tis not worth slittin' me throat over."

Further, the province has long had the lowest per capita income. And the highest rate of charitable giving! Again, as a Newfie might say, "I don't have much, but what's mine is yours."

Both of the above sets of apparently contradictory statistics bespeak an important truth. Newfoundlanders do not define their worth or self-esteem in economic terms alone. Nor are we insensitive to the plight of others. A very identifiable values set sustains the Newfoundland culture, a culture shaped by 500 years of struggle, five centuries of being our brother's/sister's keeper.

INASMUCH AS YE HAVE DONE IT UNTO ONE . . . OF THESE . . .[73]

The numbing sequence of events of 9/11 had immediate impact for untold millions of people, including tens of thousands of air passengers en route to the US. Less than an hour after planes hit the World Trade towers, pilots destined for American airports received a succinct directive:

71 Genesis 4:9, KJV

72 This became the province's official name in 2001, effected by an amendment to the Canadian constitution, at the request of then Premier Brian Tobin and the Newfoundland House of Assembly.

73 Matthew 25:40, KJV

"All airways over the continental United States are closed to commercial air traffic. Land ASAP at the nearest airport. Advise your destination."

For many dozens of pilots, that nearest landing spot was in Newfoundland. No fewer than fifty-three aircraft rerouted to Gander.

Gander and its people rose to the occasion in magnificent style. For them it was second nature, what they've always done, though never had they faced a challenge of such staggering proportions. The town's comprehensive and compassionate response, expertly choreographed by its intrepid mayor, Claude Elliott, is movingly told in American journalist Jim DeFede's award-winning book, *The Day the World Came to Town*. The role of Gander and other communities in smoothing the path for the CFAs[74] has been widely chronicled in Canadian and American newspapers, books, magazines, and TV documentaries. By far, the most high-profile recognition of Gander's shining moment in the world's spotlight is the dynamite stage production *Come From Away*, currently drawing capacity audiences and ecstatic reviews on Broadway. It won a Tony Award in June 2017 for Best Direction of a Musical.

In his book, DeFede recounts a remarkable story of two stranded passengers shopping for camping equipment at Canadian Tire, having decided they preferred a tent to the cramped quarters of the shelter to which they and 152 other passengers had been assigned. As they fished out their credit cards to pay for air mattresses, sleeping bags, and a flashlight, the cashier inquired, "You're from the planes, right?" Imagine the surprise of the two Dallas ladies on hearing store employees had been instructed not to charge stranded passengers. Over a three-day period, Canadian Tire gave away merchandise worth $30,000.

Other retail outlets, groups, and individuals also showed generosity. Fast food outlets sent carloads of food to the airport to feed deplaning passengers. The phone company set up banks of telephones on the sidewalk for free long-distance calls. Cable TV ran temporary lines to all the shelters. Pharmacies filled more than 1,000 medical prescriptions, having determined the appropriate drugs through online searches and calls to hometown doctors. A free taxi service was organized to help the visitors get around town.

And then there's the marvellous humanity of Werner Baldessarini, worldwide head of Hugo Boss, who spent three nights on a school gym floor with more than 300 other stranded passengers. When offered several bottles of the best wines and an assortment of his favourite cheeses, he declined,

74 Acronym for "come from away," widely used in Newfoundland and Labrador to refer to a visitor or resident who is not native to the province

concerned he would offend his hosts. When his Frankfurt staff lined up a corporate jet to fly him out of Gander, Baldessarini cancelled the arrangement, feeling it would be a betrayal of his fellow passengers. He had bonded with them and with the locals. He was amazed at the humanity, the community spirit, and the egalitarianism all around him.

How unusual, then, was the Gander response to 9/11? There is evidence that at least some people have been known to react quite differently when disaster strikes.

A monstrous storm slammed into the US on August 25, 2017. Hurricane Harvey made landfall in Texas three times in six days. It hovered over Houston for four days, delivering massive rainfall and unprecedented flooding.

At least 107 persons lost their lives in the hurricane and its aftermath, one in Guyana, and 106 in the United States; 103 of these were in Texas. The total destruction inflicted by the hurricane is estimated at $125 billion, ranking it one of the two costliest natural disasters ever in the US, comparable with Hurricane Katrina in 2005.[75] Harvey damaged 203,000 houses, of which 12,700 were destroyed.[76]

If stats are your cup of tea, how about these: Even as Harvey was still wreaking its merciless havoc, even as Houston and other cities were underwater, the Texas Attorney General, Ken Paxton, told the press on August 28:

> "There have already been more than 500 complaints about price gouging during Hurricane Harvey over the weekend. . . . That includes reports of up to $99 for a case of water, hotels that are tripling or quadrupling their prices, and fuel is going for $4 to $10 a gallon."

I wonder what Werner Baldessarini or, for that matter, any one of the thousands of Gander 9/11 strandees would have to say about that?

In contrast to the disgusting price hikes in Texas, New Brunswick's severe flooding in early May 2018 brought out the very best in people. How uplifting it was to learn of Rob Dekany's free ferry service for stranded Darlings Islanders and numerous other acts of generosity and compassion! Bravo!

CANADA'S WELCOME MAT

Nor was Gander the only port in the storm for the 9/11 plane people, as they were quickly and affectionately dubbed by the locals. Airports across New-

75 en.wikipedia.org/wiki/Hurricane_Harvey
76 www.thebalance.com/hurricane-harvey-facts-damage-costs

foundland and Labrador took up the challenge. Goose Bay, Stephenville, and St. John's each hosted stranded passengers and crews, as did cities elsewhere in Canada. In all, 250 planes were diverted to Canada. The day after 9/11, my late, good friend Lanier Phillips called from Washington and told me, "When I heard that all those stranded passengers had landed in Newfoundland, I had no doubt how they would be looked after."

He would have known. He was reflecting on the treatment he had received after surviving a shipwreck on Newfoundland's rugged coast nearly sixty years earlier, as recounted elsewhere in these pages. Even as Lanier voiced his prediction, the 9/11 strandees were being enfolded in unfettered kindness and generosity.

IT'S THE DNA, FOLKS!

The character of the Newfoundlander is distinctive. It is, Don Jamieson noted in his memoir, "the product of such influences as insularity, independence nurtured by necessity, fierce pride renewed constantly by adversity and a self-deprecating sense of humour . . . we were not necessarily better, only unique."[77] Ottawa author Claire Hoy has written that "the historical isolation of Newfoundlanders . . . has reared a people with some unique characteristics. The challenge of survival has imbued in them a remarkable resilience to constant hardships, deeply ingrained values of familial kinship, a striking level of unselfish warmth and hospitality and, yes, a fatalistic sense of humour."[78]

The catalyst of the generosity manifested in Gander and elsewhere on 9/11 is the Newfie take on humanity. The locals' label of their guests as "plane people" is an unintended play on words. To the Newfoundlanders, the visitors were plain people, ordinary, dispossessed human beings caught up in a vortex not of their own making. Our empathetic instincts kicked in. *There but for the grace of God go I.* The celebrated Newfoundland poet E. J. Pratt foretold, decades before the fact, how the plane people would be received by the locals.

> This is their culture, this—their master passion
> Of giving shelter and of sharing bread.

It was ever thus. I recall an incident involving a rum smuggler from Hermitage and the residents of the nearby community of Seal Cove, Fortune

77 *No Place for Fools*, Don Jamieson, St. John's: Breakwater Books, 1989, pp. 87-88
78 *Clyde Wells: A Political Biography*, Claire Hoy, Stoddart Publishing, Toronto, 1992, p. 139

Bay,[79] an outport of straitlaced Salvationists for whom booze is anathema, a one-way ticket to hell. An RCMP customs and excise squad intercepted a longliner that, ostensibly, was fishing on the Grand Banks. The police had reason to believe the boat's real cargo was hard liquor from Saint-Pierre and Miquelon, a French outpost just twelve miles off Newfoundland's south coast. Their suspicions confirmed, the boat owner was charged with tax evasion, which, depending on the gravity of the offence, could result in stiff penalties including seizure of the offender's boat and home. The case and, especially, the dire straits in which the smuggler could find himself if convicted mobilized public sympathy for him. The devout, God-fearing folks at Seal Cove sprung into action, raising money for his defence. Clearly, compassion and empathy were the motivators, not any propensity to condone the smuggler's illegal act. Put simply, it was a pragmatic application of the famous phrase from the writings of St. Augustine[80], which translates loosely as "love the sinner; hate the sin."

A most delightful application of that dictum occurred during a rancorous labour dispute. A well-known lady handed out coffee to striking nurses whose shouted vitriol was taking direct aim at Premier Brian Tobin. While the caring coffee lady recognized they needed something hot to cheer their spirits and brace themselves against the bitter cold, she certainly would not have approved of what the picketers were saying about the premier. He was, after all, her son![81] Some detractors have suggested that the gesture was not the mother's brainchild but the son's. Winston Churchill famously said, "The best spontaneity is planned." It is a credo that Brian Tobin embraces and has been known to practise when circumstances require a helpful headline. Whatever the impetus, my hat is off to Florence Tobin for responding to rage with humanity.

TITILLATING THE MASSES

In the twenty-first century, the Newfoundland culture is alive and well. It thrives in a robust oral tradition, in debating and public speaking and in vibrant live theatre.

I'm a music buff. I looked forward eagerly to my first visit to Nashville. It turned out to be a real letdown, musically speaking. Of course, the famed city's many recording venues and Grand Ole Opry put it in a league by itself. But it was the downtown live music scene that left me cold, two blocks of pubs with a dozen bands all nasally singing the same few country and western ditties.

79 Hermitage and Seal Cove are communities on Newfoundland's south coast.
80 Cum dilectione hominum et odio vitiorum
81 *All in Good Time*, Brian Tobin, Toronto: Penguin, 2002, p. 9-10

By contrast, George Street in St. John's, Newfoundland, is an eclectic smorgasbord of folk and Irish, rap and country, every taste and genre from hard rock to blues to classic. It's a lively mecca for music lovers.

In TV crime drama, Jonny Harris plays the police constable in *Murdock Mysteries*, and until recently there was *Republic of Doyle*. Harris also has his own comedy/reality show, *Still Standing*.

Canada's dean of NHL play-by-play, eighty-four-year-old Bob Cole, is a St. John's townie. National TV pundit and print columnist Rex Murphy hails from Placentia Bay on Newfoundland's south coast.

The Canadian television comedy scene is teeming with Newfies—*This Hour Has 22 Minutes*, *Rick Mercer Report*. Who can forget Mercer's "Talking to Americans" spoof, the highest-rated television special in Canadian history? He cleverly engaged George W. Bush in an exchange about "Prime Minister Poutine"[82]. Americans' familiarity with their own history was put to the test as Mercer explained that a Canadian firm had acquired the mineral rights to Mount Rushmore. Respondents were relieved and grateful to hear that drilling could be done at the rear of the iconic sculpture rather than through Lincoln's forehead!

82 The PM at the time was Jean Chrétien. Poutine is a popular Quebec concoction of French fries, cheese curds, and gravy.

PART 2
Charting a Public Course

There is a tide in the affairs of men
Which, taken at the flood, leads on to fortune;
Omitted, all the voyage of their life
Is bound in shallows and in miseries.
On such a full sea are we now afloat;
And we must take the current when it serves,
Or lose our ventures.

— William Shakespeare

CHAPTER 11
UNION MOUTHPIECE

A man only learns in two ways, one by reading, and the other by association with smarter people.
— Will Rogers, actor, vaudeville performer, humorist, and newspaper columnist, 1879–2935

The Newfoundland and Labrador Teachers' Association[83], professional association of the province's 5,000 teachers, is a phenomenal organization which has been an influential force for good in education since its inception in 1890. My involvement with the NTA dates back to my university days when I served as president of the association's campus branch. At Springdale, I continued my participation, again heading up the local branch. Following a stint as vice-president of the provincial body, I assumed the presidency at twenty-eight, the youngest person ever to hold that position.

I began my participation in province-wide issues and organizations in the mid-1960s. By then, the harsh downside of an education system predicated on segregation by religious affiliation had become a matter of ongoing dismay and grumbling, particularly among educators and parents. The duplication of facilities, especially in underpopulated areas, and the consequent added financial drain on the public purse, were taking their toll, negating efforts to offer quality education.

"Dropout and illiteracy rates were high, teachers were among the least trained in the country, and many rural students attended one-room schools that had no libraries, gymnasiums, and other facilities common in larger Canadian schools."[84]

83 The organization was known as the Newfoundland Teachers' Association until 2001, when it was changed to reflect the new official name of the province.
84 http://www.heritage.nf.ca

Senior Department of Education officials were involved in a discussion on the need for change, having realized that sizable segments of the public would be amenable to at least some tweaking of the status quo. Three men, each of whom I came to know and admire, played influential roles in fuelling a full-blown dialogue. They were John Acreman, Cecil Roebothan, and, soon after, Wilmore Woodland, respectively, the United Church, Anglican, and Salvation Army superintendents in the education ministry.

In an effort to address the education morass, the provincial government co-opted university professor Dr. Phil Warren to head a royal commission with a mandate to recommend improvements in education. Among other changes, the commission report triggered an amalgamation of the Anglican, Salvation Army, Presbyterian, and United Church school systems, and provided impetus for the passage of legislation by the House of Assembly, giving effect to commission recommendations. Of course, the consequent education restructuring had significant implications for the Newfoundland Teachers' Association, and I, as its president, and the provincial executive weighed in regularly.

Denominational schools were finally relegated to the history books in 1998. Thanks to the courageous leadership of Premier Brian Tobin, the school system was, at long last, put on a more functional footing. Premier Clyde Wells and Education Minister (later Premier) Roger Grimes also deserve credit for their pivotal roles.

The NTA presidency became full-time in 1971. I was the last but one of the part-timers. Juggling two key assignments, as school principal and provincial head of a professional association, made for a frenzied schedule. I spent many long hours throttling down the highway in the dead of night, in weather foul and fair, to meet obligations in Green Bay or the provincial capital, 300 miles away.

A frequent travel companion was Len Williams, principal of the Salvation Army high school in Windsor and a fellow member of the NTA provincial executive. A cerebral fellow who oozes humanity, Dr. Len Williams has contributed much to Canadian education, as president of the NTA and the Canadian Teachers' Federation, as head of Memorial University's teacher education program, and as chair of a provincial royal commission on education. He was named a Member of the Order of Canada in 2000 for his stellar service.

TOO CLOSE FOR COMFORT

The joint committee, an amalgam of educational leaders from government, the churches, the university, and the NTA, met monthly in the evening to address teacher training issues. My usual routine was to hit the road after the meeting, enabling me to be back at my day job at Springdale next morning. With highway traffic and police ghost cars at a minimum, I barrelled along at insane speeds, usually reaching my destination unscathed. There were exceptions. The most unnerving incident occurred in the wee hours on a straight stretch of road and, fortunately, beneath a full moon. A moose suddenly materialized on the left shoulder just ahead. I hit the brake. The right front fender missed the towering animal as it crossed my path. Whew! That was close!

But wait! A second moose followed close behind. I floored the gas and eyeballed the creature as the car inserted itself between the two animals. Just when I thought I was home free, I heard a thump and felt the rear end of the car lurch to the right. Surely, I thought, the left side of the car must be mincemeat. Yet, on inspection, I could find absolutely no evidence of the incident, save for a few moose hairs wedged in the crevice where the rear left panel butts into the bumper.

Some months later, I left the car with a salesman to get a trade-in appraisal. He called me soon after, upset that, according to him, I had tried to pull a fast one on him.

"You didn't tell me that your car was in a collision."

His mechanics had discovered that the rear bumper had shifted to the right and the chassis was twisted out of alignment. We reasoned that the moose's knee must have impacted the end of the bumper. That second animal had taken its pound of flesh after all. How's that for a close call?

I was re-elected as NTA president. However, six months into my second one-year term, I resigned due to my growing involvement in politics. My position as vice-president, then president, of the Newfoundland Liberal Party raised a red flag for some of my NTA colleagues, among them several of my respected mentors and closest friends.

An upside of old age is that you get to edit your youth, at least on paper. It's a kind of post audit of past decisions and their consequences: Did I do the right thing? Did it serve its intended purpose? What should I have done differently?

The immediate trigger of my resignation from the NTA presidency was my undertaking to manage Alec Hickman's leadership campaign. Caught up in the Smallwood-Crosbie juggernaut, many staunch Liberals, me included, pined for a third option. Hickman seemed to fit the bill, though his prospects of success were slim to none. A firm belief in Hail Marys makes me an all-too-frequent sucker for lost causes. I made the plunge, a move I have long since regretted. My precipitous decision, far from achieving its objective, was a complete dud. In the process, my action unjustifiably disrupted the NTA's momentum and disappointed many colleagues who had heretofore trusted my judgment.

I continue to be the NLTA's biggest fan. The grounding, example, and advice gleaned from my colleagues around the executive table in the '60s and early '70s have served me extremely well in the years since. Much of the success I had in public life can be traced to those adrenalin-fuelled times. How lucky was I that my mentors included guys like Dr. Sherbourne McCurdy, Cliff Andrews, Brother A. F. Brennan, Lloyd Buffett, Bill Turner, and Huts Davis, among others!

THE EMERALD ISLE

A congress of teachers convened in Dublin[85] in 1968. I went there on behalf of the NTA, affording me the privilege of treading on Irish soil for the first time. Ever since, the Emerald Isle is easily my favourite destination, other than the Rock, of course. The week in Ireland was like coming home. The spectacular coastal vistas, the laid-back pace, the comfort food, even the fickle weather and, above all, the folksy, extroverted, chatty people were therapeutic.

In 1997, my family and I vacationed in Ireland and England. The cabbie who drove us to Dublin airport treated us as long-lost friends with his non-stop commentary, one-liners, and helpful travelogue of must-see places. A couple of hours later, as we boarded a cab at Heathrow, the sullen creature at the wheel slid open the glass panel to the passenger compartment and barked, "Where to?"

Our exchange over, the sliding window slammed shut. Welcome to London! Six-year-old Stacy[86], completely bewildered, disgusted even, summed up the scene with dripping understatement: "I liked the Irish guy better!"

TRANSATLANTIC TRYST

With the Dublin teachers' convention behind me, I steamed out of Le Havre in August 1968 on the SS *France*. I was probably the most excited passenger aboard. Bound for New York, it would be my first transoceanic adventure by sea. I had soon poked my nose into every nook and cranny of the giant ocean liner. It was time to size up my fellow travellers, giving extra attention to young ladies who may be partial to a summer romance. My hands-on research soon landed me happily in the arms of a newly minted graduate

85 World Confederation of Organizations of the Teaching Profession (WCOTP)

86 Stacy and her sister, Holly, are my stepdaughters. Their mom, Darlene, and I married in 1998, parted company early in 2016, and divorced soon after.

from a Philadelphia medical school. Jo and I bonded quickly, and the six-day fling stretched into a year as I made frequent pilgrimages from Springdale to Cherry Hill, New Jersey, and rendezvoused with her in New York. It was a doomed romance, ending abruptly when her best girlfriend, whom I had also met during the cruise, said,

> "Jo, do you have any idea what your controlling, sanctimonious, narrow-minded pappa will do to you when he finds out that your Newfie heartthrob is not Jewish?"

A painful, yet graceful, parting of the ways soon followed, leaving me with great memories and, in later years, the lingering thought that my one shot at dual citizenship went up in smoke because I couldn't pass muster with Jo's dad.

Dublin, Ireland, 1968. L-R: Newfoundland Teachers' Association president, Roger Simmons; Brother A. F. Brennan, incoming president of the Canadian Teachers' Federation; Sir Ronald Gould, president of the World Confederation of Organizations of the Teaching Profession. (Author photo)

CHAPTER 12
ONE OF THE BACKROOM BOYS

The hottest place in Hell is reserved for those who remain neutral in times of great moral conflict.
— MARTIN LUTHER KING, JR.

I first laid eyes on the whirling dervish known as Joey when I was nine years old. I can see him now, just down the street from my house, as he jack-in-the-boxed out of his nondescript car, microphone at the ready, turned up the volume on his screech box, and proceeded to mesmerize the growing crowd.

The historic referendum campaign was in full swing. The upcoming vote would determine Newfoundland's constitutional destiny, deciding among three options: a return to responsible government, which had been suspended for financial reasons fourteen years earlier; confederation with Canada; status quo, a British-dominated Commission of Government, *a bureaucratic and benevolent autocracy*,[87] which had been in office since 1934, characterized by Don Jamieson as the *long night of political abnegation*[88].

Joey Smallwood was championing the confederation cause. He regaled all who would listen about the utopia that was just around the corner, provided, of course, they voted to turn their backs on Newfoundland's proud independence and cast their lot with Canada. In Bishop's Falls, he was largely preaching to the choir. Like most rural communities, the town liked what he was selling.

Many believed Newfoundland should return to self-government before deciding on its constitutional future. John Crosbie's 1946 poem, penned during college days, leaves no doubt he shared that view:

87 "Public Administration in Newfoundland during . . . Commission of Government," Susan McCorquodale, thesis, Queen's University, 1973
88 *No Place for Fools*, Don Jamieson, St. John's: Breakwater Books, 1989, p. 22

Up true Newfoundlander! Rise!
And fight once more to win proud freedom's prize.[89]

It would actually take two referenda to decide the issue. The third-place finisher in the first vote, Commission of Government, was dropped from the ballot, and Confederation with Canada won by a nose[90]. *The lost Dominion*[91] became Canada's tenth province.

The first time I got to talk to Smallwood came seven years later when I was a vagabond, not quite sixteen years old. He and I were cooling our heels in the old Gander airport terminal because a fog blanket had cancelled our respective flights. As I sat alone playing solitaire, I heard a familiar voice.

"Greg, here's a young man going places."

I recognized the two suits hovering over me. Finance Minister Greg Power had been Joey's right-hand man in the battle for Confederation. Standing next to him was, you guessed it, Premier Smallwood himself. And he was talking to me!

"Are you travelling alone? Where to?"

Smallwood and his minister were probably headed off to some distant land to coax deep pockets to invest their millions in Newfoundland's bright future. I was destined for Halifax. I had decided I wanted to travel by plane for the first time, and the Nova Scotia city was the only out-of-province place to which I could afford to fly.

I never did board that flight to Halifax, but I came within a whisker of a quick trip to Europe. By the time the fog lifted, I had passed two nights curled up on an airport sofa without much sleep. In my delirium, I responded to the wrong boarding announcement. Believing I had heard TCA, I found myself sitting aboard a TWA[92] flight bound for Düsseldorf, Germany. The bane of security screening was far into the future.

Alas, it was not to be. The stewardess's's[93] head count did me in. Back in the terminal, and now wide awake, I had to choose between globe-trotting and fending off starvation, having run out of money. I cashed the air ticket and made a beeline for the cafeteria, then the train station. I would not slip

89 *No Holds Barred*, John Crosbie, Toronto: McClelland & Stewart, 1997, p. 20
90 Confederation with Canada: 78,323; Responsible Government: 71,334. The turnout at the polls for the second vote was 85% of eligible voters compared to 88% in the first referendum.
91 *No Holds Barred*, John Crosbie, Toronto: McClelland & Stewart, 1997, p. 5
92 Trans-Canada Air Lines (TCA) is now Air Canada; Trans World Airlines (TWA) was bought by American Airlines in 2001.
93 Today, of course, the preferred term is flight attendant. What's wrong with stewardess, I don't know. Actress, mistress, princess, and seamstress have so far escaped the attention of politically correct revisionists, but don't hold your breath.

the surly bonds of earth[94] for another two years. However, I did get to meet my political idol. A few years ahead, he would become less so.

A DOTING PREMIER

There's a great story of how Joey got a glimpse of one of his idols. The Liberal road show had rolled into Corner Brook. As the platform party, including prominent developer Art Lundrigan, assembled in the holding room, Joey launched into yet another of his monologues, normally long and painfully repetitious.

This anecdote, though, is worth retelling—without the repetition. Smallwood and Lundrigan had played tourists in Rome. Just when the tour of the Basilica of San Clemente, a twelfth-century Christian edifice, appeared to be ending, the guide led them downstairs to a second church that had been converted from the home of a Roman nobleman in the fourth century and used by both early, secret Christians and pagans. Soon thereafter, the duo once again followed the guide below and came upon the ruins of a third structure, a villa and warehouse destroyed in the Great Fire of 64 AD. Smallwood recognized the lady standing in front of him and couldn't contain his good fortune. In a loud whisper, he exuded to Lundrigan: "Jackie! Jackie Kennedy! It's Jackie Kennedy!"

The manner in which he reacted to this chance sighting of an American icon and global phenomenon was revealing, significant in a way that Joey probably didn't realize. When the premier told us the story, he had to be reminded by Lundrigan to mention the name of the man standing beside Jackie—Aristotle Onassis! The Greek magnate's megabucks were no match for her beauty and celebrity. It was arguably the one time in Smallwood's political career when a gorgeous woman blinded him to his first love, a big-time tycoon rolling in dough and looking for a place to invest it.

MY WAY OR THE HIGHWAY

Ted Russell and I shared an office for two years at Memorial University in the 1960s. We were teaching speech to first-year students, though both of us had a complete disdain for the underlying premise of the course, namely that the incoming students needed to learn proper English and abandon their lilting Newfoundland dialects, the equivalent of decreeing that all Irishmen must speak the Queen's English or telling US southerners that their drawl is inferior to the lingo of New Yorkers.

94 "High Flight" by John Magee, an American aviator and poet who died at the age of nineteen in a mid-air collision over Lincolnshire, England, during World War II. He was serving in the Royal Canadian Air Force, which he joined before the United States officially entered the war.

Russell and I were mercenaries. While we didn't believe in the course, we needed the money, which, in Ted's case, might strike you as strange. He was, after all, an acclaimed writer and a pioneer in heightening an awareness of Newfoundland's distinct culture and society. But he was also *persona non grata*, at least insofar as Premier Joey Smallwood was concerned.

Beginning as a sixteen-year-old schoolmaster at Pass Island[95] in the 1920s, Russell had been, successively, a teacher, magistrate, rural development specialist, and a cabinet minister in Joey's first administration. His sojourn in the corridors of power was short-lived. Following a series of disagreements over the premier's dictatorial approach to governance and policy-making, Russell threw in the towel, the first of Joey's ministers to quit. For that, he would pay a heavy price.

Joseph R. Smallwood's middle name should have been revenge. In his treatment of Russell and the few others who had the audacity to challenge him, the premier gave new, tawdry meaning to the word vindictive. He went to great lengths to ensure that Russell didn't earn a living, threatening to disown anybody who hired Ted. Which explains why the literary icon brought home the bacon by teaching at Memorial and scriptwriting for the Canadian Broadcasting Corporation, just about the only two institutions that Joey couldn't intimidate.

As an orator, Smallwood had few peers. To make certain his message got through, he used a triad progression.

"First, I tell my listeners what I'm going to tell them. Then, I tell them. And finally, I tell them what I just told them."

His repetitive formula was as predictable as the opening bars of the Last Post on Remembrance Day, like a bugler who strikes the first note of a triad, then one after the other, the two higher notes. Even if one of the notes is slightly off-key, the listener will have heard all three. While there could be no doubt that his message was received, Joey's repetitive speaking style could sometimes induce an effect that was far less tuneful than any trumpet or piano.

Although his oratory and histrionics wowed the masses, the substance of his message, his single-minded fixation on economic development, no matter the financial and human cost, gave many the jitters. As noted, Ted Russell left the Smallwood cabinet because of policy differences. Four years later, a second minister, Dr. Herbert Pottle, resigned for similar reasons. His book, *Newfoundland: Dawn Without Light*, is a cover-to-cover condemnation of Joey's approach to industrial development and job creation. The

95 A tiny fishing village, since abandoned, on Newfoundland's south coast. Many of the characters and anecdotes in Russell's plays and radio scripts draw on his two years at Pass Island.

ex-minister's most scathing indictment is that Smallwood neglected the province's most precious resource, its people. Pottle charges that the premier squandered the opportunity to make his fellow citizens self-reliant and trained them to be wards of the state because it suited the political agenda. Far from being partners in government, the rank and file became its pawns. In Pottle's telling phrase, they were *the counters on the shuffle-board of economic development.*[96]

"Ill fares the land, to hastening ills a prey,
Where wealth accumulates, and men decay."[97]

THE ANOINTED ONE

In 1964, a paper I had written as part of my university studies came to the premier's attention. The treatise lauded advances in Newfoundland education since Confederation. Smallwood summoned me to his office and proposed my paper be expanded and published. A couple of cabinet ministers were tasked to make it happen. But the project never got off the ground—mainly, I suspected, because one of them had plans to publish a book on the same subject, which he subsequently did.

In the fall of 1965, Smallwood staged a so-called thinkers' conference that showcased several prominent speakers, including economist John Kenneth Galbraith and political firebrand René Lévesque[98]. I participated in a panel with the Canadian-born Galbraith on the role of government in a dynamic society.

The premier once again invited me to his office in early 1966 and regaled me with his vision of a glowing future in politics for me on the premise, of course, that I join his slate of candidates in the pending general election.

"Only four men are capable of taking the reins when I step down."

He then named the first three, listing their strengths but then eliminating each as he cited their weaknesses.

"And fourth, there's you!"

In his generous assessment, I was unquestionably God's gift to mankind and the only worthy successor to him. It was all very seductive, almost convincing for a twenty-seven-year-old political neophyte, until I learned that the exact same template had been used in pitching several other individuals. In each scenario, the person being courted was the only logical choice as Joey's successor.

---

96 *Newfoundland: Dawn Without Light*, Herbert L. Pottle, St. John's: Breakwater, 1979, p. 66
97 "The Deserted Village" by Oliver Goldsmith, Irish poet and novelist, 1728–1774
98 A Quebec provincial cabinet minister and, later, leader of the separatist Parti Québécois and premier (1976–85) following the party's seismic win at the polls

ONE-PARTY STATE

Ever since the 1949 union of Newfoundland and Canada, the province had been Smallwood's personal fiefdom. All decisions relating to budgetary, economic, and social policy were made by him. The choice of Liberal candidates, both provincial and federal, was controlled by Smallwood. The House of Assembly was reduced to an echo chamber for the verbose premier. On many of the major public policy decisions, the legislature didn't even get to rubber-stamp them, as Joey routinely ignored both precedent and legality to impose his vision and ingratiate himself with voters.

Corner Brook, NL, 1966. *Western Star* cartoon: Clyde Wells became Premier Smallwood's Labour minister during a nurses' strike. (Francis Hull cartoon)

In 1966, Smallwood called an election, the sixth provincial campaign since Confederation. For the electorate, it would be the fifteenth trip to the polls in eighteen years, including the two referenda and seven federal elections. For Smallwood, it would be yet another opportunity to tighten his stranglehold on power. Indeed, he seemed to be seized with the notion of wiping out the parliamentary opposition altogether. To that end, he rolled out a pie-in-the-sky platform, sweeping, audacious, and costly. And he recruited several star candidates, among them John Crosbie and Clyde Wells.

During the campaign, I was interim editor of Corner Brook's daily newspaper, the *Western Star*. The actual date of the election posed a problem for me. With the new school year getting under way, I needed to be at my desk in Springdale, more than 100 miles away, to resume my responsibilities as supervising principal. First, though, I had to discharge one final duty for the newspaper, write an editorial commenting on the election results. Except the outcome wouldn't be known until long after I had hit the road. On the completely safe presumption that Smallwood and the Liberals would once again rack up an overwhelming majority, I penned a piece decrying the small size of the opposition and its implications for democratic governance.

The task accomplished, I made a dash for the parking lot. By the time I reached my car, I had a nagging thought: What if my assumption concerning the election is wrong? To cover another possibility, I ran back upstairs and banged out a second editorial on the Smith Corona, this time lamenting there would be no opposition in the legislature, that the Tories had been wiped out. As things turned out, it was my first editorial that ran in the paper next morning. Joey won all but three seats, shrinking the Tory rump from its previous seven. The Liberal popular vote was sixty-two per cent, within four points of its support in the first post-Confederation election seventeen years earlier. Clearly, Smallwood was still the master of his fate.

Black Duck Siding, NL, 1966. As editor of the *Western Star*, Corner Brook's daily newspaper, I interviewed salmon fishermen on Harry's River. (*Western Star* photo)

THERE ARE NONE SO BLIND AS THOSE WHO WILL NOT SEE[99]

By the late 1960s, Joey had reigned as a benevolent dictator for two decades. That was about to change. The 1969 provincial Liberal convention, called by Joey to mute the growing clamour for a less autocratic regime, marked the beginning of the end for Smallwood, though few realized it at the time. If Joey himself saw it coming, which I doubt, his staggering capacity for self-delusion would have shielded him from the truth.

There were some signs. Joey's attempt in the fall of 1968 to stack the party's executive with his sycophants backfired. His hand-picks for president and vice-president were defeated by two young upstarts, Rick Cashin and me. We were a whole lot happier than Joey was! At the reception which followed, Joey pumped the hands of the party's newly elected executive members. Despite their many differences, the new president and the premier had a grudging respect for each other going back to Cashin's days as an MP[100] and beyond. So, it wasn't surprising to see them chatting up a storm just minutes after the young fox had outfoxed the old fox.

99 John Heywood, English playwright, musician, and composer, 1497–1580
100 Richard Cashin was the Member of Parliament for St. John's West from 1963 to 1968.

What happened next did surprise onlookers, though not me as I stood beside Cashin. Smallwood's handler said, "Premier, you know Mr. Simmons, I believe?"

Joey fixed a frigid stare over my shoulder, ignored my extended hand, and, without uttering a word, moved on to deliver an affectionate bear hug to one of his acolytes who had survived the election of party officers.

Smallwood had reason to pretend I didn't exist. During the 1966 election, I had published in the *Western Star* a couple of impish cartoons and penned several editorials that cut close to the bone. In reference to an ongoing nurses' wage dispute, I ran the first political cartoon featuring Clyde Wells[101]—depicting Joey's new Labour minister dressed in short pants, legs dangling above the floor, beseechingly looking up at the premier seated beside him: "And, daddy, what's a strike?"

A second cartoon was more biting. The island portion of the Trans-Canada Highway had been completed to great fanfare in 1965, facilitated largely by federal dollars and, specifically, by Prime Minister Lester Pearson. As construction proceeded, the 600-mile stretch of road from St. John's to Port aux Basques was peppered with signs which read, "We'll finish the drive in '65, thanks to Mr. Pearson!"

Paving of the final sections had been a bit of a rush job, and within months there were problems with potholes and undulating blacktop. The cartoon sketch captures driver frustration. A motorist fixes a flat tire. A nearby highway sign reads, "We'll patch and fix in '66, thanks to Mr. Smallwood!"

One *Star* editorial in particular hit a nerve. Entitled *The one-party state*, it likened Newfoundland to the USSR in its governing practices. My opinion piece was such a frontal attack on the government that I cleared it with the publisher, Wallace McKay, who predicted that the editorial would cause some waves. Sure enough, the newspaper had barely hit the streets when I got a call from a senior staffer in the premier's office. I don't recall what he said to me, but his words certainly had the intended effect. I raced into McKay's office and blurted out, "Ed Roberts just called me." My panicky tone of voice and matching body language communicated the real message. McKay, ex-military, went ballistic.

"I knew it was a mistake to bring you aboard. Whimpering nervous Nellies I don't need. If you're not up to the job, clean out your desk and make yourself scarce."

McKay's contrived tantrum saved the day. As I continued to write provocative editorials, tirades from the premier's office no longer triggered the urge to seek cover from the publisher.

101 *Clyde Wells: A Political Biography*, Claire Hoy, Toronto: Stoddart Publishing, 1992, p. 50

The relationship between the premier and me, his newly minted vice-president, would get worse. At the national level, Prime Minister Lester Pearson had spearheaded dramatic and enduring changes in social policy during his five years in the top job. Having twice failed to win a majority government, he decided to step down, setting in motion a leadership process to choose his successor.

Don Jamieson, Newfoundland's member in the Pearson cabinet, suggested I get myself elected as a delegate to the 1968 federal Liberal leadership convention. I made my intention known to two key Liberals in Springdale and was assured of their support. Joey had other ideas. At the delegate selection meeting, as soon as I was nominated, the two guys, whose blessing I thought I had, ganged up on me, one of them nominating the other, who bested me by three votes to win the sole delegate position, but not before the meeting's chairman had extolled the virtues of my opponent. The chairman was a known Smallwood henchman brought in from a nearby town, and in a delicious tidbit of finessing, he was my cousin, Wes Simms.

However, all was not lost. Jamieson, no fan of Smallwood, arranged for me to attend the convention as an observer. As I entered the Ottawa convention venue, I came face to face with Smallwood and two other Newfoundland politicians, one of whom was and is a close friend. Fred Rowe, Jr. later told me of the premier's verbal outburst when he spotted me: "Who let that little pipsqueak in here!" A few months later, commiserating with other party members about Joey's stubborn refusal to pass the torch to the next generation, I elevated foot-in-mouth disease to new heights by declaring: "What this party needs is a good state funeral!"

In no time flat, my reckless utterance reached Smallwood's ears with predictable consequences. My status as *persona non grata* was confirmed and cemented. Meanwhile, the federal leadership convention chose Pearson's successor on the fourth ballot. The new Liberal leader and prime minister, Pierre Trudeau, was a first-term MP from Montreal and had served as Justice minister under his predecessor. He had come to national prominence for his role in constitutional negotiations and his groundbreaking initiatives in justice reform. Two months into office, the new prime minister went to the polls.

If the mini-revolt which Cashin and I staged, with a lot of help from our friends, was an omen of Smallwood's loosening grip on power, the results of the 1968 federal election were a full-blown mutiny. Lifelong Liberals by the thousands bolted and cast their votes for change. Even many a Joey disciple swallowed hard and marked an X for the "dirty Tories," a term much-used by Smallwood to imply cause-and-effect between the party that formed the Newfoundland government in 1932 and the "dirty '30s."

Trudeaumania swept the nation, racking up 155 seats in the 264-member Commons. Yet, despite Smallwood's choreographed switch to Trudeau as the federal leadership convention got under way two months earlier, all but one of Newfoundland's seven ridings elected Tory MPs. "While the rest of Canada was revelling in Trudeaumania, we were swept up in Smallwoodphobia."[102]

WHY ME, LORD?[103]

John Crosbie and Joey Smallwood had a tempestuous relationship that can best be described as love-hate, not alternating but sequential. Things got off to a promising start when the thirty-five-year-old deputy mayor of St. John's and established lawyer joined Smallwood's cabinet in the lead-up to the 1966 provincial election. Even then, though, Crosbie must have cross-examined himself in the mirror the very next morning:

"What, in the name of the good Lord, have you done?"

Done, it was. And whatever misgivings the new minister may have had, campaign imperatives kept his lip buttoned, publicly, at least, until the polls closed. Almost immediately thereafter, the Smallwood-Crosbie marriage began to show ominous strains. The premier's dictatorial ways and, just as significant, his seat-of-the-pants approach to public policy and drooling fascination with industry tycoons were more than the egalitarian, rational, business-savvy Crosbie could stomach.

The Come By Chance boondoggle brought matters to a head. The breaking point for Crosbie, and for Clyde Wells, was interim financing for the proposed Come By Chance oil refinery. The premier had agreed to advance $10 million to start the project, even though developer John Shaheen had no equity in the venture. Both Crosbie and Wells quit the cabinet. That's their version. Smallwood insisted they had been given the boot.

I believed John and Clyde. I was not alone. Much of the public, but especially the pundits and insiders, had their fill of the premier's revisionist editing of the facts and his petulance.

Wells quit politics altogether, though that wouldn't be the last we saw of him. Crosbie eventually joined the microscopic Tory caucus, but not before challenging Smallwood in a riveting tug-of-war, the 1969 Liberal leadership race.

---

102 *No Holds Barred*, John Crosbie, Toronto: McClelland & Stewart, 1997, p. 74
103 Kris Kristofferson (1936–), American country music singer and songwriter

A LEG-UP FOR PECKFORD

Delegations were being chosen across the province for the upcoming leadership convention. Smallwood, Crosbie, and Alec Hickman were the main leadership contenders. I was a Hickman supporter. Each candidate's partisans were running slates, and as the delegate selection meeting in Green Bay district proceeded, it became obvious that Smallwood's list would take every position. That's when I withdrew the Hickman nominee for secretary and asked my group to vote for Brian Peckford, a Crosbie supporter. The final delegate count was Smallwood 15, Crosbie 1.

In enabling Peckford's win, I played a small yet key role in Peckford's path to the premiership. My friend was elected and soon came to Crosbie's attention, who, realizing Brian's smarts and people skills, recruited him as a full-time organizer. Three years later, Peckford was elected to the House of Assembly and would later succeed to the top job.

CROSBIE COMES COURTING

Meanwhile, Crosbie was slogging away. I flew with him in his chartered aircraft to Goose Bay, mostly to salvage some credibility as party VP after having traipsed around the province as part of a tag-team act with Smallwood and Cashin.

It was Crosbie's decision to pitch his rented helicopter on my front lawn in Springdale that made me smile and perhaps helped to burnish my image among the locals. The mountain had come to Muhammad. I had begged off on earlier entreaties to have a chat with him. Crosbie showed me the results of a poll, one of a series he had commissioned to arm him with up-to-date information on issues and on people who could impact his leadership bid.

The findings of one question in particular had me thinking vain thoughts. Having just been head of the province-wide teachers' organization and now as vice-president of the Liberal Party, I had achieved a high profile, which wasn't that difficult given the times and Newfoundland's small population. TV viewers, in the pre-cable era, had a choice of just two channels. The odds were good that most viewers were exposed daily to one or both of the news telecasts.

Here is the relevant excerpt from the Crosbie poll.

VOTER JOB RATINGS OF THE 10 BEST-KNOWN LEADERS
IN POLITICS, THE PUBLIC SERVICE AND ACADEME
JULY 1969 (EXCERPT)

	% positive job rating	Ranking
Dr. Phil Warren, Professor, Memorial University*	79	1
Alec Hickman, provincial Minister of Justice and Health	72	2
Donald Jamieson, federal Minister of Transport	71	3
Roger Simmons, President, Newfoundland Teachers' Association	70	4
James McGrath, Member of Parliament	66	5
Frank Moores, President, Progressive Conservative Party of Canada	64	6
John Crosbie, Member, Newfoundland House of Assembly	58	8
Joseph Smallwood, Premier of Newfoundland	56	12
Clyde Wells, Member, Newfoundland House of Assembly	53	15
Pierre Trudeau, Prime Minister of Canada	36	22
* Position/title at the time of the poll		

With reference to me, the pollsters noted,

> "Those who feel familiar with him give him very high marks. His job rating is seventy per cent favourable. Most assuredly Roger Simmons, if he can be inveigled into the Crosbie camp, must be used heavily . . ."

Reading the pollsters' assessment of my potential utility as an ally, it was easy to see why Crosbie was courting me. The truth is that I was quite attracted to his candidacy. The issues he espoused, sound economic development, a progressive social agenda, and fiscal probity, were all music to my ears. And I had been one of his biggest fans ever since he and Clyde Wells had stood up to Smallwood on the Come By Chance financial arrangements. But like many of Crosbie's growing army of admirers, I couldn't get past his clumsy, halting attempts at speechmaking. I had difficulty seeing that Newfoundland, where firebrand oratory is considered the requisite tool of every aspiring Moses, would embrace one so ill at ease at a podium.

My candidate of choice was Alec Hickman, Joey's Justice minister. As the Smallwood-Crosbie duel became ever more toxic and polarized, Hickman's chances, slim at the starting gun, withered with each passing day and each delegate selection meeting. By the time the leadership convention was gavelled to order, the outcome was a foregone conclusion. The first and only ballot confirmed the obvious:

Crosbie, John, 440
Hickman, Alec, 187
Smallwood, Joseph, 1,070

If there was any surprise, it was that Crosbie had fared much better than expected, given the ruthlessness and dominance of the Smallwood juggernaut.

END OF AN ERA

The six Tory MPs elected in 1968 quickly established themselves as Newfoundland's voice in Ottawa, earning themselves the nickname "The Noisy Six." History was being made, and not the version Smallwood would have written. For the first time since Confederation, Joey's megaphone, his take on reality, had to compete with, indeed was being drowned out by, a far more progressive message. It was suddenly respectable for voters, long the captives of the Smallwood agenda, to openly debate and consider their electoral options.

Frank Moores, one of the six Tory MPs, became the vehicle for change. As the new provincial leader, he quickly mobilized voter discontent with Smallwood. His first election, in October 1971, ended Joey's erstwhile stranglehold. When the votes were counted, Moores had won twenty-one seats, all but three of them gains from the Liberals. Joey got twenty seats. The rout was in full gear. Although Smallwood clung to power for another three months through a never-ending barrage of media assaults, court challenges, and constitutional musings, the writing was on the wall. Even a comical, yet pathetic, orgy of musical chairs couldn't save him. The six-term premier who had held office for twenty-three years finally gave up the ghost in January 1972. Moores, having assumed the premiership, triggered the dissolution of the legislature, clearing the way for a second general election in five months and a Tory sweep of all but eight of the legislature's forty-two seats.[104]

TOASTING THE NEW REGIME

I spent part of that very first day of a Tory government with the new premier. Sheer coincidence and Moores's legendary bonhomie made it happen. As I entered the dining room of the original Newfoundland Hotel for a late dinner, I caught sight of the only other patrons, the premier and two of his ministers. Assuming they were heavily into affairs of state, I chose a table in the far corner, but before I could take a seat, Moores bellowed across the room: "Simmons, don't like our company?" He insisted I join them for dinner, which I gladly did, surprised as I was that he would want me, a high-profile Liberal, to intrude at such a momentous time for him and his colleagues. We spent a memorable hour canvassing the events of the day and swapping stories. I raised an issue then preoccupying much of my attention, the rapidly unravelling economic situation in the Springdale area.

Premier Moores suggested the establishment of a joint committee with three representatives each from government and the Green Bay Economic Development Association, of which I was the president. Soon thereafter, the ad hoc group was put in place and tasked with exploring employment initiatives. One of the ministers at the dinner table, Ed Maynard, whose new responsibilities included Crown (public} lands, subsequently facilitated the transfer to the association of 1,000 acres of prime agricultural land which became the nucleus of a highly successful farming endeavour, which continues to thrive.

Moores's collegial approach to governance launched a whole new era in provincial politics. For me, it opened the possibility of a career in elective office.

104 I heartily recommend John Crosbie's autobiography, *No Holds Barred: My Life in Politics*, which details the unbelievable intrigue which characterized the slow-motion transition from Smallwood to Moores.

CHAPTER 13
VOICE OF THE PEOPLE

The penalty good people *pay for not being interested in politics is* to be governed by people worse than *themselves.*
— PLATO

My transition from community activist to elected politician was an easy one. Beginning with the St. Anthony outdoor rink project, I had fifteen years under my belt, reading expectations, identifying issues, working on solutions, troubleshooting individual concerns, and monitoring the public mood. Now I would get to pursue full-time what I had been doing on an as-required, ad hoc basis.

The opportunity to test the political waters popped up unexpectedly. In mid-1973, Frank Moores's year-old administration was having its first public spat. Fisheries Minister Roy Cheeseman abruptly resigned his cabinet and legislative seats. He had represented the south coast constituency of Hermitage, far removed from Springdale. Yet I was recruited to carry the Liberal Party banner into the by-election, scheduled for late fall. I would become a carpetbagger, a species upon which I had long frowned.

Yes, I had electoral assets. Two terms as the elected head of the NTA and my brief stint as president of the Liberal Party had given me a province-wide profile. As well, I was often the public face of Springdale's economic diversification initiatives and a frequent media commentator on educational matters. And just a few months earlier, my daily voice reports from a cruise ship in the Mediterranean with 1,200 Newfoundland high school students aboard had been aired on province-wide TV and radio.

My potential electability was not in question. But, if elected, how could

I effectively represent an area of the island where I had been, at best, an interloper? It was that issue that made me analyze my credentials and initially decide against entering the race. Phone calls from activists in Hermitage District, including one from the man who had won the seat for the Liberals in 1971, Harold Piercey, put my mind somewhat at ease, and I agreed to run.

Left: SS *Nevassa*, Mediterranean Sea, 1972. With 1,250 Newfoundland high school students aboard the cruise ship, I filed daily audio updates for province-wide TV and radio. (Geoff Goodyear photo)
Right: Milltown, NL, 1973. By-election campaign driver Bert Dowding and I prepare to fly to isolated communities. (Author photo)

The carpetbagger issue would raise its head during the campaign. My apprehension about it would linger, though it was tempered during the campaign as I listened to the aspirations and concerns of voters, realizing their issues were the same ones I knew first-hand from my days in St. Anthony and Springdale. And, it should be noted, the real skill of an effective politician lies not in being a walking encyclopedia but, rather, in the ability to quickly grasp the essence of an emerging issue and to know how to give strategic voice to it in a manner that brings about a satisfactory result.

THE GANG THAT COULDN'T SHOOT STRAIGHT

The government party and its candidates hold most of the cards during an election, from well-timed announcements to sod-turnings to visits by cabinet ministers. This is especially true during a by-election since the governing party's candidate, if elected, will become a member of the caucus whose party holds the purse strings.

By-elections results are seen as barometers of the government's standing in the eyes of the electorate. The by-election would be the first electoral test for the new Tory administration, and Premier Moores and his team spared no effort to influence the outcome. Hardly a day went by when there wasn't a cabinet minister popping up somewhere in the district to announce project funding, cut a ribbon, or give a speech, all designed to give the Tory candidate the edge.

Indeed, it was the unseemly lengths to which the Conservatives went that handed me and my campaign a steady stream of election fodder. The sheer number of itinerant cabinet ministers became a laughingstock. One wag in a community of 200 population scoffed, "Yesterday was a slow day; we only saw three ministers!"

Perhaps the biggest laugh was reserved for the government's ham-fisted approach to pork-barrelling. Determined to complete street paving in Harbour Breton before polling day, residents were treated to a once-in-a-lifetime spectacle: A plow scraped lily white snow off the street. Close behind, a paving machine disgorged jet-black asphalt. For once, there was no need of colour film in the camera to capture the moment for the evening TV news! In black and white, the picture was worth a thousand words and, in my case, at least as many votes. The backfire possibilities of voter bribery make it a lousy campaign strategy. In politics as in life, winning at all costs can get pretty expensive, for your pocketbook and your conscience.

Yet another silly little tactic portrayed the Tories as rank amateurs. In any political campaign, it is often not the mega announcements but the most miniscule missteps which determine the outcome. Capitalizing on the early darkness of a November evening and the absence of wagging tongues, a Tory campaigner relieved one of my youth volunteers of an armful of photo posters destined for the front windows of my supporters. The gossip network, a highly honed tool of election campaigns and rural communities, sprang into action. The rumour alleged the poster snatcher was none other than the premier's parliamentary secretary, my old bosom pal, Brian Peckford. Flattery I can handle, but that he wanted thirty photos of my smiling face is more adulation than even I can handle! The scurrilous charge against him was never proven, although my erstwhile poster distributor, an alert twelve-year-old, was certain the right culprit had been fingered. The moniker "Poster Peckford" made the evening news and quickly gained currency, both during the campaign and beyond.

STARING DOWN THE POSSE

As the campaign neared its end, published polls were encouraging for our side. That sent the Tory camp into panic mode. A vitriolic negative campaign centred on my carpetbagger candidacy took wing, demoralizing even my staunchest supporters.

Three nights before election day, I arrived at a high school auditorium for a windup rally, the very school where my Tory opponent was the principal. Parked behind the school was the mobile home in which the candidate lived with his wife, who had been not too discreetly telling her friends she couldn't wait to get out of town once the election was over, assuming of course that her husband was the victor.

I had not addressed the carpetbagger issue publicly. My workers said I had to do so or lose the election. I had mentally sorted out how I would handle the matter, so I was ready to follow their advice, though the strategy I had in mind was dicey and could backfire, since I was on the other guy's home turf. I began my speech by saying,

> "I hear there's some concern about where I was born and where I'll sleep if I'm elected. I had no say over where I was born. But I will have a say as to where I spend my time if I'm elected. I'll spend some of it here listening to you. And I'll spend the rest of it in St. John's working on your problems.
>
> "I'll tell you where I won't be. I won't be down behind this building hooking up the trailer hitch so I can get out of town."

The jam-packed auditorium erupted! Wild applause. Raucous laughter. The only times I heard about the carpetbagger label after were when constituents wanted to have a chuckle at the expense of the Tory candidate or his wife.

On paper, though, the odds favoured my opponent. If elected, he would join a government caucus with a full three years remaining in its mandate, an enticing prospect for rural electors who had been conditioned by Smallwood to look to government to address many of their problems. My election would mean three years as a member of a small opposition block.

MISCHIEF WITH A MOTIVE

Well before my entry into elective politics, I had routinely been the subject of media stories, thanks to my involvement in province-wide issues and organizations, and I had cultivated an amiable working relationship with the print and electronic outlets.

Still, as the by-election campaign was winding down, I got a bee in my bonnet about CBC TV coverage. It had its beginning the evening before polling day. The reporter had been on the ground throughout the campaign, filing daily updates, and was therefore perceived by many as a reliable bellwether. He projected a runaway win for the government candidate, despite much evidence to the contrary. The actual result showed that the CBC stringer had not read the tea leaves well or had made a clumsy attempt to impact the outcome. I believed the latter.

Far from demoralizing my troops, the prediction redoubled their resolve to mobilize our supporters while infecting Tory voters with a complacency that convinced many of them there was no need to vote if a win was already in the bag. For them, their candidate, and the government, the election night count was a most unpleasant surprise:

> Bert Meade, Progressive Conservative, 1,452
> Roger Simmons, Liberal, 2,052

I had won my first contested election, and a sweet victory it was!

During my first federal campaign six years later, also a by-election, that same reporter again polished his trusty crystal ball the night before polling day. And, once again, he confidently predicted my demise, this time opting to name the NDP candidate as the one favoured to win. The clairvoyant's horse came in a distant second.

On that latter by-election night, the CBC reporter, who richly deserves the anonymity I hereby accord him, showed up at my victory party. With a near-landslide vote in my favour, I decided to have a little fun at his expense, he who had twice written my political obituary. It requires a unique journalistic perspective to mistake momentum for rigor mortis!

Before cameras from two national television networks and a cluster of media mics, I, with sweet sarcasm, bestowed on my intrepid visionary the Roger Simmons Award for Consistency in Election Predictions.

The party faithful loved it. The press took note. Under the guise of playful mischief, but in the cause of payback, I had committed a stupid gaffe that would come back to bite me. What I had intended as a tongue-in-cheek settling of scores was seen by others, CBC on-air personnel among them, as a cheap shot at the venerable institution. Audiovisual recorders, like elephants, have long memories.

. . . A PROMISE MADE IS A DEBT UNPAID[105]

Soon after my first by-election win (1973), actually two days before Christmas, I received a late-night phone call from a distraught woman.

105 "The Cremation of Sam McGee" by Canadian poet Robert W. Service

"Roger, John is dead."

I had no idea who was on the phone or who John was. Probably sensing my bewilderment, the woman continued:

"Rev. Spencer is gone away for Christmas. You're the only one I can turn to."

The mention of the clergyman's name allowed me to narrow my frantic mental googling down to three communities where he had congregations, each of which, however, had many Johns. The question was, which John had died? The grieving woman was already at her wit's end. I wasn't about to push her over the edge by admitting I had no idea who John was. She solved my problem.

"You know, Roger, you were here in our kitchen, you sat in the rocking chair and had tea. You and John laughed a lot. When you left, you handed me a little card with your name on it. You said, 'If ever I can help you, call me.'"

Mary had no living relatives. When she got news that her husband of sixty years had passed away in a distant hospital, the sheer burden of her aloneness must have been devastating. In her most vulnerable moment, she decided to turn to someone who had promised to help her.

I spent the next day buying a coffin for John, parting with one of my suits and dispatching his corpse by boat for the trip home. It's not quite the way I would have chosen to spend my first Christmas Eve as an elected representative. But what a valuable lesson Mary had taught me! Don't make promises unless you are prepared to keep them. It served me well in the years ahead. It's surprising how many politicians never learn that lesson and, in consequence, pay the price at the polls or in defensive encounters with the betrayed.

PAYING THE BILLS

The career switch from education to politics required many adjustments for me, a major one being financial. At the time of my election, I was the highest-paid elementary/secondary educator in Newfoundland, the result of a handsome wage supplement from my school board which augmented the stipend paid pursuant to the provincial salary scale.

My new job title, Member of the House of Assembly (MHA), carried with it a dramatic reduction in my personal income. I would now earn less than forty per cent of the salary to which I had become accustomed as a school superintendent. While my lifestyle has never been extravagant, it was painfully obvious I would need to find a source of additional income just to make ends meet. Once I had settled into my new legislative responsibilities, I canvassed supplementary income options and soon landed a small, education-related consulting contract. The extra remuneration eased my immediate cash flow requirements. Some years later, though, that income would morph into a giant Achilles heel, thanks to my preoccupation with political matters, my aggressiveness as a whistle-blower, an abysmal lack of attention to my personal affairs, and, arguably, thanks to a below-the-belt settling of scores by persons with long memories and few scruples.

JOBS, JOBS, JOBS!

As noted earlier, the province has always had the dubious distinction of having the highest unemployment rate in Canada. A dearth of jobs has long been the bane of rural Newfoundland, especially in my constituency, where all but a handful of communities depend solely on the fishery. The government-ordered shutdown of the commercial cod fishery in 1992 worsened an already bad situation and hastened the near-total demise of many once thriving outports. Heads of households and youth by the thousands were obliged to look elsewhere for an income source, accelerating the ongoing exodus of workers to distant places including the Alberta oil sands, the Great Lakes, and southern Ontario

It will come as no surprise, then, that a principal preoccupation of a politician representing those one-horse towns and villages is the urgent need to maximize employment opportunities. Their isolated location and their distance from major markets render impractical the establishment of most industries, with some exceptions in the resource and information sectors.

Milltown, St. Alban's, and the other Bay d'Espoir communities in my former district are strung along a twenty-mile ribbon of road largely hugging the coastline of that scenic finger of Hermitage Bay. They boast an aggregate population of about 4,000. From the time its first non-aboriginal inhabitants arrived, the area thrived as a supplier of pit props for the mines of England providing steady jobs for hundreds of loggers. That source of employment dried up in the late 1950s, and the jobless rate skyrocketed. There was a bit of a reprieve in the late 1960s during the construction of the nearby Camp Boggy hydro power development. However, by the time I came on the scene, the area was in desperate economic shape.

STIRRING THE POT

Meanwhile, there was a battle brewing. With the completion of Stage 2 of the power facility in 1970, Camp Boggy was now fully operational. Soon after, Newfoundland Hydro implemented employment changes which didn't sit well with the community and, particularly, those directly impacted. Specifically, the utility transferred certain functions, heretofore performed at Camp Boggy, to Bishop's Falls and St. John's.

The public reaction was immediate and visceral and soon caught the attention of the press. In a radio interview, John Kealey, then St. Alban's acting mayor, gave voice to the public's frustration. He noted that some of the affected workers had worked on Camp Boggy's construction. Their insider knowledge, Kealey observed, could be used to disrupt the flow of electricity to the trans-island grid: "If you slacken a few bolts here and a nut or two there . . ."

Bay d'Espoir power is transmitted on high-voltage wires held aloft by steel lattice towers with stabilizing guy wires. It's these nuts and bolts, of course, which keep the towers from crashing to the ground. Local police had heard enough. Here, they decided, was a scarcely veiled threat to damage the power infrastructure. I got a call from the RCMP. Aware that I had scheduled a meeting, for that very evening, of community leaders to deal with the public uproar over Hydro's actions, the caller informed me that a plainclothes officer would sit in on our deliberations.

My role, the RCMP instructed me, would be to simply acknowledge the officer's presence as someone who had asked to attend as an observer, without saying who he was. During the session, I observed that our visitor was fixated on one person. Once the meeting ended, the officer shook a few hands, including the one extended by the St. Alban's acting mayor, who inquired, "Well, Sergeant, did you find your terrorists?"

"I found one, Mr. Kealey!"

AQUACULTURE GETS A KICK-START

John Kealey, my good friend and a feisty Irishman, grew up in rural Northern Ireland at Castledawson. In his late twenties, he arrived in St. Alban's to work on the Camp Boggy project. He married a local lady, the amazing Fanny, and took up residence in the town. A half-century later, he's still there, energizing and/or mesmerizing all who will listen to his rapid-fire analyses and innovative solutions. I was among those who listened.

Kealey, who had studied aquaculture in college, convinced me that salmon farming was a plausible option for Hermitage Bay. The thirty-mile stretch of sheltered waters from the head of Bay d'Espoir to the Atlantic Ocean was, according to Kealey, the ideal aquaculture location. But when I said so at a public forum convened to explore potential economic development possibilities, I was pretty well laughed out of the room. There were, fortunately, a few believers and some community leaders who, though skeptical, felt anything was worth a try. Mayor Doug Sutton of Milltown summed up the general consensus:

"What have we got to lose?"

With their guarded blessing, I secured a federal grant which funded an aquaculture feasibility pilot project, administered by the local development association, the very first such undertaking in Newfoundland. The project confirmed the potential for fish farming in the area. Shortly thereafter, three entrepreneurs, John Kealey being one of them, launched aquaculture enterprises. From that modest beginning, Bay d'Espoir is today a beehive of aquaculture activity which has become a major job generator and a catalyst for similar ventures elsewhere in Newfoundland. Province-wide, aquaculture is a growth industry and currently has an annual worth of $150 million.

JOEY AS THE SPOILER

Ed Roberts succeeded Smallwood as party leader prior to the 1972 Tory rout which left the Liberals with just eight seats in the forty-two-seat House of Assembly. Lingering anti-Joey sentiment, inside the party and out, didn't help Roberts's attempts to rebuild and reinvigorate the once-powerful Liberals. His many years as Smallwood's fixer made him suspect to many, and his four years in the Smallwood cabinet pigeonholed him as yesterday's man. The facts were quite to the contrary. Roberts and cabinet colleague Bill Rowe had begun to speak their minds and give voice to the widespread mood for change soon after they joined the inner circle in 1968.

Within two years of taking over the leadership, Roberts was obliged to put his job on the line, pursuant to the party's constitution. Four candidates contested the 1974 leadership: Roberts, of course; Smallwood, a surprise to many, but not to anyone who knew his megalomania; Steve Neary and I were the others.

My candidacy seemed presumptuous to many. I had been in elective politics just a year. What party activists and pundits didn't know was my game plan or, more accurately, Smallwood's game plan. My decision to join the race was the direct outcome of a hush-hush rendezvous with Joe Ashley, Joey's long-time confidant. Ashley told me that if Roberts led on the first ballot, as was widely expected, Joey would withdraw and support me. The strategy was driven not by any affection for me or my cause, but by Smallwood's visceral hatred for Roberts.

At the leadership convention, the first ballot results were as follows:

Edward Roberts, 337
Joseph R. Smallwood, 305
Roger Simmons, 57
Stephen Neary, 24

The moment I heard those numbers, I knew they posed a large problem for me. No, it wasn't the distant third-place finish. That was expected.

Smallwood's surprising strength, though less than Roberts's, convinced Joey he should hang in, notwithstanding his/Ashley's commitment to me. The results of the first ballot meant that Neary, as the candidate with the least votes, was obliged to withdraw, and I did so as well. While the rules allowed me to stay for the second ballot, there was no realistic reason for doing so, since in order to survive for a third round of voting, I would have had to overtake Smallwood on the second ballot, clearly not a very likely possibility. Joey's support from the first ballot held firm on the second. The result of the ballot confirmed that the once-omnipotent leader was finally a spent force:

Roberts, 403
Smallwood, 298

With a nod to W. E. Henley,[106] the *bludgeonings of chance* may have bloodied Joey's head, but it remained defiantly unbowed. His *unconquerable soul*, or, more accurately, his egomania and venom, would shortly land him yet one more time in a fight he could not win.

Frank Moores had swept the province in the 1972 general election. Just three and a half years into his mandate, he went to the polls again in September 1975. Following the 1974 Liberal leadership campaign, three of the candidates, Roberts, Neary, and me, closed ranks, and with Roberts leading the charge, the nine-member Liberal parliamentary caucus became an effective, cohesive unit. Meanwhile, the Tory government's honeymoon with the electorate was long since over. The administration's messaging had only one string in its bow, fixated solely on denigrating its predecessor, which began to wear thin with the public. Liberals had reason to be optimistic about the impending election.

There was one problem, however: The Smallwood political corpse was not yet cold. Rigor mortis set in, energizing a few last twitches which didn't bode well for the Liberal leader or for the party's fortunes at the polls. Having mounted a failed challenge to his successor and having been rejected by his party for the first time, Joey was in no mood to close ranks. Instead, he jumped ship, formed the Liberal Reform Party, and won four seats in the 1975 election. The two Liberal factions together garnered fifty-four per cent of the vote, but the split allowed the Tories to win a second majority. Slim pluralities in several seats pointed to a victory for Ed Roberts and the Liber-

106 English poet, critic, and editor who wrote the poem "Invictus"

als, absent Smallwood's treachery. I was re-elected, and my party was once again in opposition.

MAKING A DIFFERENCE

Keeping in touch with constituents between elections is any good politician's bread and butter. It is also a never-ending challenge, particularly so in rural areas where much valuable time is consumed just getting from one place to the next. A further restriction is the dearth of public venues. Other than private homes and small shops and convenience stores, the only buildings in many small communities are the post office and the church. I would often gear my arrival at a post office to coincide with the time frame when the day's incoming letters and parcels had been sorted. As my electors picked up their mail, I picked up the local pulse and constituent inquiries for follow-up.

One other routine worked well. As I drove from one community to the next, I would mentally pre-select a house at random, say, the next two-storey dwelling on the right with laundry on the clothesline. On one such occasion, my door-knocking summoned a young woman with a baby in arms and a small boy clinging to her skirt. As I sat in her kitchen and chatted, I watched her three-year-old, the same age as my son, who appeared to be hiding his right hand from my view. His mother, sensing my curiosity, took her child's hand and opened it, at least partly, to reveal a palm that had been severely burned, Tommy having fallen the previous year onto the floor furnace. She had removed the protective grating for a moment as she vacuumed. She told me resignedly, "The doctors have done all they can do."

I knew better. Rage boiled inside me at the thought that some pathetic excuse for a physician had decreed this child would go through life with a withered hand. Exercising care not to raise false hopes and armed with the mother's agreement that she was open to the possibility of getting a second opinion, I headed straight for St. John's. Next morning, I called on the province's deputy minister of Health. Dr. Lorne Klippert gave the matter the priority it merited, and in time, Tommy had a fully-functional right hand.

ANATOMY OF A SCANDAL

There is a classic yet simple template for many, if not all, government spending scandals which involve the illegal disbursement of public funds to non-government recipients. A person (or persons) in the private sector with contacts in the bureaucracy gets greedy. He/she finds a public servant who is equally greedy. They both want lots of money, and they need each other to flow the money in a manner that minimizes the probability of being found out. Their only scruple relates not to ethics or morality but to whether they may get caught.

It is instructive to note that this fraud template doesn't require the collusion or knowledge of political masters. Indeed, that would scuttle the entire scheme or require more sharing than greed would condone. Besides, government ministers get defeated at the polls. Bureaucrats, like the Energizer bunny, just keep on going.

The 1976 Auditor General's report to the Newfoundland House of Assembly contained a small but intriguing paragraph that caught my attention as chairman of the Public Accounts Committee (PAC), an all-party, post-audit panel charged with determining whether public money has been spent according to law and whether commensurate value was received. The item in the AG's report intimated that certain companies may have contravened the province's public tender legislation, enacted less than three years earlier to great Tory fanfare. The curious thing about the AG item was that the alleged perpetrators were identified only as Companies A, B, and C, which signalled to me that the Auditor General didn't have enough smoking-gun evidence to name names but, nevertheless, felt an obligation to draw the House's attention to the matter.

I paid a visit to AG David Howley's office and became quickly convinced that the obscure paragraph was fertile ground for digging and well within the mandate of the Public Accounts Committee. I also learned that many of the disbursements from public coffers related to a small kitchen fire in the College of Fisheries, a Crown property. I asked the AG, "How do I get my hands on a copy of the fire commissioner's report?"

Howley winked and said, " Maybe you'll get lucky!" When I opened my office door next morning, I stepped on a plain brown envelope. Inside was the damage assessment done shortly after the fire had been extinguished. It was but the first of many plain brown envelopes that would come into my possession in the months ahead.

The fire commissioner had estimated the cost of repairing the damaged kitchen at $17,000. The government's Public Works department had paid out more than $600,000 to two corporate entities, both controlled by the same individual, for repairs to the kitchen. The Public Tender Act stipulated that expenditures exceeding $10,000 required a competitive bid process. Lesser amounts could be authorized by work order.

In the case of the kitchen fire, one official had signed all the work orders, being careful to keep the amount of each just under $10,000 and issuing every last one to the same two contractors. The official's ostentatious oceanfront property suggested a lifestyle well beyond the capacity of his paycheque to underwrite.

The official also knew how to cover his tracks. Other than the work orders, there wasn't a single shred of documentable evidence linking him to the contractor. When the axe fell, it landed nowhere close to the official's neck. The contractor, Alex B. Walsh, wasn't quite so lucky.

BRASS-KNUCKLE SHENANIGANS

Brown envelopes were not the only intruders. On arriving at my St. John's home following the weekend at Kona Beach, my campsite facility in central Newfoundland, I faced a surprising, unnerving disarray. The upholstered sofas and chairs in my living room and home office had been slashed. The walls and carpet had also been vandalized. I called the CID.[107] I was in for another surprise or two. Next morning, I went to my parliamentary office, only to discover that a locked filing cabinet had been forced open. I made a second phone call to the CID. A day or so later, an officer, having completed his investigation of the two incidents, came to see me.

"Do you have enemies?"

"In my line of work, probably. Why? What's up?"

"The break-in at your house was made to look like vandalism, but that was to cover the tracks of the perpetrators. They were looking for something. Our examination of the contents of the filing cabinets in both your offices tells us that someone went through each file, page by page."

Bad news comes in three, they say. My third rude awakening was exactly that, a phone call at 3:00 a.m. I hustled from the master bedroom to my adjoining home office to grab the receiver before the ringing stopped.

"Are you Roger Simmons?"

"Yes. Can I help . . ."

"You have a son named Paul. He was born October 11, 1976. Do you want him to grow up?

Click. He was gone. Message delivered. I called the CID a third time. Nothing came of the three incidents, despite a commendable police effort. They and I knew the three intrusions were a classic needle-in-a-haystack case.

107 Criminal Investigation Division of the Royal Newfoundland Constabulary, the city's police force.

St. John's, 1977. I succeeded broadcaster and MHA John Nolan as caucus whip. (*Daily News* cartoon)

St. John's, 1977. Newfoundland's Minister of Public Works, Joe Rousseau, and I were the subjects of a *Daily News* cartoon.

There was no doubt in my mind, and there's none now, that the furtive filing cabinet searches and the middle-of-the-night phone threat were connected to the Public Works probe. If a couple of greedy guys had successfully conned the government out of $600,000 over a three-year period, they certainly had the smarts, motive, and perversity to pull those cowardly stunts at my expense or to instruct their henchmen to do so. Yet the lengths to which they were prepared to go to curb my legitimate legislative activities were small potatoes compared to something else which, I firmly believe, they did several years later, after I had left the provincial arena.

OUTSMARTING GOVERNMENT PATSIES

There are institutional constraints on the ability of a public accounts committee to do its job. The provision that the chair must be an opposition member does give the presiding officer a wide berth in determining the committee's agenda. However, since the ratio of government and opposition members reflects their respective House numbers, a majority government can control the committee's activities, including, importantly, its findings and recommendations.

Ottawa, 1982. On the day Queen Elizabeth II proclaimed the new Constitution Act, I chatted with a colleague. L-R: MP Stan Hovdebo (NDP, Saskatchewan), my son Paul, six, and me. (Author photo)

London, England, 1981. Schmoozing with the Iron Lady, British PM Margaret Thatcher. (Author photo)

Ottawa, 1982. Prime Minister Pierre Trudeau signed a proclamation saluting the Salvation Army's centenary in Canada. L-R: Commissioner John Waldron, Trudeau, (fellow Newfoundlander) Major Lloyd Eason, MP Roger Simmons. (Author photo)

Ottawa, 1983. I hosted a Parliament Hill reception for the honourable Don Jamieson on his appointment as Canada's High Commissioner to the United Kingdom. L-R: Prime Minister Pierre Trudeau, Jamieson, me, Barbara Jamieson, Miriam Simmons. (Author photo)

St. John's, 1987. Leadership and support staff of the Official Opposition, Newfoundland House of Assembly. L-R: Rex Murphy, Ruth Sheppard, Gloria Hibbs, Kim Ploughman, Delores Linehan, Daisy Parsons, Rosie Frey, Opposition House Leader (later Premier) Beaton Tulk, Marie Walsh, Opposition Leader Roger Simmons, Joan White, Phyllis Fiander, Opposition Whip (later Speaker) Tom Lush, Barbara Nugent, Cathy Brodie, Cindy Gollop. (Author photo)

Left: St. John's, 1987. Leader of the Opposition, Newfoundland. (Author photo)
Right: Ottawa, 1989. With Right Honourable John Turner. (J. M. Carisse photo)

Lévis, QC, 1989. L-R: My media advisor, former Newfoundland cabinet minister Steve Neary, Joseph R. Smallwood, CC, me, Hon. John C. Crosbie. (Bill Goulding photo)

Airborne between St. John's and Stephenville, NL, circa 1989. Renowned Franco-Newfoundland fiddler Émile Benoit plays a jig he composed, "The Roger Simmons Breakdown." (Author photo)

Cape St. George, NL, 1990. Chatting en français with students at L'École Notre-Dame-du-Cap. (Author photo)

Oslo, Norway, 1990. At home with the Ingstads, Helge and Anne, of L'Anse aux Meadows fame. (Author photo)

Lawn, NL, 1990. High school graduation. (Author photo)

Beijing, China, 1990. Following the 1989 Tiananmen Square student protests, three MP colleagues and I were the first elected officials from a western democracy to visit the People's Republic of China. L-R: Roger Simmons, Dan Heap (NDP, Ontario), former Speaker John Bosley (PC, Ontario), and Bob Wenman (PC, British Columbia). (Author photo)

Shanghai, China, 1990. I just couldn't resist the piano, nor the urge to teach. I soon had these three-year-olds singing the opening lines of "I'se the B'y," a Newfoundland folk song. (Author photo)

Left: Rio de Janeiro, Brazil, 1992. Just five months after her historic space flight, our focus was decidedly down-to-earth as astronaut Roberta Bondar and I teamed up to arrange seating for a Canadian NGO seminar. (Author photo)
Right: Tokyo, 1992. Federal Fisheries Minister John Crosbie and I, his Official Opposition critic, travelled to Asia and Europe for bilateral talks on foreign overfishing. (Author photo)

Portland, OR, 2000. With the Right Honourable Kim Campbell. (Author photo)

Ottawa, 1993. Taking the MP oath of office for the fourth time. L-R: My sons, Mark (14) and Paul (17), Captain Randy Hicks, Senator Phil Gigantès, Colonel Hugh Tilley, Mildred Conibear, Colonel Noreen Tilley, Deputy Clerk of the House of Commons Mary Ann Griffith, Majors Cliff and Ruth Holman. (Author photo)

Ottawa, 1994. Prime Minister Jean Chrétien welcomed General Bram Tillsley as Commissioner Maude Tillsley and I looked on. (J. M. Carisse photo)

Ottawa, 1994. I was honoured to conduct the Salvation Army International Staff Band in its Parliament Hill rendition of "Goldcrest," a jazzy march by Army officer and composer James Anderson. (Author photo)

Ottawa, 1994. At 24 Sussex Drive with Prime Minister Jean and Aline Chrétien. (J. M. Carisse photo)

Saint-Jean-sur-Richelieu, QC, 1994. Improving my oral French at the Royal Military College with MPs Jean Augustine (L, Ontario), left, and Sue Barnes (L, Ontario). (Author photo)

Ottawa, 1996. Five of the fabulous persons who staffed my offices. L-R: Janice Lane (Marystown, NL), Gwen Lomond (Stephenville, NL), and in Ottawa, Sarah Watts-Rynard, Joanne Blondeau, and Catherine Parker. (Author photo)

Ottawa, 1992. The Salvation Army's Ottawa Citadel Band posed in front of the House of Commons. L-R, front row: Eric Dinsdale, Albert Verhey, Munden Braye, Allan Bacon, Capt. David Ivany, Bandmaster Douglas Burden, Capt. Beverly Ivany, John van Gulik, Jr., Geoff Clayton, Fred Waterman, Roger Simmons, Leonard Ferguson. Middle row: Ted Venables, Calvin Wong, Kerry Brazeau, Arlene van Gulik, Kristen Hollman, Donna van Gulik, Stephanie Hodgson, Cyril Fry, Karl Rayment, Sean Wong, John van Gulik, Peter van Gulik. Back row: Brian Greenwood, Allan Weatherall, Dave Perry, Brent Ferguson, Martyn Hodgson, Jim Ferguson, Curtis Jackson, Scott van Gulik, Linda Colwell, Debbie van der Horden, Ralph Verhey. (Author photo)

Ottawa. 2001. Canada's North American heads of mission. L-R: Roger Marsham, Buffalo; Susan Thompson, Minneapolis; Colin Robertson, Los Angeles; Michael Phillips, New York; Jon Allen, DG, North American Bureau; Hon. John Manley, Minister of Foreign Affairs; John Tennant, Detroit; Astrid Pregel, Atlanta; Chris Poole, Chicago; Hon. Roger Simmons, Seattle; Allan Poole, Dallas; Keith Christie, Mexico; Marc Lortie, ADM Americas. (Author photo)

Seattle, 2002. Roger Simmons with Bishop Desmond Tutu. (Author photo)

Olympia, WA, 2002. Our eyes are fixated on a giant dragon motif suspended in Washington Governor Gary Locke's office. L-R: Canada's Foreign Affairs Minister John Manley, Locke, and Consul General Roger Simmons. (Author photo)

USS *Abraham Lincoln*, Pacific Ocean, 2003. Honorary Captain Cedric Steele, Canadian Navy, and I helicoptered to Victoria, having spent the night on the aircraft carrier. (Author photo)

Stowe, Vermont, 1996. Paul, me, and Mark. (Author photo)

North Saanich, BC, 2004. Birthday boy!
My stepdaughters, Stacy, left, and Holly. (Author photo)

View Royal, BC, 2004. African-American Lanier Phillips asked primary school students, "Should a black man have to serve a white man?" The five-year-old wearing the polkadot cap responded, "Not unless he's hurt." (Author photo)

St. John's, 2008. Memorial University saluted the achievements of Lanier Phillips with an honorary degree. L-R: Capt. Cavell Simmonds, Terry Phillips (Lanier's son), Terry's wife, Tamara, Dr. Lanier Phillips, Dr. Vonzia Phillips (Lanier's daughter), Roger Simmons. (Author photo)

Halifax, 2010. I was on hand to greet the Queen during her Golden Jubilee tour of Canada. I had first met Her Majesty nearly three decades earlier in London, England. (Author photo)

Atlantic Ocean near Great Brehat, NL, 2016. With Glorina Drodge, reliving cherished memories and making new ones. (Stephen Simms photo)

When I first raised the Public Works spending issue, the Tory majority used every trick in the book to frustrate the committee's deliberations. Every time that I, as the chair, or the clerk proposed a course of action, the four government members routinely voted it down. One of the many brown envelopes that showed up under my door included a note that read, "If I were you, I would try and reconcile the number of mercury vapour lights in the Public Works hangar with the purchase invoices."

Experience had long since taught me I would not get committee approval for a fact-finding excursion. So, I opted for a little improvisation in the interests of accountability. The moment I called the committee to order, I said, "The government hangar at Pepperrell has a whole bunch of mercury vapour lights, and I plan to find out how many. The committee is adjourned"—I banged the gavel—"and will convene in thirty minutes in the hangar."

Regina, SK, 1977. Dr. Ray Winsor, vice-chair of the Newfoundland Public Accounts Committee, and I met with Saskatchewan Premier Allan Blakeney. (Author photo)

Ignoring energetic protestations from the Tory majority, I made a beeline for the door. The government members, not about to trust me to do the counting, were already in the hangar by the time I arrived. The count completed and duly noted by the clerk, we convened for the third time that day back at our regular venue. The committee researcher read the related paid invoices into the record, revealing the government had been conned into paying for many times the number of light fixtures than had been supplied. In a friendly aside to Dr. Ray Winsor, my vice-chair, a government member and respected dentist, I said, "The jig is up. First, that very expensive kitchen fire. And now, enough fixtures to light up a cruise ship. If I were you, I'd get on the right side of this boondoggle while there's still time."

Thereafter, the committee became a relatively collaborative effort, and its report to the House documented a litany of abuses that the government could ill afford to sweep under the carpet.

FILIBUSTERING FOR A CAUSE

House of Assembly rules provided that, as the opposition spokesperson first responding to Finance Minister Bill Doody's budget motion, I had unlimited speaking time. I gave notice it was my intention to keep talking until the government agreed to establish a judicial inquiry into the Public Works spending irregularities. I began to speak late Thursday, and as of noon Friday, I was showing no signs of running out of steam any time soon. When nature called or I needed a little sustenance, my late, great friend and colleague, the indomitable Steve Neary, a past master of both parliamentary procedure and histrionics, could be counted on to incite a procedural row to allow me to attend to business.

Montreal, 1977. L-R: Roger Simmons, Quebec Premier René Lévesque, Newfoundland Leader of the Opposition Edward Roberts, and Labrador MHA Ian Strachan. (Author photo)

By mid-afternoon, the government front bench, procedurally unable to move the adjournment motion unless I yielded, faced the unpalatable choice of caving in to our demand for an inquiry or enduring, well into the weekend, my non-stop verbiage. Finally, Minister Doody, having conferred by phone with Premier Moores, who was out-of-province, rose under the guise of a point of order.

"Mr. Speaker, I wish to inform the House that the premier has agreed to set up a public inquiry. . . . Now, will the Member for Burgeo–Bay d'Espoir sit down?"

I collapsed in my seat as my colleagues thumped their desks. We had won!

The soon-appointed judicial probe and its hair-raising report would, in time, put a large dent in the government's claim as trusted custodians of the public purse, abort the careers of two ministers, and send a greedy businessman to jail. Alex Walsh was convicted of fraud and sentenced to three and a half years in New Brunswick's Dorchester Penitentiary. It would also set the stage for a settling of scores, with me on the receiving end.

CAUGHT IN THE MIDDLE

The two members of cabinet on whose successive watches the fraud had been perpetrated were hounded into resignation. Joe Rousseau's only possible sin may have been one of omission, though how he could have prevented the fraud is beyond me. Rousseau was a decent man and my long-time friend. Indeed, he and I had briefly taught school together. But he was also a political adversary, and what my party, me included, did to his reputation, and possibly his health, was shameful and unwarranted. It was easily the low point of my quarter-century in elective politics and something I will always regret.

The case of the other minister, Dr. Tom Farrell, is less clear-cut. While there was no evidence that he benefited financially from the spending scandal or was even aware of the matter until the Auditor General flagged it, his alleged involvement in another shady shenanigan led to a public inquiry and the filing of charges against him which were later dismissed. Clyde Wells acted for Farrell and received an anonymous phone call "threatening to kidnap the Wells children if the case was not dropped."[108] The inquiry judge was also targeted with a similar call.[109]

Aviation icon Gene Manion, in his 2009 book, *Flying on the Edge*, recounts a 1972 meeting with recently appointed Minister Farrell. Manion's company had won a publicly tendered bid to provide helicopter services to the province, but according to Manion, Farrell made the contract award conditional on a ten per cent donation to the minister's political party. Manion records, "I grabbed the contract off his desk, ripped it to shreds, tossed the pieces on his desk . . . and stomped out of his office."[110]

John Crosbie asserts in his autobiography that the Moores administration *put honesty back into government*.[111] There is considerable evidence to

108 *Clyde Wells: A Political Biography*, Claire Hoy, Toronto: Stoddart Publishing, 1992, p. 99
109 Ibid
110 *Flying on the Edge*, Gene Manion, St. John's: DRC Publishing, 2009, p. 194
111 *No Holds Barred*, John Crosbie, Toronto: McClelland & Stewart, 1997, p. 137

support that claim. But there were exceptions, the most egregious being the Public Works scandal. And, according to Manion, at least one minister was on the take.

UNSCRUPULOUS TACTICS

Our adversarial system of governance is soundly based and, for the most part, serves well its intended purpose of ensuring good government, adequate accountability, and transparency. Here's the "but": When an opposition member gets on a roll about some government shortcoming, the partisan political objectives are served only if linkage to government politicians can be shown or, at least, insinuated. Too often, such linkage exists solely in the fertile mind of an unscrupulous politician whose yardstick for success is tonight's TV clip or tomorrow's headline, not the fairness of the pursuit or the veracity of the accusations.

I remember well the many early mornings in Ottawa when we, the Liberal opposition strategy group, all of us skilled at finding jugulars and going for them, would gather to decide the day's line of attack during the Oral Question period in the Commons. Our House Leader, Herb Gray, could always be counted on to keep some sanity in the room: *Do we know that for sure? Do we really want to go there? Is that fair?*

Herb was no shrinking violet, to be sure. He could hold his own with the best of them in a frontal attack on the floor of the House. But, to his great credit, he never let the thirst for the kill dilute either his sterling integrity or his marvellous humanity. Deliberative bodies the world over need more Herb Grays!

MAN ON A MISSION

A distinct bonus of the political life is the cast of characters with whom you get to rub shoulders. One I came to know well and admire deeply is John Crosbie. If ever a man entered the political arena for all the right reasons, it was Crosbie. He came well-equipped. A mind like a steel trap. Independently wealthy, so he wasn't for sale. Firmly held convictions. Highly educated. Self-deprecating wit. For all his riotous display of tough partisanship, Crosbie doesn't have a mean bone in his body.

When he was first elected to the Newfoundland House of Assembly, following a stint as deputy mayor of St. John's, he lacked one essential skill, an easy command of oratory. With speech coaching, he not only transformed himself into a competent speaker with a devastating brand of humour, but also one of the most effective communicators in public life and a master of the thirty-second sound bite.

Now, if you think John Crosbie is the smartest creature on two legs, you haven't met Jane Crosbie. Feisty, acerbic, lovable Jane. She was succinctly profiled as *a spirited woman with views of her own* by Susan Riley, writing in *Maclean's* magazine.

Over the years, and particularly in the early 1990s, it was my privilege to spend time with John and Jane, sometimes in foreign capitals where we rallied support for Canada's position on overfishing of transboundary fish stocks. The three of us and two of Minister Crosbie's staff were in Tokyo. After a full set of meetings with Japanese officials, we were unwinding over dinner and John was in full oratorical flight. Jane was not buying her husband's assessment of the day's events and dramatically registered her disagreement. Sitting beside her, I became aware of her swift kick to John's shins. Communication doesn't have to be verbal to be effective!

John Crosbie and I are kindred spirits. There is, though, one area of fundamental difference. He has written that Liberals "have no principles whatever . . . no scruples and no honour"[112]. I disagree. Oh yes, I can name a few rogues who have held influential positions in the Liberal party. Equally, I have known Tories who fit the category. I do take exception, however, to Crosbie's tarring all Liberals with the same brush. Long-time senator Eugene Forsey was no rogue. Nor was Monique Begin, Iona Campagnola, or David Collenette[113]. Far from being exceptions that prove the rule, they number among an army of Liberal politicians who have served Canada well with their integrity intact. In the same vein, I have never pigeonholed Mary Collins or Ray Hnatyshyn, Flora MacDonald or Don Mazankowski[114] as morally depraved simply because they didn't belong to my party. Each of them and countless other Tories did a stellar job of pursing their mandates without ever stooping to unprincipled, venal tactics.

Conservatives, NDPers, Bloquistes[115], and Liberals are all sprung from the same root. Like fishermen and scientists, housewives and clergymen, some of them are rotten apples. The saving grace, the overwhelming truth, is that all but a sorry few are principled people, irrespective of party label or station in life.

In the Newfoundland House of Assembly, I touched off a procedural row by saying, in reference to Justice Minister Alec Hickman, that, "There's nothing worse than a reformed alcoholic!" In the context of the moment, my comment was an allusion to a well-known phenomenon. A convert to a new cause can be unbearably preachy in decrying what s/he once embraced.

112 *No Holds Barred*, John Crosbie, Toronto: McClelland & Stewart, 1997, p. 186

113 Former Liberal MPs and ministers from Quebec, British Columbia, and Ontario, respectively

114 Former Conservative MPs and ministers from British Columbia, Saskatchewan, Ontario, and Alberta, respectively

115 New Democratic Party; Bloc Québécois, the Quebec separatist party in federal politics

Hickman, a former Liberal cabinet minister, had switched allegiances and joined the Tories, as did Crosbie, which probably best explains the latter's scathing assessment of Liberals as a genre.

VICEREGAL PANACHE

En passant, I just loved Prime Minister Harper's December 2007 appointment of Crosbie as lieutenant-governor of Newfoundland and Labrador. The minute I got wind of the announcement, I emailed him my congratulations, saying his new assignment was "richly deserved and deliciously diabolical, because it will drive your few remaining detractors absolutely bonkers!"

The refreshingly irreverent Crosbie made liars of his critics as he and Jane brought new substance and class to the viceregal office. As Her Majesty's envoy, John followed in the footsteps of a long line of outstanding appointees, some of whom had made a real contribution toward the archaic institution's becoming more in step with the times and the citizenry. Crosbie's two immediate predecessors certainly qualify.

Before becoming the Queen's representative in 2002, the intellectual Edward Roberts had a successful political career spanning thirty years and has the distinction of being the only minister to sit in cabinet with Smallwood, Wells, and Tobin, the province's first three Liberal premiers. As party leader, Roberts recruited me into politics, and I am indebted to him for doing so and for his wise and unselfish mentoring during my formative years as a legislator.

Dr. Max House, lieutenant-governor from 1997 to 2002, spent thirty years as a professor of neurology. He is known worldwide as a telemedicine pioneer, having founded Memorial University's telemedicine centre, recognized internationally as the model for such systems. The Canadian Medical Association saluted him, saying, "his use of communication technology to deliver care elevated the standard of medical care in some of Canada's most remote locations."

The current lieutenant-governor is the indomitable Judy Foote, the first woman to hold the position. She's already devoted more than two decades to public service as an elected member and cabinet minister, provincially and federally. She becomes the fourteenth lieutenant-governor since Confederation, the ninety-second since John Guy took office in 1610, and number 104, if you include the dozen French appointees when France held sway in parts of Newfoundland for the half-century ending in 1713.

THE POT CALLS THE KETTLE BLACK

Newfoundlanders have gone *to the ice* since the early 1600s. The annual seal hunt has long been a source of supplementary income for seasonal fishermen and a welcome foodstuff, even a delicacy for many.

By the mid-1970s, the seal hunt was in the sights of animal rights activists and the anti-fur lobby. Each spring, St. Anthony, on the island's northern tip, was transformed into a global media centre as celebrities and spin doctors descended on the community to demonize the hunt. When two US congressmen showed up in March 1978, the media frenzy was ratcheted up a notch. Vermont's Jim Jeffords and Leo Ryan from northern California held forth in the local motel's cramped, smoky boardroom.

A Newfoundland government minister and two other Members of the House of Assembly, Opposition Leader Bill Rowe and I, were there as well, both as a courtesy to our distinguished US visitors and also to ensure their version of reality was duly rebutted, if called for. The congressmen railed at length about the alleged barbarity of the seal hunt. The minister, blunt-talking, no-nonsense John Lundrigan, got quickly past the courtesies and went straight for the jugular: "You want to save some seals? Why don't you go to the (US) Pribilof Islands[116] in your own backyard? One of these days, you're going to stick your nose in once too often!"

Little did Minister Lundrigan expect, *once too often* would come so soon and so tragically. Just eight months later, Congressman Ryan perished in a hail of bullets on the tarmac in Guyana as he attempted to leave Jonestown the day that 918 men, women, and children died in Jim Jones's diabolical Kool-Aid massacre.

St. Anthony, NL, 1978. US politicians protested the seal hunt. We treated them civilly and, their misguided arguments, firmly. L-R: Congressman Leo Ryan (D-California), Newfoundland Liberal Leader Bill Rowe, me, MP Bill Rompkey, Congressman Jim Jeffords (R-Vermont). (Author photo)

116 A group of four volcanic islands in the Bering Sea, 200 miles off the coast of mainland Alaska, with a population of 700. Subsistence hunting of seals by native Aleuts is legal.

CHAPTER 14
BAYMAN IN BYTOWN[117]

Your representative owes you, not his industry alone, but his judgement; and he betrays, instead of serving, you if he sacrifices it to your opinion.
— Edmund Burke, eighteenth-century English MP

Don Jamieson's switch to provincial politics left a vacancy in his former Burin–St. George's riding. In the late autumn of 1979, he tipped me off that the announcement setting the date of the federal by-election was imminent and urged me to seek the party's nomination. I demurred. Since our 1973 marriage, my wife, Miriam, had stood by me through a by-election, two provincial campaigns, and two party leadership races, and I didn't think it fair to her for me to get involved in yet another electoral venture so soon after my most recent trip to the polls just four months earlier.

Two weeks later, Miriam and I were listening to the radio news over lunch. The announcer reported that two parties had named their candidates for the now-scheduled by-election, but the Liberals hadn't. To my surprise, my wife suggested I should go after the nomination. That changed everything. With her blessing, I made a beeline for Jamieson's office and, in due course, secured the nomination.

BARNSTORMING IN THE BOONIES

The pace of a federal campaign in a rural riding is gruelling and non-stop. Adrenalin was the daily fuel source, discipline the watchword. With luck, I'd be in bed by 2:00 a.m. Up at five, it was time to hit the road to reach some

117 Ottawa, founded in 1826, was formerly called Bytown. Colonel John By of the British Royal Engineers supervised the construction of the Rideau Canal and laid out the city's streets.

distant community for a breakfast meeting with workers or to stand at a fish plant gate as the day shift filed past.

Motor vehicle, ferry, float plane, chopper. Whatever it took to get from A to B was employed. In winter campaigns, snowmobiles sometimes came in handy, as did ski-equipped prop aircraft.

If I wasn't on the road as much as I should have been, it's because I was in the ditch, the inevitable consequence of slippery highways, tight schedules, and a heavy foot. Almost always, I drove the car myself, often juggling a clunky radio telephone, raisin buns, and Styrofoam cups of soup and tea, all the while plotting my next move or mentally editing phrases for the upcoming speech, media interview, or campaign ad.

Sickness is not an option during a campaign. I couldn't afford to catch the flu. Of course, the frantic pace made me a prime candidate for preying viruses, and I sometimes succumbed. Even then, there was no stopping, no choice but to raid the mobile medicine cabinet and soldier on.

Yet the rewards of such a mad enterprise far outweigh the downside. Manifestations of support for your candidacy keep you buoyant, as do the encouragement of partisans, the caring of friends, and the generosity of strangers. Rarely did I encounter anything less than the utmost civility, even among those least attracted to my cause or my party. Voters practised what they believed: Take issue with the issue, not with the issuer. Often I found myself in a spirited standoff on some policy or government program. Almost never did the verbal onslaught turn personal. We agreed to disagree, such a contrast with the vitriol that has hijacked mainstream US politics and which is not entirely absent from the Canadian scene. Prime Minister Brian Mulroney's dishonest and disgusting treatment of Newfoundland Premier Clyde Wells after the collapse of the Meech Lake constitutional accord marked a new low.

I've never quite understood the notion that, if you advocate a public policy solution that is at variance with someone else's, there must be something flawed in your character, according to that someone else. A healthy democracy presumes a lively debate, not a dogmatic self-righteousness that precludes diverging views and principled compromise. No one has all the answers, well, except for Rush Limbaugh![118] Those who think they do deserve our pity, though not our rancour.

THE GIFT THAT KEPT ON GIVING

A candidate running under the banner of an opposition party has to be innovative to create and maintain a high public profile. That's right, you have to

118 American radio talk-show host and conservative political commentator

generate your own press, no easy task. But some days you get lucky and get help from the very folks who are sitting up nights trying to figure out how to ensure your demise, electorally, that is.

Just ten days before polling day, I had just such a lucky day. Indeed, it was but the first of a string of lucky days, all compliments of the Tory minister of Finance. John Crosbie, in an after-speech press interview in Toronto, was quoted as saying he hadn't received any complaints about the high price of oil, then at $35 a barrel and dramatically up from the $16 price of just eight months earlier. (The 1970 price of $1.20 was but a distant memory, not to mention sheer fantasy in the context of prices in 1979, the year the by-election was held.) I was driving, hustling from one campaign event to the next, when I heard Crosbie's unmistakable voice on the radio news.

"Nobody has complained to me . . ."

Bingo! I saw an opening and pounced. "Dear John" letters were mass-produced overnight and placed in shopping centres, corner stores, and post office lobbies across the riding. They said just two words: "I complain!"

Voters loved this chance at participatory democracy, and they flocked to shopping malls and to our campaign offices to sign the terse missives, which we promptly transmitted to Crosbie's Ottawa office. Others wired "I complain" telegrams direct to the minister. We really didn't expect an answer, but we had to give the story legs. My very shrewd campaign manager, Don Hollett, a veteran of grassroots and Ottawa politics, picked up the phone, spoke to a ministerial aide, and was told, "We are swamped. We have already received over four thousand telegrams and letters."

Bingo, again! Our press release, in time for the evening news cycle, read, "Liberal candidate Roger Simmons has been informed by the minister's office that he has been swamped by complaints of high oil prices and that more than four thousand have been received so far. Mr. Simmons added there is still time for people to make their voices heard by wiring an 'I complain' telegram to the minister."

OTTAWA, HERE I COME!

The by-election results were much to my liking:

Carter, Walter, Progressive Conservative Party, 4,308
Mackinnon, David, New Democratic Party, 4,587
Simmons, Roger, Liberal Party, 10,434

The people had spoken. I would have the rare honour of sitting in the nation's House of Commons as the duly elected Member for Burin–St.

George's, only the third person to do so since Newfoundland's confederation with Canada thirty years earlier. My predecessors had each set the bar very high. I would follow in the footsteps of two of Newfoundland's greatest native sons, two amazing men, both of whom it was my privilege to know.

Military hero Ches Carter served with the Royal Newfoundland Regiment in the First World War and survived incredible odds. He was gassed in battle, placed on the terminally ill list in an English hospital, and left to die. During World War II, he spent five years overseas with the Canadian Army and achieved the rank of Major. Between the wars, he had a distinguished career in education. In 1949, he became one of the new province's MPs in Ottawa. Elected seven times, he represented the south coast of Newfoundland for seventeen years until his 1966 appointment to the Senate of Canada, where he served for another eleven years.

Broadcaster extraordinaire Don Jamieson succeeded Major Carter as MP. A prominent radio and TV personality, Jamieson had advocated economic union with the United States during the debate in the late 1940s over Newfoundland's constitutional future. He was elected to the House of Commons in a 1966 by-election and held several senior cabinet portfolios, including the foreign ministry.

The by-election result did not just impact me alone. Would my wife, Miriam, and our three-year-old son, Paul, stay in St. John's for the time being or tag along with me? The decision was complicated by two factors. Prime Minister Joe Clark's minority government could fall at any time, sending me back door-knocking in a general election, in which case it made sense for my wife and son to stay put. Secondly, Miriam was seven months pregnant. If we were going to move as a family to Ottawa, the sooner the better. Besides, the Clark government had survived for six months, and its defeat did not appear imminent. So, off to the nation's seat of government we went, Paul and me by car, Miriam and our yet-unborn bundle of joy by plane.

DICEY ASSUMPTIONS

John Crosbie introduced the Tory government's budget on December 11, just five sitting days after my arrival in the House of Commons. The budget was the first (and the last) of the new administration, which had been in office only since June 4. The tax measures contained in the budget were widely perceived by the electorate as decidedly regressive, favouring the affluent and further impoverishing the poor.

As part of the budget's parliamentary scrutiny process, my party, the Official Opposition, moved a budget amendment to which the New Democratic Party (NDP) attached a sub-amendment. Passage of either would mean the government didn't have the support of the House. The vote on the NDP non-confidence motion was scheduled for December 13. The government was in a precarious spot.

The Social Credit Party of Canada (Socreds), a conservative-populist splinter party that had seen better days, had five MPs, enough to ensure majority support for the budget. Rebuffed by Prime Minister Joe Clark in a bid for budget concessions, Socred leader Fabien Roy and his shrinking band, a sixth member having bolted to the Tories, were in no mood to make life easy for the government. Surprisingly, Government House Leader Walter Baker and other Tory bean-counters had rationalized that the Socreds had no choice but to hold their noses and vote for the budget, the alternative being their complete demise at the polls if the government fell.

It is the usual practice of caucus whips, but especially the government whip, to order travelling MPs to return immediately to Ottawa for crucial votes. Curiously, Baker did not see fit to do so; three of their Members were abroad and/or still sulking over their failure to make the cabinet cut and would miss the crucial head count. A telegram to one of them, External Affairs Minister Flora MacDonald, revealed yet another sign the Tory high command was whistling past the graveyard:

"Despite bold talk, we believe diplomatic flu will hit Liberal benches.[119]

Insiders noticed that Prime Minister Joe Clark and his advisors passed up or fumbled several obvious salvage opportunities, any one of which would have avoided defeat.

As for Clark, he was sanguine and, from his perspective, had reason to be. Moderate Democrat Jimmy Carter was on the ropes in the US. Ultra-conservative Margaret Thatcher had been sworn in as British prime minister one month to the day before Clark himself had taken the oath of office. The evidence was clear. As Clark saw things, Liberals were on the run. The conservative brand was in style. He foresaw only two possible outcomes, both decidedly palatable. Either, his minority government would be sustained, allowing him to carry on governing "as if I had a majority," as he had vowed earlier. Or he would be defeated in the non-confidence vote, which would set the wheels in motion to win the sweeping majority at the polls that he felt he deserved and fully expected to get.

119 *Discipline of Power*, Jeffrey Simpson, Rexdale: John Wiley & Sons, 1980, p. 27

MacEACHEN MAGIC

In the regular weekly Liberal caucus the day before the confidence vote, the wily Allan MacEachen[120] made good use of his trusty crystal ball. Not only did he predict the government would lose the budget vote, he told us how and why it would happen. And he showed us how the Tory defeat would be the launch pad for a Liberal comeback, cogently detailing how we could, and would, be back in government just months after the party's bruising defeat the previous May.

That evening, the Liberal caucus held its annual Christmas bash. Jim Coutts, the Opposition Leader's principal secretary, took me in tow as he table-hopped and salivated about the impending coup. Our tour of the party venue was like a victory lap and, for me, the newbie, a graduate course in the finer points of political intrigue. The mood was electric, the optimism contagious. Incumbents were already making plans for the election campaign which the government's defeat would trigger. Some, I have no doubt, were picking their cabinet portfolios.

In the circumstances, the Liberal strategy was as simple as it gets. All we had to do was ensure that our MPs were present for the vote.

REVVING UP THE TROOPS

With the government's defeat all but a certainty, I had told my caucus whip, Tom Lefebvre, earlier in the day I had to speak in the debate before the vote was put. I just couldn't face the voters and have it said I hadn't opened my mouth since I took my seat in the House. The whip agreed.

To help me prepare for the speech, I was assigned two of the best. Barb Sulzenko had an M.A. in economic policy and was attached to the Liberal research bureau. Nate Laurie, also an economist, had recently been hired away from the Conference Board of Canada to advise Opposition Leader Pierre Trudeau. As we holed up in a Library of Parliament conference room, they did their best to school me on the intricacies of finance and taxes.

But my mind was elsewhere. I interrupted our cram session and walked down the corridor to the Commons. My intention was to ask the Liberal whip whether he thought the jig was really up for the Conservatives. As I squeezed a path through the House lobby, packed to the gunwales with opposition members, all excitedly salivating at the prospect of an imminent Tory defeat, I quickly concluded my intended query would sound naive. Fellow Liberal MP Lloyd Axworthy's impression mirrored mine:

"It's like a high school cheering section in there!"[121]

---

120 Professor, MP, minister, deputy prime minister, senator, 1921–2017

121 *Discipline of Power*, Jeffrey Simpson, Rexdale: John Wiley & Sons, 1980, p. 33

Back in the library, my inner light bulb lit up. If the government's demise was all but a done deal, this was no time for a clinical rebuttal of budget details. If my party was indeed headed back to the trenches and I was about to invade millions of living rooms across the country, this was an opportunity to rally the faithful, to soften up the skeptical, to take a few potshots at the enemy. To do that, I didn't need the coaching of the two brilliant economists sitting across from me nor the truckload of briefing notes they had assembled for me.

I opted instead for a subject I knew much better, the minister himself. For the first time on a national stage, I would get to test drive the debating template I had learned in another legislature, the fractious Newfoundland House of Assembly, where my mentors were as good as they come, Steve Neary, Ed Roberts, and Bill Rowe. Often had Crosbie and I sparred in that other arena—he, as a government minister, I, as his Official Opposition critic. I know the guy well, and I decided to try and score a few points at his expense. That would be relatively easy on this occasion, since I would have the mic. It is quite another matter if he's got one, too, as I well know from tangling with him.

The minister had preambled his budget speech with a nostalgic reference to his grandfather, Sir John Crosbie, Finance minister in a still-independent Newfoundland just before the Great Depression wreaked its havoc. In my speech, I noted that the latter-day Minister Crosbie "had spoken fondly of another Crosbie who had brought down a budget at another time in another country. . . . What the minister failed to tell the House was that, soon after that other Crosbie in that other country delivered his budget, that other country went bankrupt!"[122]

The most unpopular provision in the 1979 Crosbie budget was a six-cent tax on gasoline. This *short-term pain for long-term gain* could be mitigated, the minister recommended, by carpooling and other measures. That fateful night, in my maiden speech in the Commons, I mocked his fuel-conservation prescription:

"How does a fisherman save gas? Does he go just halfway to the fishing grounds?"

I was subsequently flattered when my consent was sought to include that quote in the Liberal Party's TV spots for the ensuing election. I was the

122 My use of "bankrupt" was poetic licence, though only technically so. Newfoundland's shaky finances, made many times worse by the Great Depression, obliged the country to seek financial help from Britain, a move which ultimately triggered the suspension of Newfoundland's constitution and the appointment of a British-dominated commission to act as a de facto government until the financial situation improved.

final speaker before the vote. I had a captive broadcast audience of millions. Alas, it was the fate of the government, not the anticipation of my oratory, that glued them to their TV sets and radios.

BACK ON THE HUSTINGS

With Clark's refusal to make concessions to the Social Credit Party, the five Socreds abstained in the budget vote, sealing the Tories' fate. With all but one of the Liberal MPs present, we watched as the Tories hanged themselves with their own rope. Ecstatic opposition MPs and crestfallen government backers created a veritable confetti shower as order papers and speech notes became airborne.

As is the tradition on such occasions, the huge main doors of the historic edifice swung open, and the assemblage poured through to spin its divergent messaging to a waiting press corps. A print journalist, referencing the fact I had been a sitting MP for just seven days, planted her tape recorder perilously close to my lips and yelled above the din, "You just got here. What do you do now?"

"The very first thing I'm going to do is wire all my workers and say 'For God's sake, don't take down the posters!'"

Crosbie was known to have leadership ambitions. A juicy bit of intrigue alleged that John had engineered Joe Clark's defeat. Three years later, I cast an amused eye back on those events, and, with apologies to hymnist John Newton, I penned a little doggerel which, thanks to the kind indulgence of Madam Speaker Sauvé, I read into Hansard under the guise of a Member's Statement (Standing Order 43):

Amazing John who, on this day just three short years ago,
Forfeited gain for short-term pain to put the boots to Joe.
Should we be here ten thousand years, we'll still recall the time
That Walter's skill at counting failed and Liberals smiled, sublime.
And so I move a Forty-Three: "That those to power inclined
Be taught to add with accuracy, have eyes in their behind."

SOBER SECOND THOUGHTS

As party hacks and politicians, the pundits and the public rejoiced or commiserated over the previous evening's drama, one question in particular popped up everywhere: Who would lead the Liberals in the upcoming election? Could a fast-tracked convention anoint a new leader? Could Trudeau be enticed back into the ring?

These were among the questions that begged answers as Liberal MPs and senators filed in for what would be a marathon caucus. First, though, once the euphoria of defeating the Clark government had receded, there was an emotional and, in my view, painfully long session of second-guessing what we had done the night before. Had we acted too hastily in precipitating an election? Were we ready for an election so soon after the last? Could the electorate be expected to give us a fresh mandate after turfing the party out of office just seven months ago?

I was the new kid on the block. I had been a member of the caucus for all of eight days. I was having real trouble figuring out what all the bellyaching was about. When my turn at the mic came, I spoke my mind. Several years later, at a private dinner party in Toronto, Monique Begin recalled the moment. She reminded Judy Erola, John Roberts[123], and me of my shoot-from-the-hip outburst the morning following the government's defeat:

"Two days ago, I stood here, looked into your eyes, and saw resolve. My mistake was not looking at your knees!"

I was surprised at the pained body language, the shell shock of MPs from the west and other swing ridings. In the caucus two days previously, they had been among the most vocal in favour of toppling the government. Since then, grim reality had set in. Certain defeat at the polls was their best-case scenario. "Nothing concentrates one's thinking like the certainty of being hanged in the morning."[124] In the subsequent election, only two Liberals were returned from the west.

If Liberal support out west was abysmally low in the 1980 election, it was simply extending a long-established trend line. Since 1957, the party's electoral performance in the four western provinces had been dismal to catastrophic, with the sole exception of the 1968 election.

1957	8 seats	1968	27
1958	0	1972	7
1962	6	1974	13
1963	6	1979	3
1965	8	1980	2

Revisionists like to assert that the Liberals' ongoing free fall in the west was caused by the 1980 National Energy Program. As you can see, the party's lack of traction with western voters predates the NEP by more than two decades, notwithstanding the Trudeau-fuelled aberration of 1968. Commentators regularly summed up western voters' antipathy toward Trudeau and the Liberals:

123 Begin, Erola, and Roberts were cabinet ministers under Pierre Trudeau.

124 Samuel Johnson (1709–84), poet, literary critic, lexicographer

> "If the PM walked on Lake Ontario, the *Toronto Star* would headline 'Trudeau walks on water.' If he walked on Alberta's Lake Louise, the *Calgary Herald* would charge 'Trudeau interferes with small boating regulations.'"

But I digress.

WHO WILL LEAD THE CHARGE?

The morning-after caucus eventually turned its attention to the question of who would lead the party in the election. Ever since he quit the Trudeau cabinet in 1975, John Turner had been seen by many as the white knight who would restore Camelot on the Rideau, but he had taken himself out of the race. The other dream candidate was former Finance minister Donald MacDonald.

As for Trudeau, any suggestion he would carry the Liberal banner into the election seemed like a non-starter. Hadn't he already said he didn't want to be leader anymore? However, at the December 14 caucus, which he attended only briefly, Trudeau admitted to the possibility of his resuming the leadership by requesting his fellow MPs to conduct a secret ballot on the issue. While Thursday night's unexpected turn of events and favourable polls opened the possibility for Trudeau to regain the reins of power, he knew the odds of that happening would be much diminished if he didn't have the full backing of the parliamentary wing.

Caucus was split down the centre. MacDonald supporters favoured a quick leadership convention. Members partial to a Turner candidacy backed Trudeau, not because they thought he could win the election; rather, they saw his return as a way to keep the position open for Turner. In the end, the Trudeau camp, myself included, prevailed. It was decided to ask the former prime minister to lead the party in the election, and four days later, he said yes.

KINDRED SPIRITS

My maiden speech in the House of Commons the night the Clark government fell in 1979 generated a flood of speaking invitations, mostly requests from federal Liberal associations to address AGMs, fundraisers, and nominating meetings. One such invite came from two Nova Scotia candidates. A Cape Breton duo, incumbent Russ MacLellan and a newcomer, the inimitable Dave Dingwall, decided I should help kick off their nominating event in Sydney. Both were elected in the 1980 vote. After serving as an MP for eighteen years, MacLellan switched to provincial politics and ably served as premier of Nova Scotia.

Like MacLellan, Dingwall would also thrive in federal politics for nearly two decades. When he held the Health portfolio, I chaired the standing committee on health. We functioned as an effective tag team in piloting tough tobacco advertising legislation through nationally televised hearings and passage in the House. Dingwall's upbeat personality, strategic genius, and off-the-wall, gotcha humour opens many doors for him and his causes. His prescience and caring saved me from a potentially problematic circumstance during my first days as consul general in Seattle. By then he was no longer a member of the government or an MP, but his watchful eye was still on the job. He later served as president of the Royal Canadian Mint. Under his leadership, the mint posted its first surplus in several years.

With Christmas upon us, polling day was delayed until February 18, making the sixty-six-day campaign one of the longest ever. Yes, another stint on the hustings lay ahead, and so soon after the last one. And, yet again, there was a jarring choice to be made. My family was now in Ottawa, our second child was due within weeks, and we had bought a house just days before. How could I disappear into the electoral trenches, incurring sizable expenses commuting between the national capital and the faraway campaign trail? The party came to the rescue, agreeing to underwrite weekly trips to Newfoundland. I would campaign four days in the riding and three close to Ottawa speaking at campaign events, as a trade-off for the party's generosity, all the while trying to predict the stork's ETA.

I was nowhere near Ottawa when my wife was rushed to the hospital with labour pains. Rather, I was in a snowbank 2,000 miles away, awaiting an arrival of a different kind, a tow truck, having lost the battle with icy roads near Marystown. Soon after, I was en route to Ottawa. As I deplaned, the airport public address system summoned me. Senator Bill Petten's spouse, Bun, herself a nurse and loyal friend, was with my wife and told me, "It'll be any time now. Get here as fast as you can." I did. But my new son, Mark, beat me to the punch, as he has so many times since. He was already Canada's newest voter-to-be by the time I hotfooted into the maternity ward of the Ottawa General Hospital.

WELCOME TO THE '80s!

The victor's opening line electrified the partisan throng packed into a ballroom at Ottawa's storied Château Laurier. The grand old hotel had often been history's backdrop, as was now the case once more, just a few weeks into the new decade.

The 1980 election results would prove to be a watershed event for Canadian federalism. Joe Clark's reckless gamble had backfired badly. The Conservatives lost thirty-three seats. The Liberals were back at the helm. Trudeau had been elected to a fourth term in five trips to the polls.

The electors of Burin–St. George's sent me to Ottawa once again, just three months less a day after they had done so the first time. Indeed, the tallied results were especially sweet. The November 1979 by-election had been a three-way contest, and I garnered fifty-four per cent of the votes cast. In the February 1980 general election, again with two other candidates in the running, my share of the total vote shot up to seventy per cent.

In a head-spinning sequence of events, Pierre Elliot Trudeau had gone from being prime minister to Leader of the Opposition to prime minister in just eight months. The acknowledged master of the one-liner was back in business. He had dished out other pithy mouthfuls over the years:

- *Just watch me,* when asked how far he would go in responding to the 1970 terrorism in Montreal
- *Why should I sell your wheat,* when western farmers were demanding his intervention
- *The Tories may even tax your mouth,* when a heckler became disruptive at an election rally
- *Zap! You're frozen!* when he ridiculed then Conservative Leader Robert Stanfield's wage and price-freeze policy
- *The government has no place in the bedrooms of the nation,* when, as Justice minister, he scripted landmark Criminal Code amendments liberalizing laws concerning homosexuality and abortion

Each retort had been a blunt broadside to those who didn't share his view. This latest one was different. *Welcome to the '80s!* It was a rallying cry, emanating from a man on a mission. He knew precisely where he was headed, and he intended to take the country with him. In the weeks ahead, he spelled out the agenda. A new energy policy. Jobs programs. A proactive industrial policy. Constitutional patriation[125] and renewal. A charter

125 The word "patriation," coined by Prime Minister Pearson in 1966, connotes the act of transferring from Westminster to the Parliament of Canada the prerogative to amend the Canadian constitution.

of rights. He told his caucus, "Fasten your seat belts, we're in for one heck of a ride!"

Not since those halcyon days after his 1968 ascendancy to the prime ministership had he been so articulate about his prescription for the nation or as determined to apply it.

A NATION TOO GOOD TO LOSE[126]

Canada's very own comeback kid was eager to tackle his new checklist of things to do. First, though, he had to deal with a major distraction and, more to the point, a serious threat to national unity. René Lévesque, the separatist Quebec premier, had scheduled a May 1980 referendum on the province's constitutional future.

The highly charged debate pitted those two larger-than-life characters against each other, Trudeau and Lévesque. The prime minister's advocacy of the federalist position, the "no" side, was complicated by three factors. His relationship with the leader of the "no" campaign, Claude Ryan, was testy. Initial polls gave momentum to the separatists. And, thirdly, the referendum question was convoluted, deceptive, even. Rather than asking whether Quebecers favoured sovereignty, Lévesque opted for a mealy-mouthed cascade of words.[127] However, Lévesque's real objective, outright separation, was known to all.

Trudeau and Ryan buried the hatchet and mounted an effective campaign which exposed the calculated deceit implicit in the referendum question. The result was a decisive rejection of René Lévesque's position. The "no" forces triumphed with sixty per cent of the vote.

DUMB, LIKE A FOX

I've long been both amused and annoyed at the attention accorded René Lévesque's refusal to support the 1981 constitutional deal. Basic common sense says he had no intention of doing so. The guy whose whole raison d'être was to dismantle Canada wasn't about to commit certain political suicide by embracing the very thing he railed against. Brian Mulroney, who would become the Leader of the Opposition in 1983, acknowledged the obvious when he

126 The title of former prime minister Joe Clark's 1994 treatise

127 "The Government of Quebec has made public its proposal to negotiate a new agreement with the rest of Canada, based on the equality of nations; this agreement would enable Quebec to acquire the exclusive power to make its laws, levy its taxes, and establish relations abroad—in other words, sovereignty—and at the same time to maintain with Canada an economic association including a common currency; any change in political status resulting from these negotiations will only be implemented with popular approval through another referendum; on these terms, do you give the Government of Quebec the mandate to negotiate the proposed agreement between Quebec and Canada?"

publicly congratulated Trudeau on achieving the constitutional deal in late 1981.

> "Lévesque's mission in life is the dismemberment of Canada . . . why should we be surprised because Mr. Lévesque has refused to agree with a concrete gesture that would prove Canadian federalism is . . . flexible and can work?"[128]

Any forward-thinking, self-respecting arsonist keeps a box of matches or a Molotov cocktail handy. The myth that the Quebec premier was somehow snookered by Trudeau and the other premiers was just the box of matches Lévesque needed. He feigned umbrage, milking it shamelessly as have his kind ever since. That's no surprise. What is mind-boggling is that federalists help to keep alive the ridiculous pretense that the avowed separatist leader had ever intended to buy into the constitutional package. It takes a very dumb mortal to sign his own death warrant. I dealt with Lévesque several times dating back to the mid-1960s. He was as mortal as the rest of us. And a whole lot less dumb than most of us.

GETTING IN ON THE ACTION

Meanwhile, I was going about my assignment as parliamentary secretary, in effect, a very junior non-cabinet minister, somewhat analogous to the British practice where only senior ministers are members of the inner circle while others pursue specific responsibilities which are integral to the overall mandates of the cabinet-level ministers.

My senior minister, the genial, scholarly, and urbane John Roberts, held two portfolios, Environment (including forestry) and Science and Technology. He was a firm believer in delegation. Short of signing authority which by law could only be his, he assigned to me all responsibility for Parks Canada, forestry, toxic chemicals, and liaison with the three granting councils which came under our jurisdiction.[129] It made for a busy two years, the term limit Trudeau had imposed on parliamentary secretary appointments, aimed at giving more MPs a chance to be part of the action.

---

128 *Clyde Wells: A Political Biography*, Claire Hoy, Toronto: Stoddart Publishing, 1992, p. 152

129 NSERC (Natural Sciences and Engineering Research Council), SSHRC (Social Sciences and Humanities Research Council), and MRC (Medical Research Council), now CHR (Canadian Institutes of Health Research)

Toronto, ON, 1981. NASA astronauts Joe Engle and Richard Truly accepted the Canadarm from Prime Minister Pierre Trudeau at Spar Aerospace, which produced the equipment. L-R: Parliamentary Secretary for Science and Technology Roger Simmons, Minister John Roberts, Engle, Trudeau, and Truly. (Author photo)

The Parks Canada file was by far the most enjoyable and, for the most part, the freest of intractable dilemmas. With twenty national parks and hundreds of historic sites[130] spread the length and breadth of the country, much of my time was spent on the road, meeting with officials, speaking at conferences, and unveiling heritage plaques, at the Anglican Cathedral and Sir Humphrey Gilbert's landing site in St. John's, on Carbonear Island, NL (where Brits repulsed French forces in 1696), at Brigus, NL (home of Arctic explorer Bob Bartlett), at Louisbourg, NS (eighteenth-century fortress), and at the Rockies' Kicking Horse Pass, AB, to name but a few.

Major events required Minister Roberts's participation. From the northern tip of Newfoundland overlooking the North Atlantic to the peak of Hawaii's Mount Kea, we set a hectic, exciting pace. We officiated at a sod-turning at L'Anse aux Meadows, Newfoundland, site of the ancient Viking encampment, the first documented arrival in North America by Europeans. Christopher Columbus, John Cabot, and Jacques Cartier would "discover" the continent five centuries later! Although Leif the Lucky and his compatriots were long gone, I did get to meet a couple of

130 Currently, there are thirty-nine national parks and 976 national historic sites.

Vikings, latter-day incarnations, Norwegian historian Helge Ingstad and his archaeologist wife, Anne.

MEETING OF TWO WORLDS[131]

It had long been thought that the first European settlement in North America was at least as far south as Massachusetts. Helge Ingstad had a different idea. In 1960, as he sat in his Oslo home, he told his teenaged daughter, Benedicte, he had a new theory about the location of Leif Erikson's North American settlement. So sure was Ingstad of his conclusion that he travelled to Newfoundland that same year, accompanied by his daughter. "I . . . carried out systematic investigations of the coasts of Newfoundland by boat and from the air."[132] His quest eventually took him to northern Newfoundland and, specifically, to the tiny, isolated hamlet of L'Anse aux Meadows.

"I would like to talk to the oldest person in this village."

Fisherman George Decker led Ingstad to a cluster of overgrown mounds and ridges that looked as if they might be burial sites or the remains of buildings. In time, archaeologists, led by Ingstad's wife, Anne, would authenticate the locale as the historic Viking settlement.

As you follow the path from the L'Anse aux Meadows interpretation centre to the Viking site, you pass under, or, more accurately, through a striking sculpture. The structure suggests a circle, except at the top there is an opening. The sculptors, Newfoundland's Luben Boykov[133] and Swede Richard Brixel, designed it that way for a reason. From the cradle of civilization, early humans had fanned out east and west. Mankind's global odyssey came full circle when the trails of Vikings from the east and aboriginals from the west intersected in northern Newfoundland. There is evidence that the two branches of civilization actually came face to face.[134] The gap at the top of the sculpture is intended to connote their spiritual bond.

The emcee for the L'Anse aux Meadows sod-turning event had a moment of panic when the time came for my speech. He couldn't find me. He should have looked toward the trombone section of the Salvation Army Band, of which I had been a charter member twenty-five years earlier. I too had come full circle.

When we met at L'Anse aux Meadows, the Ingstads mouthed the standard invitation, the kind you should never give me unless you mean it. *If*

---

131 Name given to the L'Anse aux Meadows sculpture by Bulgarian-born Newfoundland sculptor Luben Boykov and Sweden's Richard Brixel

132 *The Norse Discovery of America*, Volume Two, Helge Ingstad, Oslo: Norwegian University Press, 1985, p. 10

133 Bulgarian-born Boykov defected at Gander, NL, in 1990 when he was thirty years of age.

134 www.smithsonianmag.com/history/the-vikings

you are ever in Oslo, drop in. I did exactly that eight years later and enjoyed four fascinating hours with them in their hillside home with its panoramic view of Oslo. Their two scholarly volumes on the history and the archaeology of L'Anse aux Meadows were their parting gifts to me, which I treasure to this day.

PETTY POLITICS

A brilliant Newfoundland scholar, intellectual of the first order and reigning Canadian history expert at Memorial University, Dr. Leslie Harris was my prof for several courses, including Newfoundland history and twentieth-century Canada. Minister Roberts had delegated to me responsibility for the Historical Sites and Monuments Board of Canada. When its chair became vacant in 1981, I invited Dr. Harris, by then Memorial's president, to fill the position, which he did with distinction. But not for long.

Harris, during the 1982 Newfoundland provincial election, expressed public support for Premier Brian Peckford and his Tories. My political masters in Ottawa were not amused and decreed that Harris be unceremoniously sacked. I voiced my objection to this asinine knee-jerk reaction whereby a respected academic leader would be humiliated. And for what? For exercising his democratic right to make an electoral choice. My protestations went unheeded. And one final twist was added. I would be the one to break the news to him.

And I did. Harris, ever the class act, was gracious, though surprised. All of which ate up only a couple of minutes. So, with time on my hands and the president of Memorial all to myself, I switched gears and asked him if he would be open to a suggestion for an honorary degree. He was.

The candidate I had in mind was a truly amazing human being, retired Salvation Army officer Major Sarah Woodland. As an eighteen-year-old officer cadet, she was awed when she heard a speech by Sir Richard Squires[135], who exhorted: "Give to the world the best you have, and the best will come back to you."

Throughout her half-century of ministry, she was true to that dictum. Her spellbinding oratory was recognized early on by the Army's leadership, and at twenty-four she became the movement's itinerant evangelist, the featured preacher at week-long revival campaigns.

Major Woodland was known to Dr. Harris since her son, Bruce, was the university's public relations officer. The president liked the idea of Dr. Sarah Woodland, and he made it happen. At the celebratory dinner which followed

135 Prime Minister of Newfoundland, 1919–23, 1928–32

the convocation, I was proud to be included, the only non-family member in the room.

UPPING THE ANTE

Successive federal governments, Liberal and Tory, have routinely funded so-called make-work programs, intended to ease unemployment in communities where seasonal pursuits, such as the fishery, are the only income sources. The challenge for the MP, who decides which projects will be given the green light, is to identify those with the promise of legacy value, say, a new wharf or breakwater, a school playground or a water system.

It was part of my routine to visit such projects, both to assess their progress and to politic with constituents. On one occasion, I found the workers playing cards. The project foreman was nowhere in sight. I knocked on the door of his home. No answer. Persistent knocking eventually produced a near-comatose character busily stuffing his shirttail inside his pants. What time the guy crawled out of bed was entirely his business. But snuggling up to his sleep partner at ten o'clock on a working day was not in his contract.

I cancelled the project. Program overseers in Ottawa were apoplectic. They called to say I couldn't do that. I replied, "I just did! If my signature can approve a project, it can unapprove it."

Word of the project's fate quickly became common knowledge throughout the riding. I like to think there was a noticeable improvement in productivity. One thing is for sure, there were fewer government-subsidized poker games. At least one fewer!

In retrospect, what I had done was probably not the right thing to do in the circumstances. I could have been less draconian and sacked the foreman. Politically, my action was a no-brainer. Funding make-work projects was controversial. Many people, mainly those who had no dependence on them, felt the whole scheme was a waste of money. My action in cancelling a project sent a signal that I would not tolerate an abuse of the program.

KEEPING YOUR EYE ON THE BALL

At a Vancouver forestry conference, I watched, incredulous, as a senior BC forestry executive publicly took strip after strip off the federal government and then, in the next breath, proceeded to seek that same government's help in addressing an urgent issue in the Canada-US lumber file. If you're about to ask a guy for help, it's probably not a smart idea to smack him in the face first.

The Atlantic Liberal caucus in Ottawa routinely used a more creative approach. We left our crying towels at home and kept our bile well under control. The results were often impressive. A case in point is the Pierre Trudeau government's response to the 1982 crisis in the deep-sea fishery. A further example is the Mulroney administration's handling of the 1992 closure of the Atlantic groundfish industry, the result of strategic House interventions and ministerial meetings by Liberal MPs and, I have no doubt, by Atlantic Conservative MP advocacy in the government caucus. In 1994, Prime Minister Chrétien implemented the Atlantic Groundfish Strategy (TAGS), providing income support and labour market adjustment programs to fishermen and plant workers.

AN ORATORICAL CRAPSHOOT IN VEGAS

Following my early-morning treadmill routine in the Commons gym, I went downstairs to my office to tackle another hectic day. This one immediately became even crazier than usual when I learned Minister John Roberts was down with the flu and I would have to pinch hit for him that very evening—in Las Vegas. Three hours later, I was airborne, accompanied by the specialist from the environment department who had authored the speech I was to deliver to the Water Pollution Control Federation (WPCF). His daunting task was to transform me into a waste water expert during the flight to Vegas. I had little more than a passing acquaintance with the subject, since it wasn't part of my assigned responsibilities. But I had bigger problems. My travel companion's decidedly fractured English was further complicated by his love affair with ten-dollar, subject-specific words and an alphabet soup of acronyms. By the time we deplaned, my head was spinning, not with piercing insights about sewage disposal, but a migraine.

With a couple of hours to kill before the scheduled address, I asked him to reduce the twenty-page speech to a one-pager of three or four bullet points. Alone in my hotel room, I and my confused head wrestled with the essence of the speech and briefing notes. All too soon, it was showtime. As my WPCF handler and I approached the entrance to the cavernous Las Vegas Convention Center, I asked how large the audience would be.

"About thirteen thousand . . ."

As I regained consciousness, I heard him add,

". . . plus the closed-circuit TV viewers."

Armed with the bureaucrat's one-pager and my usual three-by-five index card containing the punchlines of half a dozen jokes, I stepped up to the podium, all the while reflecting on an apt line from holy writ, "If it is possible, let this cup pass . . ."

It did not pass. Somehow, I did. Perhaps it was the low expectation of the conference participants. The printed program touted a senior Canadian government minister as the speaker. Instead, a rookie stand-in had been foisted on them. Nonetheless, sewer experts from Montreal to Miami to Madrid seemed to like what I had to say, largely a litany of catchphrases evoking the joys and challenges of their chosen profession and some serious messaging on behalf of Canada and things environmental, interspersed with recycled jokes to drive home a point or rouse those who were nodding off.

I was due to return to Ottawa next morning, but the conference organizers had other plans. I was invited to stay over for a special event the following evening. The bureaucrat who obviously knew the nature of the event exhorted me to do so. I was now his best buddy, having read from the podium every last multi-syllable in his latest literary triumph, the trusty one-pager.

The private dinner with fifty or sixty head honchos of the world's largest sewage systems was a real blast. The powers that be had decreed my speech had been an "outstanding service above and beyond the call of duty" and merited special recognition. I was inducted into their exalted, if tongue-in-cheek, five-S society, the Select Society of Sanitary Sludge Shovellers, only the second Canadian politician to be so honoured, the first having been Jeanne Sauvé.[136] To this day, I proudly flaunt in my lapel the Society's symbol of office, a miniature gold shovel, tangible proof of my lofty international status among sewer aficionados!

PEOPLE IN GLASS HOUSES

The Las Vegas event generated other speaking invitations, including one to address a waste water conference in Perth, Australia, which Minister Roberts agreed I should accept, provided other speaking opportunities and bilateral meetings could be identified to justify the substantial cost of the trip. For that, I needed the help and support of a specific senior bureaucrat at the environment ministry. Therein lay a problem. The bureaucrat was a reputed penny-pincher who liked to wax eloquent on whatever he deemed wasteful or extravagant. From his perspective, a trip to Australia would fall squarely into that category. He took me to lunch at Le Cercle Universitaire, a gourmet dining club just a few minutes drive from Parliament Hill. Before the waiter could fill our water glasses, my host launched into an extended oration on the evils of spending government money, while taking care to note that, should my Australia trip take place, he would be the obvious travel companion. In other words, he opposed junkets on principle, that is to say, those in which he wasn't included!

His hypocritical moralizing made me snap. Contrived sanctimony does that to me. It was more than I could manage on an empty stomach. It was

136 Journalist, MP, minister, Speaker of the House of Commons, Governor General

time to focus his mind: "Lately, I've been seeing your car in my neighbourhood quite often."

This was a thinly veiled reference to a juicy bit of gossip making the rounds that the bureaucrat was indulging in extracurricular activities with a subordinate staff member. That she was simplifying her daily commute to the office by taking the government-owned car home at night was well beyond the rumour stage.

Next day, when the minister, the bureaucrat, and I met, my lunchtime sermonizer exuded a new-found enthusiasm for my proposed trip that was almost embarrassing, to him, not me. He reported he had already set the wheels in motion to secure bilateral exchanges in Canberra and to identify additional speaking venues. A focused mind is a wondrous sight to behold!

My little bit of dirty pool is a tactic I have avoided perfecting over the years. While it can have demonstrable transitory results, there is a definite downside when you face the morning mirror. But I must admit there was a nice adrenalin rush when I exploited the opportunity to remind my pontificating luncheon host of his feet of clay. And I never again saw that government-owned car in my neck of the woods.

Australia was a fascinating experience. I did a speaking tour of several cities, Sydney, Canberra, Adelaide, Melbourne, and, of course, Perth. And there were bilateral talks on toxic chemicals, heritage preservation, and culture. My Aussie handlers had kindly arranged for me to spend two nights under canvas with the legendary Harry Butler[137] and his wife, Maggie, an outing that resonates still as a highlight of the trip.

ONE STUNT TOO MANY

The members of the House of Commons' ad hoc committee on parliamentary procedure travelled to London, England, in early 1983 as part of our research to update and streamline House rules. I did a one-hand vault over a crowd-control barrier in front of Westminster's St. Stephen's Porch. I cleared the barrier; my raglan didn't. A dislocated shoulder landed me in Westminster Hospital.

Two days into my hospitalization, my fellow committee members were participating in their final event before returning to Canada, a luncheon with British Members of Parliament. Winnipeg MP, my good friend, Bill Blaikie, verbalized what was on his mind: "I wonder how Lord Straddling Roger is doing right now?" Welsh MP (later Sir) John Straddling Thomas was prompted to ask a question of his own: "Do you really have a man named Straddling in your group?" Blaikie replied, "We do now!"

---

137 Australian naturalist and TV host, 1930–2015

Whiling away the time in the hospital, my thoughts were with my colleagues, and I resolved to catch up with them. I sweet-talked a nurse into allowing me to leave the hospital for a couple of hours. As I entered the lunch venue, Murdo MacLean approached me:

"One of our MPs, John Straddling Thomas, wanted to meet you, but he left a few moments ago to keep an appointment."

Murdo was the pivotal player in the government whip's office at 12 Downing Street.

HOBNOBBING AT WESTMINSTER

At Murdo's invitation, Blaikie, BC MP Mark Rose, Toronto MP David Smith, and I went to the House of Commons' Strangers' Bar and connected with Straddling Thomas. As the Brits would say, we had a jolly good time. A full six hours sped by. Finally, Straddling hit the road to make a speech in Cardiff.

Our new friend and facilitator, Murdo, had another invitation up his sleeve: "Would you gentlemen like to go to Downing Street?"

That was a no-brainer. Except there was a problem. I was expected back at the hospital hours ago. So, my three MP buddies and Murdo headed for 12 Downing Street. I would join them later, provided I could get a physician to check me out of the hospital. The doctor delivered in a jiffy, after extracting from me a promise to get medical attention immediately on my arrival in Ottawa and handing me a Bristol board–sized X-ray image.

RELUCTANT CABBIE

With my left arm in a sling, my one usable hand is multi-tasking. Clumsily, I'm grasping a half-dozen hardcover books, the kind gestures of Jim and Marg McGrath, Don Jamieson, Allan Lever,[138] and other friends, a bag of laundry, toiletries, and that humongous X-ray photo. How do I flag down a taxi without a free hand to get the driver's attention? I dump everything on the curb, signal to the next approaching cab, and, pronto, I have wheels.

The driver, impatient to get moving, exits the vehicle to help me load my stuff. He gets to see me close up. I am not a pretty sight. Three days without a shave. My hair hasn't seen a comb since the shoulder mishap. The dangling left sleeve of my raglan is still muddied from the fall. My luggage consists of four paper or plastic bags. Within a stone's throw from where we stand, there's a psychiatric hospital. So, it's not hard to figure out what the cabbie is thinking!

138 At the time, James McGrath was a Newfoundland MP and had been Canada's Fisheries minister. He later served as the province's lieutenant-governor. Jamieson was the Canadian high commissioner in London. Lever was a Canadian diplomat posted to the United Kingdom.

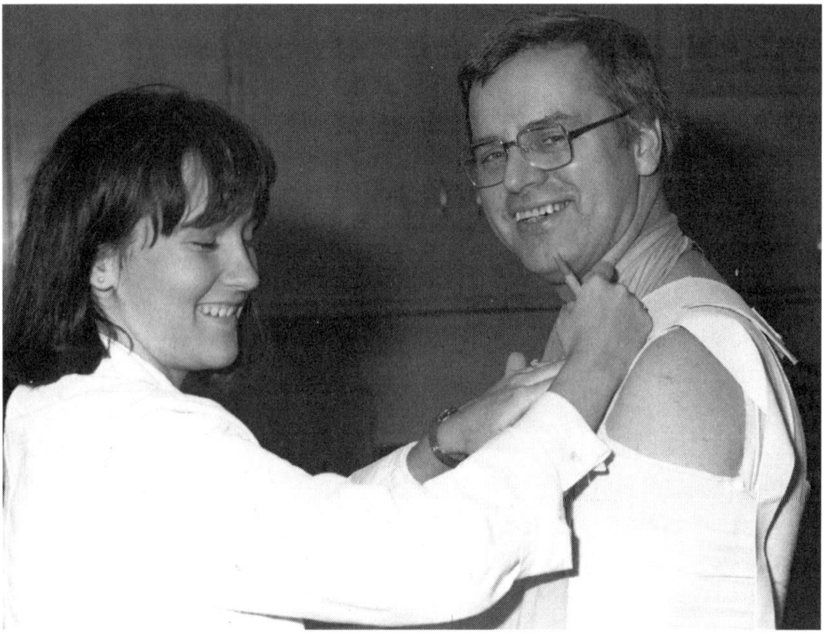

Ottawa, 1983. Let's just say that the National Defence Medical Centre nurse made an indelible impression on me! (Author photo)

I ease myself into the passenger compartment. The driver, now back at the wheel, slides open the glass panel separating us and inquires, "Where to, mate?" The cabbie is already in a foul mood. My response does nothing to improve his demeanour: "Downing Street, Number 12 Downing Street."

He loses it completely, bellowing at me in vintage cockney, "Yes, an' me lovin' mum is Maggie T'atcher! Now, where we goin'?"

Downing Street is upscale row housing. Four adjoining and inter-connected addresses figure prominently in Britain's governance: Number 9 houses the Privy Council. The official residence and office of the prime minister are next door at Number 10. Number 11 is the Chancellor of the Exchequer. Number 12, formerly the office of the government's chief whip, now functions as the PM's press office and research unit.

Everyone knows that no one goes to Downing Street in a taxi. Persons who have business there arrive in chauffeur-driven automobiles. Not wanting to drive the harried cabbie off the deep end, I deliver my next utterance in measured, robotic phrases:

"Buddy, I know this doesn't all add up for you. But I am expected at Downing Street. So, here's the deal. Take me to the security checkpoint at the entrance to the street. If the gatekeeper doesn't admit me, I'll pay you double what's on your fare meter."

Five minutes later, we pull up at the checkpoint. A London bobby pokes his head into the car's passenger section and asks, " Mr. Simmons, I expect?" My cabbie mutters a *mea culpa* and says the ride is on him. I pay and tip him nonetheless.

THE SIDE DOOR TO 10 DOWNING

Inside Number 12, all's well. Blaikie, Rose, and Smith are being royally entertained by Murdo. My arrival finds my all-time-favourite walking encyclopedia, a.k.a. David Smith, on a roll as he matter-of-factly disgorges the most obscure tidbits of British historical trivia, whether royal, political, military, or cultural. Which prompts Murdo to extend yet another invitation to his quartet of Anglofiles: "Would you like, perhaps, to have an inside look at Number 10?"

What politician would turn thumbs down on that offer? Off we went, trailing our proactive host down a corridor, transiting Number 11 and winding up in the entrance hall of the famed Number 10.

It was in the Cabinet Room, tucked away in the far back corner of the main floor, that we lingered inquisitively. We mused over whether there was a seating pecking order. Or, was there a meeting-time stampede to grab a place close to power or out of the line of fire, depending on one's presumed ranking in the eyes of Thatcher, the incumbent PM during our nocturnal caper?

Our few moments in the dining room are memorable, thanks once again to Murdo's penchant for asking all the right questions: "Would you like a souvenir?" Whereupon I relieved the china cabinet of a crystal drinking glass. Thanks a lot, Maggie! Whether or not more than one heavy tumbler got spirited away that night, I will not say. The other upstanding Canadian parliamentarians can speak for themselves.

CHAPTER 15
RISING STAR

Hold fast to dreams, for if dreams die,
Life is a broken-winged bird that cannot fly.
— American poet, novelist, and playwright
Langston Hughes (1902–67)

August 1983. It was cabinet-shuffle time in the nation's capital. Weeks of rumours and speculation about who would be dropped from cabinet, who the prime minister would invite into the inner circle. It provided, at the very least, a distraction during the dog days of summer.

For some of us, though, it was far from a slow summer. The ever-worsening crisis in the deep-sea fishery kept me on my toes from early morning to bedtime. In a twenty-page report to my constituents, I documented the issues in play and summarized steps taken by the federal government to mitigate the impact on fishermen, plant workers, and communities.

I also took a few swings at the Peckford government for talking out of both sides of its mouth. The premier told a national television audience that some trawler plants would have to close. Soon after, he said that "not one fish plant can be allowed to permanently close." Clearly, the left hand didn't know what the right hand was doing. The livelihood of tens of thousands of plant workers and fishermen hung in the balance.

DRAFTED TO THE A-TEAM

Only the prime minister knows if and when there will be a cabinet shuffle. But even here, Newton's immutable first law of physics applies, figuratively speaking: A body in motion will continue in motion unless acted on by an outside force. The intruding factor may be a resignation from cabinet, an underperforming minister or two, or a nagging realization that the government needs to reset its compass.

Once such an occurrence gets the ball rolling, a time-honoured public ritual preludes every cabinet shuffle, whether in Ottawa or a provincial capital. Immediately, the press goes into overdrive, speculating on which ministers will be shown the door and who will replace them. Body language, perceived slights, the foot traffic at 24 Sussex[139]—all are parsed and scrutinized for clues to the new cabinet lineup. Day in, day out, media pundits confidently issue ever-changing winners' and losers' lists.

For the insider, reading the tea leaves is often not that difficult. If, for example, there's a cabinet vacancy, just knowing the ex-minister's home province or region is enough to make an educated guess as to which of the remaining MPs from that province will be invited to join the A-team. Long-standing practice mandates that each province gets at least one seat at the cabinet table. As Abraham Lincoln noted, "If the twelve Apostles were to be chosen nowadays, the shrieks of locality would have to be heeded."

Hopeful MPs and eternal optimists stay close to the capital, certainly close to the phone, convinced their time has arrived. Every MP sees him/herself as obvious cabinet material. I admit to being no different. But I am also a realist. Newfoundland and Labrador's small population usually means just one seat at the cabinet table, and that one was filled, ably so, in my view. My late, good friend Bill Rompkey, selected by the PM following the 1980 election, seemed to have a lock on the position. He had fostered an excellent rapport with his fellow Newfoundland MPs and had a respectable batting average in ensuring our province got its fair slice of the federal pie. Dreamer though I am, a realist I can be.

So, as the clock ticked toward the shuffle, I had no real expectation I would get the call. In the home stretch, as speculation reached fever pitch and the mess in the deep-sea fishery continued to dominate the headlines, pundits and insiders alleged that Rompkey was all but absent from the fisheries debate and surmised that could spell trouble for his sojourn in cabinet.

My phone rang. It was early evening, August 11. The PM's deputy principal secretary, Gordon Ashworth, was on the line. Could I be available to take a call from the boss next morning? Well, yes!

I talked to my wife about the call, and we canvassed the implications. Miriam raised a recently concluded Revenue Canada[140] investigation into

139 The official residence of the Prime Minister of Canada
140 Now the Canada Revenue Agency (CRA)

my income tax affairs. I noted that the matter had been resolved seven weeks earlier. I pointed out that the very fact of Ashworth's call was confirmation that the tax issue was no longer in play, since I had obviously cleared the requisite screening process which precedes every cabinet shuffle.

By morning, the impending call from the PMO was the furthest thing from my mind. In deference to the stifling hot weather, I opted for shorts and golf shirt. Well before 8:00 a.m., I settled in behind my desk in the Confederation Building to confront, yet another day, the latest bad news. Those days, it was all about the fishery. And it was all bad. The one-and-a-half-hour time difference with Newfoundland aggravated matters. It was already mid-morning back on the Rock. Playing catch-up was my daily routine.

Around eleven o'clock, Ashworth was back on the phone: Would I come over to Langevin?[141] The PM wants to talk to me.

"Gordon, how much time do I have? I'm wearing shorts!"

"He needs to see you now!"

As I was ushered into his office, the prime minister, standing behind the desk in his trademark gunslinger pose, extended his hand in greeting. Straight to the point, he invited me into his cabinet, then explained why. The *why* was the fishery. My tongue deserted me. My mind raced at warp speed:

Fisheries portfolio! He can't be serious! Oh well, I will sink or swim on the fish file, with or without the title.

Trudeau picked up on what must have been a kaleidoscope of non-verbal signals—surprise, then inadequacy, bravado, acquiescence.

"Roger, what is it? Don't you want to know what I have in mind for you?"

By then my thoughts had sprinted ahead once again.

"Where does this leave Rompkey?"

"I spoke with him. You will be my new minister of state for Mines, working with Chrétien[142] and keeping us on our toes concerning the offshore fishery and Newfoundland."

As the PM stood and extended his hand, signalling the end of our brief chat, he gestured toward my naked knees and, with that impish twinkle in his eye, said, "And try and find a pair of pants for the swearing-in!"

141 The now-renamed Langevin Block, a four-storey Second Empire–style sandstone edifice located directly across the street from Parliament, houses the Office of the Prime Minister (PMO) and the Privy Council Office (PCO). Sir Hector-Louis Langevin was a Father of Confederation and an architect of the infamous aboriginal residential school system. Prime Minister Justin Trudeau announced in June 2017 that Langevin's name would be taken off the building, responding to persistent aboriginal protesting.

142 Jean Chrétien, minister of Energy, one of several portfolios he held while Trudeau was PM

ROGER WHO?

As the guy from the Privy Council Office (PCO) began administering the oath of office to the first of my colleagues, Collenette, it was evident to all that English was not the official's first language and would not soon become his second language. That, and the nervousness occasioned by this, his debut at swearing in cabinet ministers, got me thinking: *Why is this fellow administering the oath? Where is the Clerk of the Privy Council, who would normally do it?* That would have been Gordon Osbaldeston, who, I later learned, was holidaying in the US. It would prove to be a very expensive vacation—for me.

Post-ceremony, there was the requisite kibitzing and congratulations all around. After all the intervening years, it is a Trudeau one-liner which stands out. As I was exiting the ornate Rideau Hall ballroom, the PM shouted a special goodbye in my direction: " Roger, you'll be fighting the other guys, right?"

It was a private joke, an allusion to our morning meeting when he had lauded my combative style. I took it as a compliment, an affirmation he was pleased to have me on his side. There was no doubt that I was elated to have him on my side, where, without even a nuance of equivocation, he steadfastly remained in the difficult months ahead.

My elevation to cabinet got mixed reviews. Friends and political soulmates thought it was the best thing since sliced bread and wished me Godspeed; my detractors, not so much. Newfoundland's Premier Brian Peckford was at his gratuitous best, insisting that we "are not that good friends." Caustic. And, given the verb tense he chose, true. Otherwise, reaction in Newfoundland was favourable. The now-defunct St. John's *Daily News* heralded the appointment.

> Simmons will acquit himself well. . . . He has a reputation for thoroughness, is tough-minded, but also has the ability to be a conciliator.

The national press largely ignored me, opting instead to profile my urban colleagues, deemed more newsworthy copy in the big-city dailies. I did rate a little ink in regional newspapers where mining was key to the local economy and in mining industry publications. In truth, though, I was largely an unknown to the Ottawa press entourage camped outside Rideau Hall. That reality was succinctly captured in the whispered query I overhead as I navigated the forest of cameras and microphones:

"Which one is Simmons?"

I felt the urge to answer the question. To myself only, I muttered, more in mild put-down than prediction, "You'll know soon enough!" Even I didn't realize just how soon that would be, and not for the right reasons, either.

MESMERIZED AND MOTIVATED

Next morning, Saturday, reality quickly set in. Now, not only was I the MP whose riding was bearing the brunt of the deep-sea fishery crisis, I was Newfoundland's representative in the federal cabinet. Now, the buck stopped with me. Already, expectations were being voiced that my seat at the table could translate into better times for the troubled sector. Besides, the fishery problem had languished far too long. It was time to craft a consensus on what needed to be done. That wouldn't be easy. Premier Peckford and his Fisheries minister, Jim Morgan, both articulate wordsmiths, had launched a war of words, pinning full blame for the fishery woes on the feds. My friend and colleague, federal Fisheries Minister Pierre de Bané, and I had lobbed a few verbal grenades back at the province. It was time to can the rhetoric and seek common cause.

Quite apart from being the new broom, I felt there were additional reasons why I might be able to inject some new momentum into the fisheries stalemate. I knew all the key players well, Peckford best of all. Our university days as fellow student leaders, six years together as educators, and vacationing on Florida beaches had forged a solid personal relationship that thrived until the insanity of partisan politics got in the way. Fisheries Minister Morgan and I had spent several years taking each other's measure across the floor of the House of Assembly, but also swapping our best jokes between sittings and socially.

My admiration for and friendship with Richard Cashin, fiery, cerebral head of the fishermen's union[143], can be traced back to the mid-1960s, when as young turks we successfully challenged Joey Smallwood's slate of candidates for the provincial Liberal Party executive positions.

Despite my fractured relationship with Premier Peckford, there was an ace in the hole. Two of his defining attributes are integrity and compassion. I was confident that he would not allow tribal one-upmanship and rhetoric to trump an opportunity to get the deep-sea fishery back on a sound footing. And there was a second ace. Trudeau was seized with the urgency of resolving the dispute. He wanted the file off the table. This he made clear to me during our brief tête-à-tête just hours before the swearing-in ceremony. With the PM at my back and Cashin potentially onside, it was time to forge ahead.

143 Newfoundland's Fish, Food & Allied Workers Union (FFAW)

My first activity as a member of cabinet was a one-on-one with my senior minister, Jean Chrétien. He warned me against allowing bureaucrats to snow me under with lengthy memos and briefing notes. He pulled open a desk drawer and retrieved a single sheet of letter-sized paper.

"That's a briefing note. If they can't fit it on one page, they don't know what they're talking about. Send it back!"

Then, after a get-acquainted session with my new deputy minister, a phone consultation with Deputy Prime Minister Allan MacEachen, the signing of documents giving effect to a cabinet decision, and a ride to the airport with my new driver at the wheel, I was off to the Rock. My wife, Miriam, and I, accompanied by our sons, Paul, approaching seven, and Mark, three, were headed for a previously arranged, ten-day vacation in Newfoundland's picturesque Codroy Valley.

Energized by the adrenalin flow of my new responsibilities, preoccupied with mapping a strategy for the task ahead, and sobered by the seemingly intractable dimensions of many of my immediate challenges, the Codroy Valley served only as a change of venue, not a change of pace. All weekend, I pumped the phone, dictated memos to colleagues, interlocutors, and staff, digested mounds of briefing binders, and rejigged my upcoming schedule based on the new reality. Among my very first actions as minister were two important telephone conversations. Peckford and Cashin each agreed to meet with me the following week. By mid-week, I had internalized, more in hope than confidence, my new mantra: "I can do this!"

FATEFUL PHONE CALL

All too soon, my readiness for the job at hand would be the least of my worries. As the week wound down, my world fell apart, though I didn't realize it at the time. The clerk of the Privy Council, the same Gordon Osbaldeston whose absence from the August 12 swearing-in had caught my attention, called me from Ottawa. He alerted me to an urgent matter which had arisen, and it was imperative, he advised, that I return immediately to the nation's capital. What Osbaldeston told me didn't square with the facts. I didn't need any persuasion to hightail it back to Ottawa.

CHAPTER 16
TAXPAYER IN THE CROSSHAIRS

Our lives begin to end the day we become silent about the things that matter.
— Martin Luther King, Jr.

My high-profile brush with the taxman should have been a minor footnote in Revenue Canada files and my career. Indeed, it was well on the way to becoming such when some hardball politics got in the way. The facts of the case are simple. In the course of an audit, it was determined that I had failed to report certain income on my annual tax returns. The amount of unreported income was $28,000, spread over four years, which translated into unpaid taxes of $5,142.

In the summer of 2010, I ran into David Vardy, an old friend whom I had briefly taught many years before when I was fulfilling my teaching practicum at a St. John's high school. He subsequently emailed other members of that class, reminiscing about the good ol' days and mentioning my name. A respondent's email showed up, inadvertently, I assume, on my laptop: "Isn't that the fella who was a rising star up in Ottawa and then he screwed it all up?"

She was right, of course. I did screw it all up. And that was certainly the near-unanimous public perception at the time. Here's what the public didn't know when my case was making headlines and, clearly, what the writer could not have known when she wrote that email: My screwing up was not a solo act. I had tons of unsolicited help from RevCan.

The sentiment expressed in the above-mentioned email goes to the heart of why I decided to put pen to paper and give my perspective on those long-ago events. Few people know the backstory. The following pages will, I trust, rectify that and allow the reader to draw whatever conclusions that seem appropriate.

HAM-FISTED FISHING EXPEDITION

Once the matter of the unreported income was brought to my attention, I offered to pay up and asked what the financial penalty would be. I had good reason to believe that would be the end of the affair. There are, after all, countless thousands of precedents in which Canadian taxpayers in circumstances identical to mine have had the matter fully resolved by remitting the relevant unpaid taxes and the assessed financial penalty.

However, the tax agency had decided that, in my case, it would not be that routine. In meeting after meeting, two investigators badgered me, alternately offering to go easy on me if I "came clean" or threatening to lower the boom if I didn't. My problem was that I didn't know what I was supposed to come clean about. The tag team from RevCan acted like they were on to something. In three successive sessions, they kept flashing a cheque, saying it was payable to me, but refusing to tell me the amount or who had signed it. Their messianic fervour and persistence almost convinced me. Thanks to their tactics, I have an understanding of why suspects under police interrogation sometimes confess to crimes of which they are innocent.

The more these guys waved the cheque at me, the more I racked my brain for long-forgotten misdemeanours. Surely, I told myself, a dose of wilful blindness must be shielding me from some nefariously sordid act in my past. Pocketing $50,000 for making someone disappear? Receiving a $10,000 bribe to look the other way? As hard as I tried, I came up empty. At long last, Sherlock and Watson relented and showed me the cheque. It was a donation to my Liberal Party provincial leadership campaign a full five years before. Mistakenly, the donor had written just my name on the cheque, rather than "Roger Simmons Campaign," which, had they flipped the cheque over, was plainly stamped under the words "Deposited to the account of."

There was no ambiguity about the amount the donor contributed: $50,000? $10,000? Not quite! The cheque was for $300! Had it been personal income, it would have yielded precious little to the RevCan coffers. Despite the persistent efforts of its investigators, RevCan had drawn a blank, and for good reason: There was no other unreported income of which they were not already aware.

FISHERMEN ON THE HOOK

The timing of the audit of my tax returns is central to an understanding of the issue. In 1982, RevCan launched an audit of fishermen's incomes. The approach was brutal. The fishermen's audits covered a five-year period. The blatant unfairness of the audit and the overly aggressive manner in which it was conducted were mind-boggling, unforgivable. Thousands of law-abiding citizens were maligned and railroaded into difficult financial predicaments. Being the MP for the electoral riding most affected, I took up their cause, in the House of Commons with questions and speeches, in the media, in meetings with and letters to the tax agency.

I suggested to RevCan, as did several other MPs and the fishermen's union, a way to mitigate the issue without inflicting undue hardship on the affected fishermen and their families. The quantity of fuel fishermen consumed to get to and from their fishing grounds could have been easily approximated, based on type of engine and distance travelled, and a dollar value assigned. Similarly, in the absence of receipts for food and other supplies, a reasonable per diem could have been allowed. Instead, RevCan persisted in applying a much more arbitrary yardstick. It disallowed all expenses which could not be supported by receipts, saying, in effect, "We have proof of your income. Since you can't prove you had expenses, we assume that you had none. So, pay up and shut up!"

The results were predictably horrendous. Fishermen, like so many others, are not known for their bookkeeping skills. Yet they were required to produce a paper trail for their income and for the expenses they had claimed on annual tax returns. Documenting the income was easy. Fishermen sold their daily catches to one or two buyers, and they (or RevCan) could readily obtain the necessary information from the fish buyers. Documenting claimed expenses was a more difficult and, in most cases, an impossible challenge. Many fishermen had not been diligent in saving their receipts; some didn't even realize they needed to do so.

A REASONABLE PROPOSITION

Indeed, RevCan could have taken quite a different tack. The fair approach would have been to give notice to fishermen that, effective immediately, fishermen would be expected to have on hand full documentation of expenses incurred in prosecuting the fishery. In other words, the agency could have injected a little humanity into its enforcement practices, acknowledging in the process that fishermen's inability to document their fishery-related expenditures was not a wilful act. Alas, anyone who has been audited by RevCan will tell you that humanity is not its strong suit! Nor would this approach have swelled the public coffers as did the unconscionable onslaught visited on the fishermen. Which brings to mind an interesting question: Is the first priority of RevCan to ensure tax law compliance or to maximize revenue collection?

Did RevCan have the legal authority to take the actions it did against those fishermen? The answer is an unequivocal yes. But that cannot be the end of the matter or a justification of the harassment that was perpetrated, and the pulverizing financial pain that was inflicted on innocent people. Good democratic tradition and practice require that there must be fairness in applying the law. There was no fairness in what was done to these fishermen. The high-handedness, callousness, and perverseness of RevCan's actions boggle the mind and have no place in a democratic society.

CLOAK-AND-DAGGER TACTICS

Ron Huntington[144], a right-wing Conservative MP from Vancouver and, therefore, someone with whom I had little in common, ideologically speaking, was a member of the Commons' Standing Committee on Finance, as was I. We were also fellow members of an ad hoc committee on House of Commons procedure. In the course of our committee work, including pre-budget hearings on the road and a trip to England, Ron and I developed an enduring friendship.

One afternoon in the House during the fall of 1983, Ron signalled across the floor for me to join him, which I did. He showed me a list of seventeen MPs who were then under RevCan audit. My name was on the list, of course, since by then my case had mushroomed into a very public affair. The other names on the list included Liberal government backbenchers and members of both opposition parties, Conservative and NDP. I was in good company. It is inappropriate to recite the names on that infamous list, since their audits were private matters between them and the tax agency.

Huntington pointed out that all seventeen persons on the list had at least one thing in common. All had raised concerns about the fishermen's audit in the daily Question Period or had otherwise spoken publicly in defence of the fishermen and had taken exception to RevCan's tactics in its conduct of the audit. It was clear to Ron and me that the tax mandarins didn't take kindly to such meddling by mere MPs and decided to focus the minds of a bunch of zealous politicians who, in the view of the tax moguls, got too big for their boots.

Nor did RevCan draw the line at federal MPs. At least one provincial politician attracted the agency's attention and was placed under audit. Jim Morgan is a law-abiding citizen who, like me, was simply doing his job as an elected representative. But, like me, he had committed one unforgivable transgression: He had tweaked RevCan's nose. He had publicly voiced alarm at the *"Gestapo-like tactics"* employed in auditing Newfoundland fisher-

144 A lieutenant commander in the Royal Canadian Navy during World War II, Member of Parliament (1974–84), Minister of State for Small Business and Industry in Prime Minister Clark's administration, 1979–80

men[145]. And why not? He was, after all, a legislator with a sizable fishing constituency—and the province's minister of Fisheries.

RevCan saved its most brazen deed for the one MP who could rain on its parade. In an outrageous instance of insubordination and kneecapping, the tax agency took direct aim at its very own minister, Bill Rompkey, whose unwarranted humiliation at the hands of his deputy is well-documented. Stephen Clarkson and Christine McCall, in the second volume of their award-winning bestseller, *Trudeau and Our Times* recounts that,

> In retaliation for complaining against him to [Privy Council Clerk Michael] Pitfield, the deputy minister [Doug Rutherford] launched an audit of fishermen in Rompkey's riding.[146]

PAYBACK TIME?

In my case, there may well have been an additional agenda in play, aimed at settling a score dating back to my days in provincial politics and, specifically, my role in exposing a Public Works spending scandal and dispatching Alex Walsh to a cell in New Brunswick's Dorchester Penitentiary for three and a half years after being convicted of fraud. Even an elementary understanding of human nature and familial loyalty would suggest that Walsh's ignominious fate, largely at my hands, would not have been far from his close relative's mind each time that relative, one of my two RevCan tormentors, turned his attention to my file.

But that linkage can be no more than a strong hunch. I have no direct evidence which would confirm that the relative's persistence in advancing my file was driven by anything other than his obligation to ferret out tax abuse. Yet I couldn't help but notice that he was light years ahead of his fellow investigator in his manic zeal to trip me up, and I do abhor the ends to which both of them went in my case. The charitable interpretation is that they were simply following orders from their superiors.

Still, it may be instructive to know just how Walsh's relative became involved in my audit. Did he ask to be assigned to it? Or was it just the luck of the draw? If the latter, integrity and normal practice should have constrained him to recuse himself because of an obvious conflict of interest.

Indeed, by his own admission, the Walsh relative saw recusal as an option he was prepared to exercise, should circumstances warrant it. As part of the probe into my tax file, he travelled to Corner Brook to solicit

---

145 *Globe and Mail*, March 13, 1984. Morgan also told a task force on Revenue Canada activities that the agency had leaked his income tax information to the press.
146 *Trudeau and Our Times: The Heroic Delusion*, Vol. 2, Stephen Clarkson and Christina McCall, Toronto: McClelland & Stewart, 1994, p. 493

information from my brother Dave. It was only when they met that the investigator realized that here was the same Dave Simmons with whom he had played hockey as members of a team twenty years earlier. Which prompted him to say, "If I had known Roger was your brother, I could have recused myself."

It is a bit of a stretch, to put it mildly, to believe that, while he mused aloud about his long-ago acquaintance with my sibling as potential grounds for recusal, he saw no such ramification in my role in Alex Walsh's fraud conviction. Did the investigator lack the judgment required to recognize so blatant a conflict of interest? Or did he know full well that there was a gigantic conflict of interest and chose to ignore it in order to pursue a vendetta against me? The other possibility, diabolical as it is, is that he was assigned my file because of his conflict of interest.

The events I have recounted happened over thirty years ago. The harshest indictment of today's CRA[147] is that only its name has changed. The decades-old Gestapo mindset which Jim Morgan fingered is alive and well. CRA's public pulverizing of a British Columbia businessman, initiated with a routine 1996 audit, continued unabated for twenty years. The shocking case of Irvin LeRoux is a TV-documentary-in-waiting. His ordeal may have finally ended in 2016, when the BC Supreme Court ruled that CRA was culpable.[148]

As recently as October 2017, there was public evidence that the tax agency continues to act as a law unto itself. It announced that employee discounts would be treated as taxable income. The move would have significant tax implications for employees and would saddle employers with new administrative responsibilities. Not surprisingly, the CRA announcement precipitated anti-government protests across the country. In fact, the government was unaware of CRA's action. Not even the agency's own minister, Diane Lebouthillier, was in the know. To its credit, the government immediately nixed the scheme.

SELECTIVE LENIENCY

So, the question remains: How did my failure to report income amounting to $28,000, surely a miniscule matter in the context of other RevCan files, become such a big deal? The manner in which the agency handled my case takes on added significance when viewed through the prism of other actions it took at the time and subsequently, for example:

147 Canada Revenue Agency

148 *Global News*, Justin McElroy, January 9, 2016

- Journalist and consultant George Radwanski was forgiven almost $540,000 in unpaid taxes one day before becoming Canada's privacy commissioner.[149]
- John C. Doyle *had received preferential treatment from Revenue Canada over a period of twenty-seven years.*[150]
- *Revenue Canada . . . agreed to tax only half of the $225,000 the former prime minister (Brian Mulroney) received from Karlheinz Schreiber in a now-infamous series of cash-stuffed envelopes.*[151]

Mulroney informed the agency of the unreported income in 1999[152]. That was more than five years after he had received the initial $75,000 payment. The sequence of events and the nature of the payments were both acknowledged by Mulroney in his testimony before a House of Commons parliamentary committee in 2007:

> "In August 1999, Mr. Schreiber was arrested. . . . This stunning new development put in serious doubt my relationship with him. I thought the best way to deal with this situation was to declare the entire amount as income, although I had only used it for expenses—absorbing the expenses myself and compensating myself for the fees to which I was entitled. Accordingly, I then instructed my advisors to contact the income tax authorities and to ensure that the full amount received in this private transaction was declared by me as income and all applicable taxes paid."[153]

If Mulroney's failure to report more than $200,000 for several years could be viewed by RevCan as an oversight, surely it is not unreasonable to suggest that my unreported income of $28,000 should have been treated in a similar manner.

Further, as noted above, Mulroney got a heavily discounted repayment rate by going "cap in hand to Revenue Canada. . . . It was a bargain to die for—at least to anyone who has neglected to declare sizable amounts of income."[154] The fifty per cent discount, pursuant to a windfall provision that was only available to Quebec taxpayers, was "routine" at the time, according to RevCan spokesperson Christine Sauvé[155].

---

149 *Iron Man*, Lawrence Martin, Toronto: Penguin, 2003, p. 419
150 *No Holds Barred*, John Crosbie, Toronto: McClelland & Stewart, 1997, p. 158
151 *Maclean's*, June 8, 2009
152 *Globe and Mail*, December 13, 2007
153 House of Commons' Information and Ethics Committee, December 13, 2007
154 *Maclean's*, June 8, 2009
155 Ibid

From the above, it can be concluded that RevCan's treatment of me was driven by something other than standard procedure, precedent, or the leniency it was selectively extending to others. Clearly, ulterior motives were in play, which, I submit, were tied to my active advocacy on behalf of the audited fishermen. I also believe that my role in exposing a fraud artist when I was in provincial politics may have been a driving factor in the investigation.

The two RevCan investigators, my accountant, and I met for what would be the final time on June 20, 1983, in my Parliament Hill office. They informed us that I would be required to pay the taxes attracted by the unreported income plus a financial penalty for failing to report the income, and that would be the end of the matter. Imagine my relief on hearing that! My relief would be short-lived.

CHAPTER 17
SHOOTING STAR?

If you can trust yourself when all men doubt you,
But make allowance for their doubting too . . .
Yours is the Earth and everything that's in it.
— RUDYARD KIPLING, ENGLISH JOURNALIST, POET, AND NOVELIST, 1865–1936

Fall seven times; stand up eight.
— JAPANESE PROVERB

My stint in Pierre Trudeau's cabinet was brief. Revenue Canada saw to that. A personal income tax issue, which I had been given to understand had been resolved, fuelled by a payback vendetta aimed at several MPs, me among them, postponed, and ultimately derailed, my opportunity to play a meaningful role in government. In less than two weeks, I went from rising star to a potential shooting star.

The sudden reversal of fortunes is a twisted tale of brazen treachery. RevCan had thrown in the towel, shut the book on my tax issue. Then, from their warped perspective, the fertile minds in the tax agency got lucky. Their saving grace was my appointment to cabinet and, even more significantly, a monstrous gaffe by another government agency. In the blink of an eye, RevCan fixed on a whole new, bold strategy: metamorphosis. Transform a high-profile politician into a poster boy for its cause.

In response to Gordon Osbaldeston's August 18 phone call, I immediately returned to the nation's capital. On Sunday, August 21, I drove to Val Morin, Quebec, north of Montreal and 200 kilometres from Ottawa. There, I met with the PM's principal secretary, Tom Axworthy.

Trustworthy, affable, and a brilliant mind, Axworthy ranks easily as one of the most competent and committed public servants to ever grace the Langevin Block[156] edifice. As deputy principal secretary and, then, in the top job, he ran a tight ship. Among MPs, he had a solid reputation for keeping his ear to the ground and for being a ready pipeline to the PM.

Tom and I got quickly to the subject at hand, reviewing the bizarre sequence of happenings that had culminated in that moment, analyzing my conundrum and canvassing options. The meeting served as a valuable preparation for my meeting, the following day, with the Clerk of the Privy Council.

THE RIGHT DECISION

I met with Osbaldeston Monday morning. Up until that time, I was firmly of the view that there had been some mix-up which could be straightened out. The Clerk quickly disabused me of that notion when he indicated that RevCan had informed him there was a fifty-fifty chance that charges would be preferred against me. The moment I heard that, it was crystal clear what I had to do. Resignation from cabinet was the only appropriate course of action. I asked Osbaldeston to immediately be in touch with the prime minister, who was travelling abroad, and to convey my decision to him. The Clerk placed the call, spoke with Trudeau, then handed me the phone. Asked by the PM to summarize the issues in play, I did so. He expressed himself "astounded" by the turn of events and said, "If you believe it's the right decision, I accept your resignation."

He concluded our conversation by indicating that he would be in touch when he got back to Ottawa. The prime minister called me Saturday evening, September 4, soon after returning from his overseas trip.

In theory, at least, there were options other than resigning, but whether survival in cabinet was possible is entirely beside the point. As I told my House of Commons colleagues on September 12, the first sitting day following the summer recess,

> "There is only one way to be in cabinet: Because you have legitimacy, because you have the full right to be there. When I was sworn in, I had legitimacy. Once the circumstances which triggered my resignation arose, I no longer had unabridged legitimacy. Questions would arise: Should I be in cabinet in those circumstances? If the answer is 'no' or 'maybe not' or even 'maybe,' unless the answer is an unqualified 'yes,'

156 In June 2017, the building was renamed the Office of the Prime Minister and Privy Council.

> my full legitimacy as a minister would be circumscribed, compromised, emasculated. . . . I felt it would be wrong to continue in cabinet once I had learned that the legal aspect of the tax matter was still outstanding, irrespective of whether a charge would ultimately be laid or not.
>
> And there was a fairly easy pragmatic choice to be made: to somewhat damage my credibility by resigning from cabinet so ridiculously soon after my appointment, even if my reasons never became public, or to ultimately destroy my credibility altogether by continuing in a position for which I lacked unbridled legitimacy."[157]

As I spoke, Senator Eugene Forsey sat in the gallery opposite. The retired parliamentarian, a Newfoundlander, native to my electoral riding, and a valued friend and mentor, was one of the foremost authorities on the Canadian constitution. Not normally given to hyperbole, Forsey wrote me later that day to say that my statement to the House had been a "masterpiece of erudition, concise yet comprehensive, candid, by the book."

Ottawa, 1989. L-R: Steve Neary, retired senator Eugene Forsey, and me. (Author photo)

A few days prior to my House of Commons intervention, I spoke in similar vein to the Liberal caucus, noting that I had rejected the option of remaining

157 House of Commons Debates, September 12, 1983

in cabinet, of "hanging on by my fingernails," in which case, "staying in cabinet becomes an end in itself, rather than the vehicle by which to do certain things."

To the prime minister and cabinet, the MPs and senators—in all, about 200 politicians—I said, "My decision to resign was an important one, yes, wrenching in its implications for me and others. But it was not an especially difficult decision. . . . I believe I did the right thing in the circumstances, just as I believe I did the right thing ten days previously in accepting the prime minister's kind invitation to join his cabinet."

MEDIA CIRCUS

The requisite news release disclosing my resignation went out from the PMO on August 22. My departure from cabinet so soon after being appointed could be expected to set off a brief media feeding frenzy. I believed the news would be nothing more than an overnight wonder. The days ahead would thrash that assessment as the press drilled down, determined to get the story behind the story. Five days after the news broke, an Ottawa daily ran in its weekend edition no fewer than ten stories related to the resignation, ranging from the results of a national poll, to reaction from constituents, past and present, to a detailed profile on "Simmons, a private man who chose a public life."[158]

Shortly before the resignation became public, my good friend Herb Metcalf and I holed up in a downtown hotel, monitoring the press until the news cycle had run its course. Before doing so, I instructed my staff to phone about twenty people, my family members, close friends, colleagues, and key supporters, before the story hit the airwaves and to pass on a carefully worded message: "Roger has asked me to call you to say that you can expect some news in the next couple of hours. He suggests that the nature of the news will be such that you may want to go somewhere with a radio or TV and collect your thoughts before talking to anyone."

Why did my resignation receive such saturation press coverage? The best explanation is that it was the height of Ottawa's silly season, the lazy days of late August. Media scribes couldn't find something more substantive to write about. The press needed a story, any story. The job of the press wasn't made any easier by the advice I had received from lawyers not to divulge the reason for my departure from cabinet. But, here again, the accommodating folks at RevCan were more than willing to lend a hand with a well-timed press leak. They were breaking the law, of course. But that wouldn't have bothered a bunch of zealots who believe they are a law unto themselves.

---

158 *Ottawa Citizen*, August 27, 1983

"A law is only as good as those who enforce it," I told the House of Commons on September 12. "I can only express the hope that the 'highly placed government source' who discussed my private tax affairs in public has a more competent, less malicious understanding of his other responsibilities and of the legal parameters within which he is supposed to operate."

Left: Ottawa, 1983. With Prime Minister Pierre Trudeau. (J. M. Carisse photo) Right: My lawyers advised me not to disclose the reason for my cabinet resignation. This cartoon by Jim Phillips ran in the *Toronto Sun* daily newspaper on August 29, 1983. (Author photo)

The press kept probing my psyche. Was I angry? Sad? Embarrassed? No, I was focused. One of my redeeming traits is that I do not panic under pressure. As reporter Greg Weston noted,

> "The only time this week that Simmons publicly showed any signs of anger was in a face-to-face confrontation with a *Citizen* reporter. . . . He wasn't mad that the paper had broken the story. . . . He was angry that a reporter had knocked on the door of his home. . . . That, he claimed, was 'harassment' of his wife, Miriam."[159]

The *Citizen* reporter was none other than Weston himself. Ironically, at the very time his journalistic instincts were making life miserable for me, I

159 Ibid

gained a grudging admiration for him. He could have skewered me in the article. Instead, he showed self-discipline and integrity, two must attributes of any good news reporter.

I've never shied away from a reporter who knows how to get the story right. As a former journalist myself, I couldn't help but applaud Weston's diligence in chasing down the story, but I did feel he crossed the line when he came to my suburban Ottawa residence, in the process inflicting unwarranted trauma on an innocent party, my wife.

A man's home is his castle, and the uninvited should not breach the moat unless the castle's occupants are in imminent physical danger or it conceals evidence of illegality. Neither applied in my circumstance, as the journalist well knew. In the years since then, I have been delighted to watch Weston blossom as a respected scribe. Arguably, he learned a helpful lesson from his misstep that August night.

While the sheer volume of media coverage was excessive, I had little reason to complain about the substance of the reporting. With a few glaring exceptions, including the one mentioned above, the press handled the issue with the persistence and responsibility which ought always to be its trademark.

Notwithstanding, mainstream media has been known to indulge in tabloid journalism to hype a story. In the days following my cabinet resignation, there were two CBC TV reports where sensation trumped the facts. The anchor conjectured that my failure to report $28,000 income on my tax returns could net a jail term of "up to ten years," a preposterous fabrication which fuelled a barrage of frenetic phone calls from family and friends who assumed the network knew what it was talking about.

And, in a story aired on the night of August 23, CBC declared my office was shuttered and I was nowhere to be found. That was a barefaced lie. The public network had merely resorted to one of the oldest journalistic tricks in the book: If you can't get the facts, make 'em up, improvise, run with something that sounds plausible. Apart from those incidents, I've not had any scores to settle with the media, including the CBC.

Except for four hours immediately following the resignation announcement, I was on Parliament Hill and, for the most part, in my office every day during the week of August 22 and was regularly intercepted by members of the media as I moved between meetings. Indeed, one commentator suggested that I was too available to the press, that I was somehow enjoying the whole media circus. While it wasn't a particularly fun experience, I didn't see the need to skulk about like a fugitive. If reporters were determined to keep asking the same questions, I was not averse to giving them the same answers.

PICKING UP THE PIECES

My conveyor belt odyssey in cabinet behind me, I turned my focus to charting the uncertain course ahead. I wasn't yet aware whether Justice would lay charges against me, but I had to be ready just in case. More immediate, it was imperative that every conceivable angle be explored to see if the matter could be put to bed by an appropriate approach to RevCan. It was with that objective in mind that I engaged the services of a top-notch tax lawyer.

A year or so earlier, I had addressed the Law Society of Upper Canada[160] at the behest of its treasurer[161] and Allan Lutfy[162], the PM's in-house legal counsel. It was Lutfy who, on hearing of RevCan's reversal, gave me the legal advice I needed: Get the best tax lawyer in the country, he exhorted. And I did, again thanks to Allan.

Heward Stikeman, co-founder of the highly respected law firm of Stikeman Elliott, had all the right credentials. He had been deputy minister at RevCan, had authored the definitive bible on Canadian tax law, and was a friend and former colleague of several senior RevCan personnel. I tracked down Stikeman by phone the day after my resignation, and I met him five days later at his summer getaway at Rideau Ferry, just over an hour's drive from Ottawa. His opening words were, "Before you even called me, I saw you on the TV and I thought, 'That guy's got a tax problem!'"

We spent the next three hours together. I talked. He listened, posed questions, and cross-examined. He scrutinized the documents I had brought. Then, he stood, extended his hand, looked me in the eye, and said, "I believe you! Absolutely, and without qualification!"

Two days later, on August 30, Stikeman came to Ottawa to meet with a senior RevCan official, then with me. His account of the meeting with the official confirmed what I already knew to be the case. He quoted the official as saying, "Don't worry about it. Obviously there's been a monumental screw-up here."

Within twenty-four hours, Stikeman was summoned back to RevCan to receive a very different message. Here again is my lawyer's account of what the official told him:

> "Simmons's investigation was complete. A decision had been made to assess a penalty and close the file. However, when your man went into

160 Renamed as the Law Society of Ontario by its governing body in November 2017

161 An organization usually refers to its head honcho as chairman or president. Not so with the lawyers! Their top dog is the guy/gal who holds the purse strings! Who said lawyers aren't smart?

162 He was appointed as a federal court judge in 1996, where he served for fifteen years, eight as chief justice.

> cabinet, we had a problem, a—uh—perception problem. How could we ever explain that the file had been taken off the desk *before* he became a minister? So, we decided to put the file back on the desk. We solved our problem. Now, it's his problem."

In a further meeting, sometime during the week of September 5, between the two men, the official told my lawyer that, "If this thing goes to court, it will be thrown out the same day."

If Stikeman was a believer after our first encounter, by our third get-together he had become my champion. He was deeply offended by RevCan's about-face and spoke repeatedly of the official's duplicity as a betrayal of their long friendship.

Skipper, my dad, was always good for a story, usually one that was true and had an unexpected twist, like the following. A father and his three grown sons worked as a unit harvesting logs for the paper mill. Early one morning a freak accident took the life of the eldest son. Not surprisingly, the two devastated brothers assumed the tragic turn of events meant an immediate cessation of their logging. The father had other ideas. He commanded them to lay out their brother on the log pile. Then, he addressed the lifeless body of his firstborn: "Jim, my son, you're gone. Taking you home now won't bring you back. And would you want us to lose a day's pay?"

Whereupon the father picked up his bucksaw and tackled another tree. Two flabbergasted siblings took the hint. The deceased had to await the end of the work day for his last ride home!

There are times when the practical thing to do is definitely not the appropriate course of action. From RevCan's perspective, the practical solution was to "put the file back on the desk," while turning a blind eye to the gross indecency of its action.

SEISMIC BLUNDER

The absence of the Clerk of the Privy Council from Ottawa at the time of the August 12 cabinet shuffle was the pivotal element in my dramatic reversal of fortunes. Long-standing practice and common sense dictate that, before the prime minister invites someone to join the cabinet, the Clerk initiates a thorough screening of the candidate to ensure the candidate has no legal, financial, or other skeletons in the closet. It was that certainty which underpinned my assurances to my wife during our conversation the night before the cabinet shuffle. Astoundingly, in Gordon Osbaldeston's absence, no such screening was done. None of the four ministers who joined the cabinet that day had been vetted[163].

Consider what would have transpired if the requisite screening of prospective cabinet members had been undertaken. Simple logic dictates that there could have been two, and only two, possible outcomes insofar as my screening was concerned. Either charges were pending—a finding which would have eliminated me from cabinet consideration—or there was nothing to abort my cabinet candidacy, confirming, de facto, that there was no intention to lay charges, which was in fact the case.

That's what I was told on June 20. And that syncs with Stikeman's account of his August 30 meeting with the senior RevCan official and, specifically, the latter's statement that the file was "off the desk." That finding would have been the green light for the PM to invite me into the cabinet and, crucially, would not have allowed RevCan to "put the file back on the desk" as the official confessed to Stikeman during their August 31 meeting.

Either of the two possible findings would have saved the public purse several hundreds of thousands of dollars and spared me and my family from astronomical legal bills and unjustified humiliation.

In hindsight, I should have raised the issue with the PM in our morning meeting on August 12. That retrospective is not a new insight. I realized my error the moment I learned that RevCan had, in the official's words, "put the file back on the desk" and the reason for doing so. Despite my disgust at the ruthlessness of RevCan during the fishermen's audit, I could not have fathomed it could stoop to the kind of treachery acknowledged by the official in his August 31 meeting with Stikeman.

"A FRIEND IN NEED IS A FRIEND INDEED"[164]

From the time of Osbaldeston's August 18 call to me until Stikeman reported to me on his second (August 31) meeting with RevCan, I remained optimistic that the matter could be resolved quickly. That frame of mind and my belief in the rightness of my decision to resign kept me buoyant. That second Stikeman meeting with the agency changed everything.

Reeling from RevCan's kick in the guts, I needed to talk to someone who could make some sense of what was happening. A one-on-one chat with my good friend David Smith was just the therapy required. So, off to Toronto I went.

A crackerjack corporate lawyer and a former deputy mayor of Toronto, Smith was the MP for Don Valley East. At the very first post-election

163 Prime Minister Trudeau later confirmed that the standard security check was not done prior to the August 12 cabinet shuffle. (Canadian Press, September 15, 1983)
164 Quintus Ennius, Roman poet, dramatist, and satirist, 239 BC–169 BC

caucus get-together in 1980, as I took my turn telling the bartender my beverage choice, a voice over my shoulder inquired: "Salvation Army or Pentecost?"

Overhearing my request for a Diet Sprite, David Smith had deduced I must be a teetotalling evangelical. And so began my enduring friendship with an amazing guy. David comes by his knowledge of Pentecostalism first-hand, his dad having been the elected head of the Pentecostal Assemblies of Canada for seven years and served another seven as president of its seminary at Peterborough, Ontario. David's impressively large collection of Salvation Army brass band and choral recordings attests to his affinity for the Army, and they routinely fill the air during my visits to his den.

Heather Smith is, like her husband, David, a delightful host and a loyal friend. A long-time judge of Ontario's Superior Court[165], she is a woman of flawless circumspection with a practised ease at staying above the fray. David and Heather Smith's cozy nest in Forest Hill became my port in the storm where empathy, advice, and a willing ear worked miracles in sharpening my focus for the battles ahead.

TAKING IT ON THE CHIN

The phone call I was most dreading came soon after my resignation from cabinet became public. Don Jamieson was among the close friends my staff had called. Serving as Canada's high commissioner to Britain, he was back in Newfoundland on vacation and wasted no time in tracking me down. I was right to be apprehensive, but for the wrong reason. I was fully expecting a stern dressing-down for the sequence of events which culminated in my resignation. Instead, he threw me a curve, though the surprise was no less painful:

"Resignation! That's the last thing you should've done. Stupidity personified! Why didn't you call me before you committed suicide? It's a whole lot easier to keep the lid on than to put the genie back in the bottle. You've played into their hands. Now that bunch of reprobates in Revenue has all the cards. Your goose is cooked!"

Cooked or not, Jamieson insisted I come to see him without delay, which I did ten days later. The eyeball-to-eyeball reprise of his telephone rant was no more palatable. After unloading on me at length, he turned his attention to a review of the facts and next steps. Like Trudeau and Stikeman, Jamieson was incredulous when I told him the details of my

165 Madam Justice Heather Forster Smith began her legal career as a Crown prosecutor with the federal Department of Justice. She is the current Chief Justice of the Ontario Superior Court of Justice, having been appointed to that position in 2002.

tax case. He insisted there had to be more to it, that I was holding back something.

"No one gets dragged into court for five thousand dollars in unpaid taxes. No one quits cabinet over such miniscule piffle. What are you not telling me?"

He chewed me out royally. I told him of the PCO oversight in not screening the candidates for cabinet and of Stikeman's two meetings with RevCan. Jamieson exploded yet again.

"Those nefarious, low-life, self-serving, cowardly gangsters in Revenue. Your cabinet appointment gave them an opening. By quitting, you handed them your head on a platter!"

In full flight now, his renowned broadcaster's cadence kicked in as he paced the floor, repeatedly slashing the air for emphasis. Then, slumping into his favourite recliner, he went silent, except for asking me to turn up the volume on the stereo. *"Louder! Put her up on blast!"* The deafening roar of Sir Edward Elgar's "Pomp and Circumstance" transformed the room and Jamieson. I knew from previous visits that gorging on ear-splitting music, often the very piece now playing, was how he recharged his batteries and pondered tough issues. At long last, he spoke, quoting the lyrics behind the music:

"'Thine equal laws, by freedom gained, have ruled thee well.' It was stupid politicians, lawmakers, like us who gave these charlatans the noose. Now, let's see if we can get it off your neck. There's got to be a way to get you out of this mess."

Matter-of-factly, Jamieson canvassed the facts of my case, drilled me some more, and spelled out likely scenarios. I came away from that unforgettable, marathon evening with many ideas, angles, and options to put to my lawyer. More importantly, Don did me an invaluable service by succinctly mapping out a way forward and steeling my resolve. In subsequent phone calls and visits, his broad shoulders and wise counsel were a key source of strength in the rough weeks and months which followed[166].

Decades later, to hear "Pomp and Circumstance" is to fondly remember a larger-than-life, blunt-talking, astute friend, Don Jamieson.

166 As we say in Newfoundland, Jamieson was no slouch at speaking his mind, peppering every phrase with colourful descriptors, some of them printable. Anyone who knew him will recognize that I have sanitized or omitted his more graphic characterizations. Otherwise, the above quotes reflect the tone and essence of his utterances and are extracted from notes I made during and immediately after our session.

LOWERING THE BOOM

Immediately after his second RevCan meeting, Stikeman told me he had no doubt that my tax file would wind up in court:

"This is now so high-profile. They have to charge you to sustain their tough-guy image, to show the public that not even a prominent politician can get away with trying to beat the taxman, as they allege you've done. You are now RevCan's poster boy."

Therein lay the essence of Don Jamieson's reason for maintaining I should not have quit cabinet. My action had introduced a public dimension, allowing RevCan to take advantage of the changed circumstance. I believe that, whether I had remained in cabinet or not, the agency would have ensured that my case became widely known. In the lingo of computerese shorthand, there's an app for that. It's called a RevCan press leak, illegal[167] but effective. The income tax moguls are its past masters.

Stikeman's prediction came true within days. It's rare to find an MP on Parliament Hill when the House is in recess. Nonetheless, my continuing preoccupation with two issues, fisheries and my tax case, kept me late at the office on most days. Friday, September 9, was such a day. At 6:40 p.m., the phone rang. It was RevCan's deputy minister, Doug Rutherford. Justice would be laying charges on Tuesday, he told me.

RevCan's public version of events was that it recommended to Justice on July 24 that charges be laid. That doesn't square with, indeed directly contradicts, what the official told Heward Stikeman during their meetings on August 30 and 31. Nor does the July 24 date make sense in the context of what Osbaldeston told me during our August 22 meeting. He had been informed by RevCan on August 18 that a decision to prosecute had not been made.

It's also intriguing to note that, if the recommendation to prosecute was indeed made on July 24, the failure of the Privy Council Office to screen cabinet candidates prior to the August 22 shuffle was an omission of monumental significance.

What, then, caused RevCan to change its mind between June 20 and August 18, the day that Osbaldeston was informed of my tax issue? The answer is simple, and it's right from the horse's mouth. The RevCan official told Stikeman on August 31 that, "When your man went into cabinet, we had a problem."

We also know when RevCan changed its mind or, perhaps more cor-

167 "CRA (RevCan) officials are forbidden by law from discussing the filings of individual taxpayers." – *Globe and Mail*, October 31, 2007; updated March 27, 2017

rectly, when the official became aware of his department's new stratagem. It had to be sometime subsequent to the August 30 (first) meeting between the official and my lawyer.

What is crystal clear is that RevCan changed its mind because of one piece of new information, and one piece only: I had become a cabinet minister. That had the potential to create an awkward public perception problem for the tax agency. In the official's own words, "How could we ever explain that the file had been taken off the desk before he became a minister?"

RevCan had a solution to the problem. Make it my problem, which it did immediately and in spades.

GENTLE GIANT

Heward Stikeman was nearing the end of a brilliant career when he immersed himself in my troubles. I owe him a great debt for his helpful advice and, especially, his unwavering belief in me and my cause. He counselled me through six meetings and numerous phone consultations. He travelled three times to Ottawa from Rideau Ferry and once to Montreal on my behalf.

Having long since quit the courtroom, Stikeman arranged for John Sopinka, a partner in Stikeman Elliott's Toronto office, to spearhead my defence. Catherine Chalmers, Sopinka's Toronto colleague, joined the defence team, as did my long-time friend, St. John's lawyer Norm Whalen.

Stikeman, Sopinka, and I met in Montreal on September 15. It was immediately obvious that Sopinka enjoyed both a cordial relationship with Stikeman and his complete confidence. That trust was clearly not misplaced: Just five years after Sopinka acted for me, he was named to the Supreme Court of Canada. He died much too soon in 1997.

When the time came to settle up with Stikeman, he refused to take a dime. "This one's on me. Besides, someone has to keep an eye on that gang." Stikeman was certainly right about that. He passed away in 1999. I hadn't had the opportunity to reconnect with him for several years. The last time we spoke, RevCan's betrayal of him, and me, was still a raw wound for both of us. Ten years after his passing, a tribute in the *Globe and Mail* saluted "his gentleness, intellect, zany wit, and single-mindedness of purpose." Dr. Glenn D. Feltham, former tax law professor and president of the Northern Alberta Institute of Technology, said of Stikeman, "No individual has had a more profound effect on the development of tax in Canada."

Once, twice, maybe three times in a lifetime, you get to know a truly great human being. Heward Stikeman fit the bill to a T.

Given my long involvement in Newfoundland education and politics and the resulting high profile, the challenge for the St. John's court administration was to assign a judge to my case who didn't know me personally. The choice of Judge John Trahey was ominous. The following day, I ran into Gord Seabright, a close friend dating back to my Springdale days and an imposing, flamboyant character with a verbal bluntness that could shatter windowpanes. Seabright, like Trahey a provincial court judge, took me aside at a reception. His candid assessment of Trahey's new assignment was far from reassuring: "Yesterday was not your lucky day! Trahey's notion of consistency is 'Convict all of 'em!' Once in a blue moon, he acquits—just to keep his batting average respectable!"

The other shoe dropped when I learned that RevCan had fingered superstar lawyer Clyde Wells to prosecute my case. Up until then, I had enjoyed a friendly relationship with Wells stretching back nearly two decades to our Young Liberal days. Indeed, he had acted for me in a real estate transaction some years earlier.

Clyde had a well-deserved public persona as a successful lawyer and as a guy to watch. Joey Smallwood had recruited him at age twenty-eight to join the provincial cabinet. As Joey soon learned to his sorrow, his new Labour minister was, to quote British Prime Minister Margaret Thatcher's descriptive self-assessment, "not for turning." Brian Mulroney and all of Canada would learn the same lesson during the Meech Lake shemozzle. Wells's stick-to-it-iveness on any position he espouses is legendary. Compromise and flexibility do not figure prominently in his vocabulary or way of operating.

Recalling our past association as political fellow-travellers and friends, I was understandably taken aback at the news of Clyde's impending role in my case, as were some of his law colleagues—though I understood that, from his perspective, this latest assignment was all in a day's work for a lawyer with his credentials.

ENCOURAGING SIGNS

With the court proceeding set to get under way on October 24, 1983, I had reason to be optimistic. I had the best legal team I could have wished for. I felt there was no substantive case against me.

John Sopinka asked me to indicate my preferences for character witnesses. Several friends and former work colleagues had already come forward offering to take the stand on my behalf. I chose Clarence Wiseman and Don Batstone, both of them men of sterling character and reputation. General Clarence Wiseman, my fellow Newfoundlander and long-time role model, mentor, and friend, had been worldwide head of the Salvation Army (1974–77). He flew in from Toronto for the court hearing. Don Batstone, my former school board chairman in Green Bay, had recently retired from a distinguished career in RCMP counter-intelligence. Both knew me well, both had plenty of experience doing character assessments, and their long public service careers ensured they wouldn't be intimidated by the vagaries of the court process or wilt under the pressure of a baiting prosecutor.

I was buoyed by the fact that the prime minister had not filled the cabinet vacancy created by my resignation, which I interpreted as tangible evidence both of his confidence in me and his resolve not to prejudice the outcome of my legal battle. I was also encouraged by several conversations I had with the PM, often sitting beside him in the Commons chamber, while my tax problem wended its way through the court.

My spirits were certainly lifted by the many dozens of phone calls, countless one-on-one conversations, and hundreds of letters and telegrams from friends and strangers alike. Here's a sampling:

"I continue to be a strong admirer and friend."
— Future senator Michael Kirby, Montreal, August 24

"Those of us who know you will miss the enthusiasm
you could have brought to the cabinet table."
— Senior advisor to federal cabinet minister
John Roberts, Ottawa, August 25

"May strength, quietness of spirit, and deep inner peace be with you."
— Clergywoman and former university colleague, Toronto, August 29

"I will always remember . . . the night of the 22nd. All around you might have been going bad, but you stressed the importance of looking only to the future."
— Ever so briefly, my ministerial chauffeur, August 30

"The widespread support is a tribute to your ability and integrity."
— Future colleague and prime minister, Paul Martin, Montreal, September 9

"Our priest asked the congregation to write you urging you to be strong."
— Joan White, constituent and ex-member
of my House of Assembly staff, October 3

"Claire and I . . . want you to know that we hope you have the strength to overcome these difficulties."
— Lily Shreyer, Rideau Hall, Ottawa, October 10

The caring, handwritten note from Her Excellency was especially appreciated. It had been my pleasure, three months earlier, to spend several days aboard a Coast Guard ship with Governor General Ed Shreyer and his wife. Authors Farley and Claire Mowat, close friends of the Shreyers, also made the trip.

The incoming mail wasn't all pleasant to read. My circumstance, both before and after the court's decision, unleashed a small torrent of abuse, ridicule, and hatred, impugning everything from my party affiliation to my morals to my sanity.

As matters took their course in the provincial courthouse in St. John's, it became ever more obvious that the case mounted against me, aided by the interventions and body language of the presiding judge, would be deciding factors, not what I knew to be the truth. Wells, skilled courtroom performer that he was, played Judge Trahey like a compliant fiddle. Even the come-from-away domicile of my two Toronto lawyers was fair game as they were repeatedly admonished with "That's not how we do things here' put-downs.

Throughout the four-day proceeding, I was rarely ill at ease or frustrated; focused and engaged, yes, but not panicky or distraught. My defence team did a superb job of presenting our case, refuting prosecution claims and blunting surprises from the other side.

With the benefit of hindsight, limitless moments of reflection, and lots of Monday morning quarterbacking, I do second-guess my defence team in one respect. The entire thrust of its strategy was centred on the issue of wilfulness on which the Justice charge was predicated. The vendetta which, I believe, was at the heart of RevCan's audit and investigation of my tax file, and the agency's duplicity in putting the file "back on the desk," were not canvassed during the court proceeding. In particular, sworn testimony by the iconic Stikeman concerning the substance of his meetings with RevCan would have been persuasive evidence of the tax agency's real agenda.

As well, my lawyers and I were not aware, at the time of the court proceeding, that there was a key relationship between one of the RevCan investigators and Alex Walsh, the businessman serving prison time for his role in the Newfoundland Public Works spending scandal which I had exposed as chair of the Public Accounts Committee.

IF YOU CAN BEAR TO HEAR THE TRUTH YOU'VE SPOKEN TWISTED BY KNAVES . . .[168]

My blood pressure shot up when the two investigators' recounting of what transpired during our several meetings bore little resemblance to the facts. Their charge that I had been reticent in admitting I had received the unreported income was a complete fabrication, a blatant lie, tailored to shore up their claim that I had deliberately failed to report this income. As soon as I was made aware of the income and its source, I immediately indicated the approximate sums I had received.

I had seen no need to have someone in those meetings with me who could later attest to the truth or otherwise of what was said. Indeed, I naively thought that would have been interpreted as an admission of guilt.

As a takeaway from my ordeal, I maintain that good tax law should stipulate that, in any such meeting during which evidence is sought which may be subsequently used in a prosecution, the taxpayer should be required to have a lawyer or other corroborating witness in attendance. Conversely, the statute should provide that evidence obtained in a meeting where no such witness is present is inadmissible in prosecuting a case.

In the absence of such protection from unscrupulous fishing expeditions, I was a lamb to the slaughter. It was my word against that of two others, not exactly a balanced formula for establishing truth, particularly if they have an agenda and are seeking to advance it. I believe the outcome of my case would have been quite different had I been able to rely on a witness who could affirm that significant elements of what the investigators alleged didn't square with the facts. *The truth shall set you free* is a good guidepost. In my case, though, the more I told the truth, the deeper I dug the hole because my interrogators cherry-picked the facts that suited their narrative.

A case in point and the final irony is the following: In addition to the $28,000 in the court documents, I had other unreported income during the same years. And I told the tax investigators about it. Dozens of forty-foot accommodation trailers had become surplus to housing requirements in Churchill Falls, Labrador. I bought ten of them and had them shipped, at considerable cost, to my Kona Beach property, forty miles north of Grand Falls, Newfoundland. I sold two of them, but the others were rendered unusable in a severe windstorm. The sales revenue was dwarfed by the financial bath I took on the damaged units.

---

168 Rudyard Kipling, English journalist, poet, and novelist, 1865–1936

The tax investigators informed me they had decided not to factor the trailer income and expenses into their reassessment of my returns. At the time, I thought they were doing me a favour. Their real motive was something far less helpful. My losses in the trailer affair essentially offset the unreported income to which I had already admitted. As well, my failure to claim these losses buttressed my explanation of negligence while undermining the investigators' thesis of wilful tax avoidance. How could they argue that I was out to beat the system if I had not seen fit to claim offsetting expenses?

At the conclusion of the four-day proceeding, Judge Trahey reserved judgment, ultimately handing down his decision a week later. He ruled for the prosecution, and I was fined $3,500.

It goes without saying that my biggest faux pas was neglecting to report the $28,000 income on my annual tax returns. But it was other naive mistakes I made subsequently which helped to seal my fate. Meeting with the two investigators, in the absence of a corroborating witness, was, without a doubt, my second biggest blunder.

My case set a precedent as the smallest in dollar value of unreported income ever to be prosecuted[169]. All others of similar or less size have been mitigated by assessing a financial penalty, including cases where there was clear evidence of a wilful act of tax evasion.

STAMPING OUT RUTHLESS FISHING EXPEDITIONS

It is not hard to draw the conclusion that my income tax ordeal was less about compliance than about good old-fashioned payback. I don't have a martyr complex. I am not a likely candidate for self-immolation. But if a guy is towering over me swinging a baseball bat toward my head, I know he's not here to play ball with me. Whether or not a second vendetta, fuelled by my role in unearthing the Newfoundland Public Works scandal, added to my troubles, others will have to decide.

An arm of government should not have the licence to purposely inflict misery on its citizens. Yet that is the daily option of the Canada Revenue Agency, and, in my experience both as a taxpaying citizen and a veteran politician, I can attest that it is all too often the agency's way of carrying out its business.

It is not bureaucrats as a whole who are at fault, though if duplicity and malevolence are communicable diseases, RevCan/CRA has infected a whole

169 *Clyde Wells: A Political Biography*, Claire Hoy, Stoddart Publishing, Toronto, 1992, p. 122

generation of well-intended public servants. The real culprit is the system itself. In Canada, as in other jurisdictions, the imperative to ensure that no one is above the law has, irony of ironies, unwittingly spawned a horde of bureaucrats who are not only beyond the reach of the law, they get to de facto rewrite the law to suit their warped agenda and to rewrite it yet again as that agenda changes.

The challenge for duly elected lawmakers, not the self-appointed legislative drafters in tax agencies, is Olympian. Whether in Canada or elsewhere, the impossible task is to put the genie back into the bottle, to craft a tax law enforcement regime which achieves its legitimate purpose, while thwarting unscrupulous zealots who self-righteously rank their misguided mission above any consideration of the real intent of the legislation. The tragic result is the unjustifiable and continuing harassment, yea, the ruin, of law-abiding taxpayers such as the fishermen who were vilified in the 1982 audit, such as BC's Irvin LeRoux and untold thousands of others.

What's needed is a tax law enforcement arbiter. Oh, I'm aware that Canada already has an income tax ombudsman. However, that office is mere window dressing; it has no power, no teeth. The ombudsman's involvement is after the fact. What I propose is an arbiter who is a parliamentary, not a government, appointee and whose decisions are binding. Tax agency stratagems would have to pass muster with the arbiter to guard against mindless, malevolent fishing expeditions and unethical ploys by tax investigators to cover their tracks when some diabolical scheme blows up in their faces. A tax arbiter may not have saved my seat at the cabinet table. But an arbiter would, at the very least, rein in the ruthless excesses which are the stock-in-trade of CRA.

RETROSPECTIVE

Every cloud has a silver lining, even an ominous monstrosity that blocks the sun and darkens the sky. That is an apt metaphor for my tax troubles. And yes, believe it or not, I have found the silver lining, again and again. My doctoral-level seminar in personal financial management, treachery, and kneecapping has reaped untold dividends. I believe I am a better person, more organized, less procrastinating, certainly less trusting, more alert to demented con artists who think that making life miserable for law-abiding citizens is an honourable way to earn a paycheque.

And I now know who my friends are.

News of the court decision unleashed yet another flood of mail, telegrams, phone calls, and one-on-one conversations. The outpouring of empathy and support was overwhelming and uplifting. From all walks of life, from every corner of the nation, expressions of support poured in.

Not that all of the mail was reassuring or pleasant to read. Partisans of other party stripes, armchair experts, self-appointed executioners, and, in a few cases, certifiable hate-mongers and sickos all took their pound of flesh at my expense.

The option to appeal Judge Trahey's finding was, of course, open to me. After consultations with friends and tax lawyers, I reluctantly decided against launching an appeal. The overriding reason was financial. To date, I had racked up legal bills of more than $70,000, and I was effectively bankrupt. The appeal, I was told, could double my indebtedness. In reality, there was no decision to make. I just didn't have the money.

I've recently reviewed my entire file on the tax issue, including the hundreds of letters, first of congratulation, then of condolence, support, puzzlement, ridicule, and judgment that my cabinet appointment and its aftermath spawned. My abiding reaction is just how completely I let so many people down by my carelessness. I shall go to my grave lamenting the pain and the dashed hopes I inflicted on others by my inattention to my personal affairs and the havoc it caused.

In January 1984, soon after I had forfeited my right to appeal, the PM reappointed my predecessor, colleague and lifelong friend Bill Rompkey, as Newfoundland and Labrador's representative in the federal cabinet. Bill's outstanding political career spanned nearly forty years as an MP, minister, and senator, a position he held until his 2011 retirement. What a wonderful guy! His humanity and bonhomie touched many lives. Sadly, Bill passed away in early 2017. We miss him dearly.

THE VOTERS WEIGH IN

Prime Minister John Turner convened his first caucus the day after assuming the Liberal leadership in 1984. He canvassed the views of members on the timing of an election call. With the Liberals leading by ten points in the polls, should he opt for an immediate trip to the ballot box or delay a few weeks until he could put his own imprint on the government? I was among those who favoured the latter option and said so. Then, I added, "However, if you decide to pull the plug now, don't worry about me. If I lose my seat, you won't get forty." Turner opted to pull the plug. I lost my seat, and we got forty!

My narrow defeat in the 1984 federal general election was the first following my public mauling at the hands of RevCan. It is unclear to what extent the tax issue was a factor. The election night figures placed me just one per cent or 299 votes behind the victor while holding most of my support from the previous election, when the final count had ranked me among the top five vote-getters nationally. Across the country, my party lost sixteen per cent of the popular vote in 1984 compared to the 1980 election results and dropped from 147 to 40, a staggering 107 seats. Forced to choose between Brian Mulroney's liberal Tories and the Liberal Party's toryism, voters across Canada opted for hope over exhaustion. My narrow defeat appears to have been part of a referendum on the national Liberal brand.

The income tax issue may well have helped my campaign. My constituents were well aware of its essential elements, including the tax agency's unprecedented decision to prosecute such a low-dollar case. They were equally cognizant of my aggressive role concerning the fishermen's audit, and many of them saw linkage between the two matters. Further, thousands of fishermen who had been mercilessly run into the ground by their RevCan audits and their families had an axe to grind with the agency. My axe became their axe. Often, during the campaign, I was told by electors that their reason for supporting me was directly related to what RevCan had done to them—and to me.

Discharged by the electorate and out of politics for the first time in more than a decade, I looked for other opportunities and quickly found one, or, more accurately, it found me. *As one door closes, another opens* is a creed I live by. The glass is always half full.

CHAPTER 18
LEADER ON A SHORT LEASH

A genuine leader is not a seeker for consensus,
but a moulder of consensus.
— Martin Luther King, Jr., American Baptist minister
and civil rights leader, 1929–1968

For twenty-four years, with just one short interruption, I held elective office or was seeking election. That one brief interlude followed my narrow defeat in the 1984 federal election when my party was reduced to forty seats by the Mulroney steamroller.

Our election night wake in Marystown lasted into the wee hours, an opportunity to commiserate with friends and supporters, to show my appreciation for their loyalty and hard work and to reminisce about happier times. Then it was time to get behind the wheel for the four-hour trek to St. John's airport and the early-morning flight to the nation's capital to see family and wind down my Parliament Hill operation before my official eviction in ten days' time.

THE PRIVATE SECTOR COMES CALLING

I was at my suburban Ottawa home before mid-morning. My wife, Miriam, handed me a business card, saying some guy named Ron Marsland wanted to talk to me. Unlike the crazy schedule that had ordered virtually my every waking moment during the past several years, my appointment calendar was now blank. I tracked Marsland down that very afternoon. His opening words to me were, it seemed for a moment, inauspicious: "I'm one of the people who hoped you would be defeated—but not for the reason you think."

Ron proposed that we merge our skill sets in a consulting business. Less than twenty-four hours after the voters had told me my services were no longer required, I became Ron's corporate partner. We would peddle productivity, his specialty, and government relations.

The next six months were a roller-coaster series of fits and starts as Ron and I hustled for a piece of the action. There were some successes. Canada Post and Honeywell engaged our services. Halifax businessman Harry Steele[170] had me canvass the merits of acquiring a stable of weekly newspapers. My recommendations led to his purchase of thirteen Newfoundland weeklies, the launch of a St. John's paper, and the hiring of crack journalist Michael Harris as its editor.

BACK IN THE SADDLE

Then came news from the Rock. A Newfoundland provincial election had been called. Liberal Leader Leo Barry was on the phone asking me to be a candidate. So soon after my federal loss, I asked myself if a return to the hustings was a wise move. To help me decide, Marsland and I became instant polling gurus. I wrote the questions. He pumped the phone.

My in-house pollster soon had the evidence I needed. I was off and running. It would be my ninth campaign of one sort or another in less than twelve years. Barely seven months after my federal defeat, I was back in the Newfoundland House of Assembly. And, as in my first provincial incarnation, I was a member of Her Majesty's Loyal Opposition.[171]

The leader of the majority party, and thus the premier, was again Brian Peckford, wily, focused, and affable, and my friend, though the myopia of partisan politics had weakened the bond.

THE POT CALLS THE KETTLE BLACK!

As the opposition Finance spokesman, I was speaking in the Address in Reply to the Speech from the Throne which outlines the administration's legislative program for the just-convened House session. A government backbencher and erstwhile friend, having opted for partisanship over camaraderie, heckled me repeatedly. When you have the mic, interjections from the other side of the chamber are not a problem, indeed they can energize your delivery. The other guy is the one with the problem. His mic is off, pursuant to House protocol.

My adversary kept hurling taunts across the floor, referencing my troubles with RevCan two years earlier. His persistence gave my House Leader, Beaton Tulk[172], an idea which might silence the noise from the far corner. Tulk held up something and gestured that I should give it to the heckler.

170 Retired Navy admiral, entrepreneur, last chairman of Canadian Airlines
171 This formal title for the Official Opposition dates back to 1826 at Westminster and usually refers to the second-largest party in the legislature.
172 Educator, MHA, minister, premier of Newfoundland and Labrador, 2000–01

The reality was that my self-righteous taunter may have had a little baggage of his own. His ailing motel had recently burned to the ground in a mysterious fire. Corridor gossip informed us that the police were investigating. Arson was suspected. The scuttlebutt said that the owner, my heckler, wanted to collect the fire insurance.

As Tulk held his item aloft, I pretended to ignore him until I was sure his antics had the attention of the House and the public galleries. Then, in a mock scold, I said, "Beaton, put that lighter away or someone will want to torch this place, too!"

Immediate, dead silence from the far corner. It was the first time I saw a guy plead guilty without moving his lips. The non-verbal *mea culpa* easily trumped his earlier rantings. Like Marley in Dickens's Christmas classic, my tormentor had forged the chain himself, link by link.

Quebec, QC, 1987. As Newfoundland Leader of the Opposition, I paid a courtesy call on Quebec Premier Robert Bourassa. (Author photo)

CHANGING OF THE GUARD

The Leader of the Opposition, Leo Barry, was a former Conservative Energy minister who had rowed out with Premier Peckford over policy issues and crossed the floor, joined the Liberals, and, soon after, became their leader. Despite his early success in growing Liberal strength in the House from four to fifteen members in the 1985 general election, he soon got into trouble with his caucus. What he lacked, according to his fellow Liberal MHAs, were a willingness to listen, the common touch, and the ability to be in two places at the same time. He was in Boston when his caucus felt he should have been minding the shop in St. John's. In truth, though, the Boston trip was merely the proverbial straw. Barry had lost the confidence of his parliamentary team. Indeed, all fourteen members of his caucus signed a letter demanding a leadership convention.

To this day, I believe the caucus did the right thing in the circumstances, and not because I succeeded Barry as Leader of the Opposition. The caucus decision to ask me to step into the role came as a surprise. Undoubtedly, an element in its choice was the fact, well-known to my colleagues, that I hoped to return to the federal arena at the first opportunity and, therefore, didn't aspire to the leadership of the provincial party.

CELEBRATING CANADA AND JOEY

I assumed the leadership of the Official Opposition on March 25, 1987. The anniversary of Newfoundland's joining Canada was just six days away. I was appalled to learn that nothing had been planned to mark the occasion. It was no surprise that the Conservative government had chosen to ignore the milestone, since any celebration would inevitably remind voters of the central role played by their nemesis and punching bag, Joey Smallwood, in bringing about Confederation. It was disconcerting, however, to realize that the Liberal Party was also taking a pass. The reason may well have been that Leo Barry had himself been a Tory just three years earlier and harboured a visceral dislike for anything connected to Smallwood.

The former premier had suffered a debilitating stroke in 1984, leaving him partially paralyzed and unable to speak. The volatile, verbose talking machine had become mute Joey, surely the cruellest oxymoron of all, certainly for him and his dwindling band of admirers, acolytes, and defenders. For his detractors, critics, and professional hate-mongers, it was a providential reprieve, an answer to prayer that the megaphone that walked like a man had been silenced at last.

An eleventh-hour attempt to organize an event to fete our thirty-eight years as Canadians was worth a try. And I knew the two people who could make it happen. I met with Mrs. Liberal herself, Joan Cook[173], and Steve Neary, who had served in Smallwood's last cabinet, and we set the wheels in motion for a mammoth celebration. Liberals and other rank-and-file Newfoundlanders swelled the St. John's Holiday Inn ballroom to make merry, reminisce, and get a little face time with the guest of honour, Joey. It was his first public ap-

173 Senator, 1998–2009; Joan, a dynamic, focused political activist, played a pivotal and much-appreciated role in my first electoral campaign.

pearance since his stroke, and he did not disappoint. Standing at the podium, tears rolling down his cheeks, he responded to the sustained applause of 700 proud Canadians by flashing a thumbs-up, waving his hand, and mouthing repeated thank yous. Though age and illness had taken their physical toll, his mind and his personality were as responsive as ever.

The district Liberal association in Goose Bay, Labrador, staged a fundraising roast with me as the roastee. The usual cast of characters lined up to take their best shot. As well, the organizers had arranged for a mystery roaster. Imagine my surprise and initial skepticism when a teenager was paraded on stage. Sixteen-year-old Seamus O'Regan brought down the house with his witticisms, one-liners, and twists of the knife. His intervention was easily the highlight of the evening.

St, John's, 2017. With long-time friends, former premier of Newfoundland and Labrador Kathy Dunderdale and Seamus O'Regan, Canada's minister of Veterans Affairs. (Author photo)

Roast organizers have not been the only ones to recognize O'Regan's skill set and potential. At age ten, O'Regan was a regional correspondent for CBC. In 1999, *Maclean's* magazine named him as one of 100 Young Canadians to Watch in the twenty-first century. Following stints as a political staffer on Parliament Hill and speechwriter for Premier Brian Tobin, he co-hosted CTV's *Canada AM* for ten years before becoming a correspondent for *CTV National News*. Currently, O'Regan is the MP for St. John's South–Mount Pearl, having successfully contested the 2015 federal election. And in August 2017, Prime Minister Justin Trudeau invited him to join the cabinet as Newfoundland and Labrador's representative in the federal cabinet and minister of Veterans Affairs.

When Clyde Wells became leader of the Liberal Party, some of my caucus colleagues were apprehensive that his adversarial role in my tax prosecution would make for a rocky transition. Wells would succeed to the position I held, Leader of the Opposition, as soon as he won election to the House of Assembly. My friends need not have worried. From the moment he declared his leadership candidacy, Wells was always upfront, indeed cordial, in his dealings with me. I actively campaigned for him, at his request, during his successful by-election campaign which allowed him to take his seat in the House.

Near Grand Bruit, NL, 1993. Premier Clyde Wells and I visited the Hope Brook mine. (Author photo)

During the handover of opposition leadership responsibilities, Wells invited me to his home for debriefings, and once he took over, he involved me as a key member of his team. Indeed, we briefly shared the leader's office until alternate office arrangements were made for me. When Wells led the party in the 1989 provincial election, I campaigned for several of his candidates.

The Tories had been in power for fifteen years when Wells assumed the Liberal leadership. The provincial economy was on the ropes. A once-vibrant fishery struggled as cod stocks were on the brink of collapse. The jobless rate was skyrocketing. Provincial coffers were all but bare. Premier Peckford decided it was time for a Hail Mary and badly fumbled the ball. He knew better. After all, how often had he railed against the very strategy he now embraced, Joey Smallwood's quick-fix approach to economic diversification?

The provincial government partnered with a Calgary businessman to establish a giant greenhouse facility in Mount Pearl near St. John's. Philip Sprung, the late Alberta entrepreneur, would use his hydroponics process to grow cucumbers to supply local consumers and the export market while Newfoundland would get some jobs. That, we were told, was the plan. Things didn't quite work out that way, however. The project, dubbed by CBC as "Premier Peckford's pickled palace," was cursed from the start with construction snafus, cost overruns, and production delays.

The real problem, though, was the absence of a sound business case. The first cucumbers grown at the new facility cost $1.08 a cuke to grow at a time when a consumer could buy the same item for a quarter in Boston[174]. Overall, the 800,000 cucumbers produced at the greenhouse cost Newfoundland taxpayers $27.50 each.[175]

Two years after the project was launched with great fanfare and the promise of 150 permanent jobs, the Sprung greenhouse, having burned through $22 million in taxpayer dollars, went into receivership.

Provincial politics had been a tough slog for my party. Liberals, for twenty-three years the party of government, had been reduced to a corporal's guard in 1972 and, with the exception of the 1975 election, had not come close to regaining power. By 1988, the Tories had been in government for sixteen years. The baggage of power and an increasingly arrogant posture of entitlement were beginning to take their toll.

Our new leader, Clyde Wells, was orchestrating a disciplined, effective opposition in the House and making significant strides with the electorate. Indeed, just months into his leadership, we scored a by-election victory in the Tory heartland, winning a metropolitan St. John's seat, Gerry Ottenheimer's[176] old bailiwick. My great friend and future premier, Beaton Tulk, managed the campaign, and I headed the poll organization. For the first time in thirteen years, the Liberals had a real chance at forming the provincial government.

But my political heart was in Ottawa. The countdown to the 1988 federal general election had begun, and I was determined to once again be the Liberal standard-bearer in Burin–St. George's.

Newfoundlanders went to the polls in a provincial election in 1989. Clyde Wells and his reinvigorated team squared off against the newly minted premier, my good friend Tom Rideout[177], who had succeeded Peckford.

Wells led the Liberals to a resounding victory, winning thirty-one seats to the Tories' twenty-one. Two weeks later, he took the oath as the province's fifth premier since the union of Newfoundland and Canada.

The current premier, Dwight Ball, is Newfoundland and Labrador's thirty-second[178] head of government throughout its several stages as colony, quasi-independent country, dominion, and province. The first, Phillip Francis Little, assumed office in 1855.

174 www.heritage.nf.ca/articles/politics/sprung-greenhouse.php

175 *Failures and Fiascos: Atlantic Canada's Biggest Boondoggles*, Dan Soucoup, Halifax: Nimbus Publishing, 2013

176 Member of the House of Assembly (MHA), Leader of the Opposition, minister, Speaker, senator

177 Educator, MHA (Liberal, then Conservative), minister, premier

178 Including the three men who served as Chair of the Commission of Government (1934–49)

CHAPTER 19
ITINERANT TRIBUNE

Tribune: An officer of ancient Rome elected by the plebeians to protect their rights from arbitrary acts of the patrician magistrates; a protector or champion of the people.
— TheFreeDictionary

The year 1988 marked my fifteenth in elective politics, ten in the Newfoundland House of Assembly and five in the House of Commons. Each arena had given me many satisfying moments, wrenching heartbreaks, and lasting memories. Having tasted national politics, that's where my preference lay, and I was determined to get back to the House of Commons at the first opportunity. By mid-1988, it was widely assumed that Prime Minister Mulroney would go to the polls before the year was out.

To have a shot at once again becoming the honourable Member for Burin–St. George's, I first had to win the Liberal nomination, which I fully expected would be contested, as indeed it was. In American parlance, I had to survive the primary. That was going to take some fancy stickhandling and hard work. I was ready for both.

For months before the party nomination process was set in motion, I carried in my pocket a copy of the Liberal Party's official nomination form and invited voters to sign it. The party rules required twenty-five signatures. I secured 3,000. These included a healthy majority of party activists and community leaders.

By the time my opponent declared his intentions, I effectively had the nomination sewn up. Even his closest friends, who would have certainly been in his camp had they known earlier of his planned candidacy, were telling him instead, "Sorry, but I already gave my word to Roger."

YON CASSIUS HAS A MEAN AND HUNGRY LOOK[179]

With the nomination in the bag, there was one more hurdle, though at the time I regarded it as a mere formality. The Canada Elections Act stipulates that a candidate running under the banner of a political party needs a letter of endorsement signed by the party's leader in order to have the party's name appear on the ballot. I had won the Liberal nomination fair and square, so how could there be a problem? Simply put, an incumbent Newfoundland MP, and a Liberal one at that, didn't relish the notion of my returning to Parliament. Indeed, I was already aware that he had raised thousands of dollars to underwrite the campaign costs of my nomination opponent. When that investment didn't yield the hoped-for return, the MP bent the leader's ear, invoking my income tax problem, which had been put to bed five years earlier, to try and persuade John Turner not to sign my nomination.

Shortly after the 1988 election, Turner hosted the caucus at a reception at Stornaway[180] and invited me to hang back for a one-on-one chat. He was in a talkative mood. He told me of the abortive attempt to prevent me from running as an official Liberal candidate and gave me some advice: "Watch your back."

Turner referenced the caucus revolt against his leadership a few months before the 1988 election, telling me that the dissidents had been plotting their mutiny when one of their number slipped out of the meeting. It was the same MP who had tried to trip me up. Turner told me, "(He) came to my office. He pretended to be on my side, speaking of the seventeen conspirators as 'they,' trying to give the impression he wasn't one of them. Of course, he was just covering all his bases. There are snakes in the grass around here, lots of them." Indeed, the landscape was even more infested than Turner realized. Eventually, letters demanding his resignation were signed by twenty-two of the thirty-eight members of his caucus.[181]

The 1988 federal vote has become known as the free trade election. Prime Minister Mulroney had signed a free trade agreement (FTA) with the US in January 1988. In so doing, he had done a complete about-face. During the 1983 Conservative leadership campaign, Mulroney ranted forcefully against "opening the floodgates"[182] when leadership contender John Crosbie spoke in favour of such an agreement. Mulroney pontificated, "Free trade affects

179 *Julius Caesar*, William Shakespeare, Act 1, Scene 2
180 Official residence of the Leader of the Official Opposition
181 *Divided Loyalties*, Brooke Jeffrey, Toronto: University of Toronto Press, 2010, p. 116
182 *No Holds Barred*, John Crosbie, Toronto: McClelland & Stewart, 1997, p. 212

Canadian sovereignty and we will have none of it, not during leadership campaigns or any other time."[183]

However, when the MacDonald Royal Commission, appointed by Pierre Trudeau, recommended in 1984 that the government pursue a free trade agreement with the United States, Mulroney—having succeeded Trudeau as PM—embraced the idea. During the 1988 election, the Liberal Party campaigned against the bilateral pact. Protecting Canadian sovereignty became our messianic mantra, our *cause célèbre.*

We warned of subjugation by the behemoth on our southern flank. In so doing, we were mounting the very arguments Mulroney had employed against Crosbie.

At an all-candidates rally in Stephenville, I finished my speech, the final one of the evening, with a confident prediction of Liberal vindication at the polls. Then, I strolled over to the onstage piano. "In the unlikely event we lose the election, get used to this." The first six notes of "The Star-Spangled Banner" filled the hall. The crowd loved it. It became the coda of several subsequent speeches, usually with similar effect. I'm not saying my less-than-melodic tickling of the ivories did the trick, but I won the 1988 election with a thousand votes to spare:

Joseph Edwards, New Democratic, 2,299
Joe Price (incumbent), Progressive Conservative, 17,488
Roger Simmons, Liberal, 18,527

SNATCHING DEFEAT . . .

The 1988 federal election was the Liberals' to lose, and lose it we did. Mulroney's honeymoon with the electorate was long since over. Having had to stare down several scandals during his first mandate, Mulroney and his Tories were vulnerable. As well, he had to fend off accusations by his detractors that he was still saddled with or, worse still, comfortable with the branch plant mentality that had been his stock-in-trade as president of Iron Ore Company (IOC), a subsidiary of Cleveland's Hanna Mining. His maudlin public love-in with Ronald Reagan fuelled perceptions of Pavlovian submission to all things American. Canadians want their leaders to cultivate a good working relationship with their US counterparts, not a cozy sleeping arrangement.

Leadership became a factor during the campaign, according to political scientist Jon Pammett.[184] Though voters had their fill of Mulroney's bluster and brinkmanship, many didn't see Turner as a plausible alternative, undoubtedly influenced by media stories of caucus disaffection with his stew-

183 *Divided Loyalties*, Brooke Jeffrey, Toronto: University of Toronto Press, 2010, p. 56
184 Ibid, p. 162

ardship. CBC, "*with no hard evidence of any kind*"[185], aired a story asserting there was an organized move afoot to force John Turner out.

I was far removed from the fray, busily knocking on doors in Monkstown, Margaree, and McKay's. Yet even in those places, remote from the centre of action, prospective supporters were exposed to the media's almost daily chronicling of Turner's alleged troubles, and they frequently raised the matter with me.

Despite a strong performance by Turner, Mulroney won a second majority, the first Conservative prime minister to do so in a century. Party standings were as follows:

Progressive Conservative, 169 seats, 43% of the popular vote
Liberal, 83, 32%
New Democratic, 43, 21%

The FTA was ratified soon after, even though a majority of electors had voted for parties opposing the deal.

BRICKS AND BOUQUETS

Consigned to the opposition benches for another four years, the Liberal caucus met in St. John's in early 1989 to lick its wounds, second-guess its election performance, and regroup for the battles ahead. There, I got to see Paul Martin in action for the first time. My initial impression was that, for a rookie MP, he was getting ahead of himself.

Nonetheless, during the ensuing years, I watched with admiration as Martin's expertise and energy were deftly applied to his MP responsibilities and to his key role in readying the Liberal Party for the 1993 election. Subsequently, his stellar performance as Finance minister earned him well-deserved accolades far and wide. Martin's brief stint as prime minister would be a far different story.

Brussels, Belgium, 1989. With Ross Reid, parliamentary secretary (later minister) for Fisheries and Oceans. (Author photo)

185 Ibid, p. 148

New York, 1991. Canada-France maritime boundary arbitration. L-R: The Honourable Yves Fortier, Canada's ambassador to the United Nations, Francois Mathys, agent for Canada, and me. (David Gray photo)

Rio de Janeiro, Brazil, 1992. The House of Commons' Official Opposition delegation at the Earth Summit. L-R: Marlene Catterall (Ontario), Roger Simmons, Christine Stewart (Ontario), Charles Caccia (Ontario), Paul Martin (Quebec). (Author photo)

In the lead-up to the 1993 election, Opposition Leader Jean Chrétien tasked Martin with co-chairing a policy platform committee. As opposition Fisheries critic, I presented a policy paper entitled "Shoals & Shenanigans," which reflected a consensus of my associate critics, (later Minister) Lawrence McAuley and Ron MacDonald, and me. Among other issues, it mapped out a strategy for dealing with the biggest threat to the fishing industry. The first Throne Speech following the election committed the new government to decisive action "to ensure that foreign overfishing of east coast stocks comes to an end." That initiative was straight out of the proposals my two colleagues and I had advanced, and I was especially delighted when the new Fisheries minister, Brian Tobin, took dramatic and effective steps to deal with the problem. The arrest of the *Estai*, a Spanish trawler, after shots had been fired, immediately galvanized international action and eventually led to a more equitable fishing regime.

Rio de Janeiro, Brazil, 1992. At the Earth Summit, MP (later Prime Minister) Paul Martin and I chatted with (later Sir) Shridath "Sonny" Ramphal, former Secretary-General of the Commonwealth. (Peter MacLellan photo)

DAY OF RECKONING

As Brian Mulroney neared the end of his second mandate, his best years, certainly insofar as elective politics was concerned, were behind him. The public's antipathy toward him was palpable. No dummy, he read the writing on the wall and gave notice he would pack it in.

The ensuing race to succeed him soon became a coronation as party heavyweights such as Perrin Beatty, Barbara McDougall, and Michael Wilson, inexplicably cowed by the unlikely candidacy of rookie MP and Defence Minister Kim Campbell, opted not to contest the leadership. Within months of being acclaimed as the new PC chief, Campbell, savouring a tempting post-convention bump in the polls, dissolved Parliament, and the 1993 election was on.

The Liberal leader, Jean Chrétien, ran a near-flawless campaign, fielding an impressive slate of candidates and strategically dribbling out elements of a comprehensive policy platform, all neatly packaged in a so-called Red Book. Meanwhile, Campbell's condescending forays were aggravated by a disingenuous effort to disown the Mulroney legacy, botched advertising, and a foot-in-mouth virus that cost her votes almost every time she spoke.

Ottawa, 1991. Waiting for a roll-call vote, I raised an issue with Prime Minister Brian Mulroney. Former Prime Minister Joe Clark is beside me. (J. M. Carisse photo)

The low point in the campaign was a Tory ad which was widely construed as a below-the-belt jab at the Liberal leader's facial deformity, the result of Bell's palsy when he was a child. The public backlash was electric and sustained. If the ad made voters think twice about getting on board with the Tories, it was Chrétien's masterful handling of the incident that really upended their campaign bus:

> "God gave me a physical defect. . . . When I was a kid, people were laughing at me. But I accepted that because God gave me other qualities, and I'm grateful."

A further reference to the "face ad" was classic Chrétien:

> "It's true, that I speak on one side of my mouth. I'm not a Tory; I don't speak on both sides of my mouth."

Ostensibly, the electorate's choice was between Campbell and Chrétien. In reality, the election was a referendum on the Mulroney legacy, and voters were in a judgmental, unforgiving mood. When the dust settled on polling day, the Tory bloodbath was unprecedented, the worst electoral defeat in Canadian history. Only two of the party's 295 candidates survived. Even the prime minister lost her seat.

There was a certain biblical déjà vu in the Tory results—two MPs, one male, one female; one francophone, one anglophone; one minister, one backbencher; a moderate and a right-winger. As with Noah of old, voter-inflicted retribution for past transgressions was tempered only by the imperative to continue the species. The ultimate wisdom of the electorate should never be underestimated.

Chrétien and the Liberals won a resounding victory, and, for the fourth time, the great people of Burin–St. George's decided I should be their advocate in Ottawa. The seat numbers told the national story:

Liberal 177, Bloc Québécois 54, Reform 52
New Democratic 9, Progressive Conservative 2

If the drubbing of the once-mighty Tory Party was a watershed event, the electorate's choice of Her Majesty's Official Opposition was also an eye-opener. Lucien Bouchard's separatist party, the Bloc Québécois, had edged out the Reform Party, whose overnight emergence as an electoral player heralded a seismic realignment in the body politic.

ARSONISTS IN THE FIRE BRIGADE

Recently, while addressing a group of US students visiting Canada and wanting to learn about our political system, I noted there are four parties represented in the House of Commons and quickly rhymed off three, Conservative, NDP, and Liberal. Then, I drew a blank. I could not for the life of me name the fourth party. Really, why should I? Mine was, revealingly, a mental "bloc." You see, I've never been able to get past the incredulity of a taxpayer-funded presence in Parliament of a party whose avowed objective is to destroy the institution and the country it is elected to serve.

For seven of my fifteen years in the House of Commons, I sat opposite or next to Bloc MPs. During four of those years as chair of the standing committee on health, my vice-chair was a Bloc member, my late good friend, the congenial, upbeat Pauline Picard. I travelled on parliamentary junkets to China and Ukraine with members of the Bloc caucus. In Seattle, I hosted House of Commons committees including Bloc MPs. In other words, I've seen those guys and gals close up. I made many friends among them. A finer assemblage of humanity, intelligence, and good humour you couldn't find.

But, as politicians, they have an agenda, one which is diametrically opposed to mine and to Canada's. I went into Parliament with the notion that my presence could improve the lot of those I represented and otherwise contribute to fostering a better country. Bloc MPs go there to tear the country apart. After more than twenty years of trying their best to do so, their scheme is in tatters. It's high time they threw in the towel. Yet they linger. Why? The pay is good. Pension entitlement gets better by the day.

CALCULATING, COMPETITIVE, CARING

I have known Brian Tobin for more than forty years. I was one of the three caucus members who interviewed him for his job as a press aide to the provincial Leader of the Opposition, first Bill Rowe, then Don Jamieson. His energy, clear-headedness, and people skills closed the deal for him then, as they have consistently done ever since. Tobin's foresight and his ability to see the larger picture, his lightning grasp of complex files, and a decisive approach to resolving issues have well served him and Canada. I have greatly admired his fierce competitive streak, though, if truth be known, I was sometimes the one outfoxed by his wiles.

Ottawa, 1995. Going head to head. L-R: MPs Roger Simmons, Ron Fewchuk (L, Manitoba), Brian Tobin. (J. M. Carisse photo)

Brainy, articulate, fast on the draw, take-no-prisoners. That's the Brian Tobin Canadians see. Yet there's a whole other dimension to him which may not be readily obvious to those who know him only as a public figure and business entrepreneur. From the first time he and I met, when he showed up on my doorstep to offer support for my 1977 provincial Liberal leadership run, I've often had the good fortune to be on the receiving end of his generosity, humanity, and empathy. During my 1983 hospitalization at Ottawa's National Defence Medical Centre, Brian was the only MP to drop by. While he was a federal cabinet minister and, then, premier of Newfoundland and Labrador, he and I collaborated on many files aimed at benefiting our constituents. When I lost my 1997 re-election bid, he was on the phone that very night from Toronto, taking time out from his gig as a national TV election analyst. In early 2004, as I was trying to make a go of my new consulting business, it was Tobin who lined me up with a Calgary developer with whom I secured a long-term contract.

Tompkins, NL, 1993. "First lady of the accordion." With the talented Minnie White, CM, and her daughter, Barbara. (Author photo)

As a member of Parliament's ingenious Rat Pack, Brian Tobin had distinguished himself as a skilled debater and strategist. When the Tories won power in 1984, he and fellow Rat Packers Don Boudria, Sheila Copps, and John Nunziata kept government ministers on their toes and cemented the Liberals' profile as a proactive, effective opposition. Brian was a key Chrétien activist during the 1990 Liberal leadership campaign and the Liberals' 1993 election victory. His well-earned status as a valued Chrétien player, coupled with my blotted copybook in the 1983 RevCan affair, meant that Tobin, not I, would be a shoo-in for Newfoundland and Labrador's seat in cabinet.

Like legions of other Canadians, I was deeply disappointed when Tobin abandoned his 2003 Liberal leadership campaign in the face of the Paul Martin juggernaut. John Crosbie's promising candidacy in the 1983 Tory leadership was torpedoed by his inability to speak passable French. Crosbie and Tobin had racked up enviable track records as leaders, both in Newfoundland and Labrador and nationally. Oft has it been said of Robert Stanfield[186] that he was among the best prime ministers Canada never had. John Crosbie and Brian Tobin belong to that exclusive club.

LOOSE LIPS SINK SHIPS

Some days, it's best to keep your mouth shut, one of the many lessons I've learned the hard way. In 1993, I was one of several MPs who let their names stand for the House of Commons Speakership. I had positioned myself well for a serious bid. The several Liberal colleagues who were also candidates could be expected to garner the lion's share of caucus support. My strategy, while not neglecting my Liberal friends, was to focus on the other caucuses and, specifically, the Bloc Québécois and Reform MPs.

A bit of sheer good luck gave me a kick-start. I found myself at the same Calgary hotel as the new batch of Reform MPs who were convening for their first caucus since their dramatic success at the polls, going from a single seat in Parliament to fifty-two. For two whole days, I had a captive audience of newbies, all friendly, most of them anxious to have corridor conversations to glean insights on the finer points of life on Parliament Hill. I subsequently met in Ottawa with the entire Reform caucus. I came away with many assurances of support and believed I would do very well among Reform MPs, a conclusion confirmed by my good friend John Cummins[187], a Reform member from BC who was partial to my candidacy.

As I had done prior to my session with the Reformers, I thoroughly briefed myself on MPs in the other caucuses as though cramming for a final exam. My trusty researcher, Catherine Parker, would sit across the desk quizzing me on the names of constituencies and their respective MPs until I could match every last electoral riding with its MP's name and photo.

The Bloc Québécois was a special challenge. My oral French capability was limited, especially in a meeting with fifty-four MPs whose mother tongue was Quebec French with its rich idioms and nuanced intonations, noticeably different than the international French I had studied. Here again, Lady Luck was on my side. The scheduled fifteen-minute question and answer session went on for more than an hour. I believe I understood most of what was said to me, and either the Bloquists comprehended my responses or they were awfully polite in not saying otherwise. At the conclusion of the

186 Lawyer, premier of Nova Scotia (1956–67), leader of the federal Progressive Conservative Party, and Leader of the Opposition (1967–76)

187 British Columbia MP, 1993–2011; leader of the BC Conservative Party, 2011–13

meeting, my assessment was that most of the Bloc MPs were comfortable with my candidacy. One in particular, Claude Bachand[188], an early supporter, was optimistic that most of his colleagues would vote for me.

With what seemed like solid support for my candidacy in the two largest opposition caucuses and the assurance of a smattering of votes from my own caucus, it looked like I would be a viable contender for the Speakership.

It was then I made my big blunder. I opened my mouth. On the afternoon before the Speaker vote, members of the Liberal caucus went to the Commons chamber to get a first look at the new seating assignments. Two cabinet ministers and I mused about the upcoming vote, and I mentioned the presumed strength of my support in the Bloc and Reform caucuses. The telltale body language which my bragging triggered in my two colleagues instantly made me regret my confident strutting and ego-tripping. All too soon, I would know why.

Early next morning, just a couple of hours before the vote, I got two phone calls in quick succession. John Cummins called to say that his Reform colleagues couldn't support me because of my "*continuing income tax problems*." That matter had been fully resolved ten years earlier, a fact that got omitted from the overnight smear job. Minutes later, Claude Bachand was on the phone saying that his leader, Lucien Bouchard, had it from "a reliable source" that I was "recklessly anti-Quebec."

The fix was in. Quick-thinking Liberal colleagues, with agendas different than mine, had torpedoed any chance I had of becoming Speaker. But it was my wagging tongue that had launched the missile.

I am not suggesting that, but for some creative overnight mischief-making that decimated my potential Bloc and Reform support, I would have been chosen. The man elected that day, the late Gilbert Parent, and his successor, Peter Milliken, also a candidate in 1993, were formidable contestants and, like a fourth candidate, the late Jean-Robert Gauthier, were highly respected, active Members of Parliament. Each of them had large followings, not only in the government caucus but on all sides of the five-party chamber. I do know, however, that my failure to button my lip when it mattered and the mischief it spawned ensured I would be nothing more than an also-ran. Yet another valuable lesson learned.

Though I wasn't a happy camper at the time, I didn't feel betrayed. Instead, my real anger was directed toward my glibness and strategic stupidity. I regarded the incident as just a couple of guys who faced a choice between friendship and political considerations. All politicians make that choice almost daily. John Crosbie notes, "Friendship count(s) for less in politics than

188 Quebec MP, 1993–2011

in any other field"[189]. And, according to Brian Tobin, "Friendship in politics must be peripheral to other concerns"[190]. Just about all the opponents I faced in nomination and election battles have been among my good friends. I've never thought of friendship as cloning.

Ottawa, 1994. My seatmate, Ottawa–Vanier MP Jean-Robert Gauthier, and I were candidates for Speaker of the House of Commons. When my name was dropped from the ballot, I joined my colleagues in cheering him on. (Andy Shott photo)

Port aux Basques, NL, 1995. Me, MHA Bill Ramsay, Mayor Aneitha Sheaves, provincial Minister John Efford. (Author photo)

POLITICS, A BLOOD SPORT

There was one pivotal incident that breached the usual civility that is the hallmark of electioneering in Newfoundland. The event was pivotal because, I believe, it single-handedly transformed my 1997 election candidacy into a lost cause.

189 *No Holds Barred: My Life in Politics*, John Crosbie, Toronto: McClelland & Stewart, 1997, p. 63

190 *All in Good Time*, Brian Tobin, Toronto: Penguin, 2002, p. 66

At a Port aux Basques public rally, a man stepped up to the floor microphone and, interrupting my response to a question, shouted "Liar! Liar!" The aggressive intervention was timely in at least one respect. Jim Carrey's popular movie of the same name was in theatres and, obviously, gave rise to the wording of the interjection.

The audience was justifiably exercised over the shortage of doctors in rural areas. My party, on assuming office four years earlier, had taken an axe to the outrageously high deficit inherited from the previous administration. The resulting government cutbacks in funding to the provinces for health care had struck a nerve with the public, indeed, had become a dominant issue in the campaign. "Liar, liar" mobilized the audience's anger over the health issue. There was thunderous applause. At that moment, standing at the onstage mic was a very lonely vigil.

Things got worse in the days ahead. A CBC video camera had captured the moment, including the blood-drained stare on my face, and the clip was aired repeatedly, not only in the next day's news bulletins but for the rest of the campaign whenever a promo for election night coverage was shown. The "liar" incident and its frequent reruns on TV helped to energize the health protest vote and had, I believe, an adverse impact on the chances of every Liberal candidate in the province. For me, and for my fellow Newfoundland MPs, election night counts told the tale as our massive Liberal margins of previous campaigns shrunk dramatically.

Did I think the "liar, liar" intervention was unfair? Of course. I had the facts to refute the charge. But no one was listening. Reasonable politics is an oxymoron. Political fortunes can turn on a dime. "Liar, liar" was my dime.

It was all downhill after that. The incident telegraphed that I was vulnerable in what was considered a safe Liberal seat. In the previous election, four years earlier, I had garnered seventy per cent of the votes cast, the fifth-highest percentage of all 1,500 candidates across Canada. It would be a very different story this time.

SHOOTING THE MESSENGER

There's a time-tested adage that says, "Four things come not back—the spoken word, the spent arrow, wasted time, the neglected opportunity." With deadly skill, I managed to trample the wisdom of that cautionary line by opening my trap when I should have clamped it shut. In a media interview soon after that game-changing night in Port aux Basques, I let go with a one-liner, "The CBC got out of the news business years ago."

Yes, the "liar" story had created a big problem for me and my campaign. But it was I who compounded the damage by trying to shoot the messenger.

You must never taunt the guy holding the mic, especially if he gets to use it on television every day. That valuable lesson was learned too late to salvage my plummeting electoral fortunes. But it was learned.

On reflection, it was my journalistic instincts, shaped during stints as a daily newspaper editor and a magazine and weekly publisher, that put the incident in its proper context. The CBC video journalist had done exactly what I would have done. Beyond the size of the crowd and the issue that drew them to the hall, there wasn't much about the event that would make it to the evening news. The "liar, liar" outburst was pure gold for the reporter. He got his story and, from his perspective, a captivating film clip to go with it.

CLOSE ONLY COUNTS IN HORSESHOES AND HAND GRENADES[191]

What turned out to be my last kick at the can, electorally speaking, wasn't the roaring success I dearly wanted it to be. I came up short. My long stint in politics was over. What an amazing experience it was! For close to a quarter of a century, I had the honour of being the voice of the best people on the planet. I am proud and grateful beyond words, and will ever be.

A week or so after the election, I attended my last caucus. Defeated incumbents and MPs who had not sought re-election were each presented with a plaque of appreciation and invited to say a few words. By the time my turn came, I had to dig deep for something that had not already been said:

> "Driving here today, as I caught a glimpse of the Peace Tower, my reaction was not regret that I will no longer be here, but pride that I have been.[192] The opportunity of representing one's fellow citizens is a unique privilege. It gives me great satisfaction that I was able to do so.
>
> "As a teenager, I ran away from home. My first night on the lam, I slept on a concrete dock. Thirty years later, I was having dinner with the Queen. On both occasions, my first thought was exactly the same: *What am I doing here?*
>
> "Each of these incidents taught me a valuable lesson which has since served me well. I commend them to you, especially new MPs. First, set a high personal standard. And two, take full advantage of every opportunity, however fleeting or unusual."

---

191 Frank Robinson (1935–), baseball player, first African-American manager of a major league team, Baseball Hall of Fame member

192 A similar sentiment is a proverb frequently attributed to American author Theodor Seuss Geisel (1904–91), pen name Dr. Seuss, but also to Gabriel García Márquez (1927–2014), Colombian writer and journalist: "Don't cry because it's over. Smile because it happened."

PART 3
Navigating the Wider World

I may not have gone where I intended to go, but
I think I have ended up where I needed to be.

— Douglas Adams, English author,
comic, and musician, 1952–2001

CHAPTER 20
NEWFIE DIPLOMAT

To say nothing, especially when speaking, is half the art of diplomacy.
— Will Durant, American writer and philosopher, 1885–1981

My electoral loss in the 1997 vote was a surprise to many. Prime Minister Chrétien called from his Shawinigan home early next morning to express his disappointment over my defeat, offer condolences, and talk about the future. He asked that I touch base with him the following week in Ottawa. Which I did.

Our get-together was, as always, cordial. Chrétien's agenda caught me off guard. He proposed several public sector positions, any of which would have allowed me a continuing role in government. While appreciative of his confidence in me, I begged off. As I took my leave, the PM's parting words alluded to a whole new possibility: "Roger, if you won't work for me in Canada, maybe you will do so outside the country."

SUMMONED TO SERVE ABROAD

Six months later, Foreign Affairs Minister Lloyd Axworthy buttonholed me at the Liberal caucus Christmas party to say, "The boss wants to put you back in harness as a foreign service officer, heading up one of our missions abroad."

In a subsequent phone call, Chrétien mentioned four possible postings, two overseas and two in the US. Meanwhile, I had entered into a consulting arrangement with Hill & Knowlton, a global public relations company. In late June 1998, I flew from Ottawa to Newfoundland on behalf of a client. As I deplaned in St. John's, a phone message summoned me back to Ottawa. The two-week orientation for new heads of mission had begun that morning. And that's how I learned I was being posted to Seattle as Canada's consul general.

The weeks leading up to my August departure for the US Pacific northwest had me juggling many balls. Winding down my consulting practice, putting the house on the market, and absorbing almost daily briefings by Foreign Affairs personnel left little time to focus on the job ahead. I did ask my soon-to-be Seattle colleagues to pre-arrange a few courtesy meetings with key business, political, and academic leaders so I could hit the ground running.

Because of my long involvement as a Liberal Party politician, I wanted to send early signals of my determination to be scrupulously non-partisan. I saw to it that my day-to-day mix of activities reflected my new sanitized status. For example, a meeting with a Democratic office-holder would need to be balanced with a call on a Republican. In that spirit, I hit pay dirt on my first two outings.

GETTING ACQUAINTED

Ralph Munro is the quintessential class act. And a gentleman. And a visionary. I could go on. Other descriptors are equally apt: mischievous, loyal, generous, affable.

It was my good fortune to make his acquaintance soon after my arrival in Seattle. Indeed, he was the very first dignitary on whom I called in my capacity as Canada's representative in the US Pacific northwest. When we met, in his Olympia office in the state capitol, he had been Washington's secretary of state for close to twenty years. A moderate Republican, his collegial, egalitarian demeanour endears him to people in all walks of life, irrespective of political stripe or ideology.

Ralph's impressive knowledge of Canada helped pave the way to a productive working relationship between us and a great, enduring friendship. I quickly found I could rely on him for sound strategic advice and for helpful analysis on a wide range of issues. The ultimate networker, he opened many doors for me in the interests of cementing the Canada-US bond. And there were countless invitations to his home, where the hospitality was always top-shelf and fattening and the mix of guests eclectic and stimulating. Later, when I was handing out citations to persons who had excelled in promoting the Canada-US relationship, Ralph's name came quickly to mind.[193]

193 Go to smashedbrick.com to see names of Companions of the Order of the Smashed Brick.

BIRDS OF A FEATHER

Congressman Jim McDermott's office was just around the corner from the Consulate[194], and a brief get-acquainted session with the seasoned[195] Democrat was confirmed. The meeting did not go well at first. McDermott seemed distracted and bored as he and his staffer kept checking their watches. My newly minted diplomatic credentials were not having the expected impact, so I took a different tack: "I was an elected politician for twenty-four years."

McDermott stood up, excused his staff member, and shut the door. The scheduled fifteen-minute meeting lasted two hours as we swapped war tales from the electoral trenches. The friendship spawned that August afternoon in 1998 thrives to this day.

A member of Congress gets hundreds of guest passes for a presidential inauguration and one VIP seat for his/her spouse. Republican George W. Bush's first oath-taking in 2001 held no magic for McDermott's wife, Thérèse. Jim graciously decided that I should get the VIP treatment, so I was delighted to take in both of Dubya's inaugurations. When Thérèse decided to attend the first Obama inauguration, she pulled rank and got the front-row VIP seat. I had to settle for one a dozen rows from the podium.

VALUED MENTOR, RELIABLE FRIEND

Going from elective politics to diplomacy can be a steep learning curve. While many of the required skills are similar, success or failure as an interloper in the foreign service rides on other factors. Career diplomats do not, generally speaking, take kindly to the arrival in their midst of an outsider, especially a former politician.

All too often, it is the newcomer who creates problems for him/herself by strutting, or treating the posting as a sinecure. Occasionally, the career diplomat decides to make life difficult for a political appointee, and, in a recent case, the career foreign service officer didn't let up until his nemesis, the outsider head of mission, had been run out of town or, to phrase it more diplomatically, had been posted elsewhere.

I was fortunate. Robert Poetschke, the quintessential foreign service officer, is a dream. With a doctorate in history, thirty years as a career diplomat, and an enviable imperturbability, Poetschke had been, in effect, my im-

194 Canada's Seattle mission is a Consulate General, which means it offers the full range of programs and services, in effect, an embassy not located in the host country's national capital. The term Consulate connotes a mission which provides some but not all of the services. The Anchorage, AK, Consulate opened during my tenure as consul general and, on my recommendation, functioned as a branch office of the Seattle mission. Notwithstanding, the term Consulate is routinely used to reference a Consulate General, as you will note in these pages.

195 Congressman McDermott, a medical doctor and Vietnam veteran, served twenty-eight years as a US Representative, until 2017, having been elected to his fourteenth term in 2014.

mediate predecessor. When the previous consul general, the respected Tom Boehm, died in office several months prior to my arrival, Robert assumed responsibility as acting head of mission or, in the enigmatic jargon of the diplomatic world, *chargé d'affaires ad interim*.

A prince of a man, Poetschke quickly became my mentor and trusted friend. He deserves much of the credit for the relative ease with which I was able to shoehorn into my new role. We worked together for four years. When he was reassigned to Ottawa, he left a big vacuum. I sorely missed his wise counsel and valued camaraderie.

O CANADA!

Representing Canada abroad has got to be just about the best job there is. That is especially true if you are posted to the US west coast. There is a long-standing love affair between the peoples of western Canada and the American northwest. They see themselves as a transboundary regional entity dubbed Cascadia. Like Europe's Basques and the Kurds of Iran, Iraq, Syria, and Turkey, Cascadians share a value set, a community, and a world view. Unlike these others, there is no political agenda, just a desire to do business and to intermingle socially without the impediment of counterproductive cross-border constraints.

A necessary element of being a Canadian diplomat is keeping abreast of issues back home, especially those that impact relations with the country in which the diplomat is posted. If the assignment is next door in the US, staying up to speed is relatively easy. In Seattle, I had access to Canadian television plus frequent cultural, academic, parliamentary, and business delegations from Canada and regular occasion to slip back into the country for speeches, bilateral meetings, and downtime.

I got far more invites than I could handle to address Canadian service clubs, chambers of commerce, and cross-border fora, or to visit manufacturing plants and resource extraction venues. I devoted a good slice of my time to such activities. If your job is to sell Canada abroad, you must know what you're selling.

My ready access to American officialdom kept me up to speed on emerging issues and in touch with policy-makers. Such intelligence and proximity were key to the Consulate's mandate to represent Canada's interests in the US Pacific northwest, including ongoing liaisons with its congressional delegations, the senators, and House members who represent the region in Washington, DC.

I always jumped at the chance to take the pulse of mainstream America, to mingle with ordinary folks, and get a sense of their concerns, their knowledge, and awareness of Canada. I drew on a practice from my political days, asking my staff to build a meet-the-people activity into every out-of-town trip.

From salmon catchers in Newport, OR, to furniture makers in Ferndale, WA, to Alaska's Prudhoe Bay offshore oil workers, I acquired a sense of what makes Americans tick and gained an appreciation of the dynamics of the US economy.

Seattle, 1999. At the World Trade Organization (WTO) meeting. L-R: Me, Pierre Pettigrew, Minister of International Trade, and Sergio Marchi, Ambassador to the WTO. (Author photo)

Seattle, 2002. With (L-R) Seattle City Councillor Martha Choe, US Senator Maria Cantwell (D-WA), MP Sophia Leung (L-Vancouver Kingsway), and Jeff Morris (D-40th District, WA). (Author photo)

Vancouver, 2002. L-R: US Consul General Hugo Llorens, Vancouver, me, and US Ambassador to Canada Paul Cellucci. (Author photo)

Calgary, 2000. L-R: Idaho's Governor Dirk Kempthorne, Consul General Roger Simmons, Ralph Klein, Premier of Alberta. (Author photo)

A STITCH IN TIME

I had barely landed in Seattle before my embryonic diplomatic skills were put to the test. News reports and the information feed from Foreign Affairs in Ottawa alerted me to a fast-developing border confrontation. In violation of NAFTA and WTO provisions, North Dakota, South Dakota, and Montana had placed restrictions on imports of livestock and grain from Canada, citing health safety concerns. Canada believed the real reason was to protect market share for US farmers who were plagued by oversupply and low prices. Montana and North Dakota farmers were blocking trucks from Canada carrying cattle, hogs, and grain from crossing the border.

My approach to problem solving is proactive. Wherever possible, I try to deal with a small issue before it mushrooms into a bigger one. I surmised that the border incidents would soon be replicated in Idaho. So, off to Boise we went, Robert Poetschke and me, to see the governor. Phil Batt was winding down his term in the top job. He received us cordially in the presence of a dozen officials, including his director of Agriculture, Pat Takasugi, who confirmed that the Idaho cattle fraternity was gearing up to join the border blockade. Poetschke and I spelled out the Canadian position. Governor Batt, an onion farmer, was sympathetic to our concerns. Thanks to him and our timely intervention, Idaho farmers refrained from border protests. Of course, the larger supply and pricing problem took much longer to resolve.

CRUISING DOWN THE RIVER

I paid a courtesy call on Washington Governor Gary Locke[196] soon after my arrival on the Pacific coast. It would be the first of many visits to his Olympia office. The most memorable time I spent with Locke was during a cruise down the Columbia River. The governor and his cabinet were touring eastern Washington, and he kindly invited me to join them. It was an enjoyable and informative three days.

There was a steady stream of Canadian politicians coming my way, and most of them needed a little face time with the governor. Premier Mike Harris of Ontario, Alberta's Ralph Klein, and BC's Gordon Campbell came calling, as did several Ottawa ministers. Provincial ministers also dropped by, as well as municipal politicians from St. John's, Fort McMurray, and Prince George.

A MAN OF FEW WORDS

John Kitzhaber extended his hand in greeting, smiling on cue. The Oregon governor was in his usual uniform, sports jacket and open shirt, tight jeans and cowboy boots. Alberta Premier Ralph Klein and I had come to do a little business. I had given Klein a heads-up on what to expect. In initial encounters with a stranger, Kitzhaber can be a man of few words. At such times, it's hard to engage him, to determine his position, or get a commitment.

Today would be such a time. Preliminaries over, Klein went through his agenda, item by item. The governor uttered the occasional, all but in-

196 Locke, the only Chinese-American to serve as a state governor, joined the Obama cabinet in 2009 and was US ambassador to China, 2011–2014.

audible "um" or nodded and didn't show his hand on any of the matters raised. The painfully useless session was winding down, and we all stood to shake hands.

I decided it was time for a Hail Mary. Both men had well-earned reputations as avid sports fishermen, and the governor had previously shown me his impressive array of salmon flies, every last one of which, he was proud to say, he had tied himself.

"Governor," I interjected, "the premier might enjoy seeing your salmon flies."

Kitzhaber was transformed. Someone had finally raised a subject which interested him. Retrieving his handiwork from a cabinet, the erstwhile mono-syllabist launched into an oration on the joys of fly tying, ending by inviting Klein to choose a couple of flies for later use on the river.

The premier and I left the governor tidying up his precious collection. Neither of us had a clue where Kitzhaber stood on several bilateral issues, but we had laid bare his Achilles heel, which would reap dividends for Klein and, even more so, for me in future encounters with the governor, whether on Alberta's oil sands, Pacific salmon quotas, softwood lumber, or Saskatchewan potash. At Governor Kitzhaber's second swearing-in, I was a guest, and, during the inaugural ball, he swung by my table two or three times to chat. It was the Salvation Army's William Booth who said, "The way to a hungry man's soul is through his stomach." If you can discern a person's passions, the rest is doable, sometimes a piece of cake.

THE CASE OF THE RELUCTANT GOVERNOR

The coverage area of the Canadian Consulate at Seattle comprises the states of Alaska, Idaho, Oregon, and Washington. An early priority was to make courtesy calls on each of the four state governors. Within weeks of my arrival, I had met three of them. The fourth, Tony Knowles of Alaska, was a bit elusive. Each approach to his office staff came up empty. He was busy; he was out of town. Our suspicion that we were being stonewalled gained credence as I was walking from the Alaska state capitol to my Juneau hotel. Knowles drove by, the very governor who was out of town, according to information from his staff just two hours previously.

A Seattle friend with good access to the governor's office interceded for me and determined that a senior staffer had resolved that Knowles "would not be embarrassed by Canadians a second time." The first occasion, according to my source, occurred after a meeting some months earlier with then BC premier Glen Clark. I was told that, with Governor Knowles standing beside him, the premier had taken a decidedly confrontational approach during the media scrum.

Now that we knew what the problem was, we just had to find a way to fix it. The opportunity came soon afterwards. In the absence of Canada's consul general responsible for Wyoming, I was asked by Ottawa to pinch hit at the National Governors' Conference in Jackson Hole. At the pre-dinner reception, I spotted Governor Knowles and introduced myself. His body language screamed that Canada was not his favourite word, and he quickly moved on to the next handshake.

As my good friend Mike Harcourt[197] would say, it was time for Plan B. I was aware that each governor would host a dinner table and that, otherwise, it would be open seating. I entered the dinner venue, still empty but for a hotel staffer or two, and determined where the Alaska governor and his wife would be sitting. I neatly printed my name on a place card, switched it with hers, and assigned the next seat to her.

I spent much of the dinner chatting up Susan, a delightful, worldly-wise conversationalist. Every time the governor wanted to speak to his wife, he had to talk past me. By evening's end, Susan and I had bonded and she was telling her husband he should invite "this nice man" to an upcoming Anchorage event. He did, and I went. It was but the first of many such invitations from my new friend, the Governor of Alaska.

Coming between husband and wife is a dicey diplomatic ploy and one not mentioned in the briefing books. Clearly, it is justifiable only if it's in Canada's national interest!

ALASKAN HOSPITALITY

US Senator Frank Murkowski succeeded Tony Knowles as Alaska's head of state in December 2002. After the inaugural formalities were over, Governor Murkowski invited me to celebrate with family members, Republican Party strategists, and key supporters. His gem of a wife, Nancy, took a Horizon Air executive and me on a delightful room-by-room tour of the historic twenty-six-room mansion. All too soon, it was time to catch my plane to Seattle, but the wintry weather was iffy. Standing in the doorway, the governor's parting words to me as I boarded the taxi were, "If you don't make it out, come back for the night." The marvellous Murkowski hospitality was always on offer. On that occasion, though, I didn't need to accept. I was back in Seattle by bedtime.

---

197 Premier of British Columbia, 1991–96. In 2002, Harcourt suffered a near-fatal fall which resulted in a severe spinal cord injury. His astonishing recovery is chronicled in his brilliant book, *Plan B: One Man's Journey from Tragedy to Triumph.*

FRIENDS IN HIGH PLACES

It was the rainy season in Seattle. My first few months in the city were miserable, weather-wise, especially from October on. For a record sixty-nine days straight, there was precipitation.

The opportunity to escape the foul weather couldn't have come at a better time. A trip to Boise was just the therapy I needed. Indeed, it was only after landing in the state capital that I realized just how recuperative the visit could be.

Not only did I put distance between me and the Seattle doldrums, I was in the midst of a no-holds-barred, statewide celebration. US Senator Dirk Kempthorne[198] had been elected governor, succeeding Phil Batt, and was about to take the oath of office. I had been invited to join the festivities.

Activities got under way with an early-morning church service. The governor-elect's family and key advisors were there and practically nobody else. Except me. I felt like I stuck out like a sore thumb and began to wonder if, maybe, I had unwittingly intruded on a private moment. My apprehension was short-lived. A couple of friendly types took me under their wing. Obviously pleased that the Canadian consul general had elected to share their thanksgiving, my new-found acquaintances gave me the red-carpet treatment over the next three days and showered me with invitations that kept me busy, happy, and sleep-deprived.

Following the church service, I met several of the key players who would be my Idaho contacts during the subsequent five years on files ranging from academe to trade to border issues to agriculture. The several friendships that got kick-started that day and during my earlier meeting with Governor Batt are among the fondest of my entire tour of duty in the American Pacific northwest.

Governor Kempthorne and his outgoing and savvy bride, Pat, never missed an opportunity to identify with Canada or to show us great hospitality and warmth. When I arranged for Newfoundland's Alan Doyle and his Great Big Sea band to headline the annual Boise River Festival, the Kempthornes joined me in the front row. When the governor flew north to Coeur d'Alene in the government's Beechcraft King Air, I was invited along. When the local hockey team squared off against visiting Portland, OR, two Consulate colleagues and I sat in the bleachers as Kempthorne's guests. He asked me for which team I would be cheering. I replied, "Does it matter? Most of the players are Canadian anyway!"

The governor and I spoke at an economic conference. A county commissioner named Roger Simmons was also in the room. From the podium,

198 Former mayor of Boise, ID, Kempthorne was a US senator. Following two terms as Idaho governor, he was Secretary of the Interior during George W. Bush's second administration.

Kempthorne deadpanned, "I was going to ask the commissioner to sit with the consul general and me, but Roger would have been beside himself!"

Boise, ID, 1999. Hockey night in Idaho! L-R: Governor (later US Secretary of the Interior) Dirk Kempthorne, me, and two colleagues, Trade Commissioner Rod Johnson and Immigration Consul Brian Springgay. (Author photo)

HOBNOBBING WITH DEMOCRATS

Al Gore came to town in early September 1998, a month or so after my arrival in Seattle. I got wind of the vice-president's visit just two days in advance. He and western Washington's Democratic contingent in DC were scheduled to hold a by-invitation-only forum on salmon. That told me that King County's who's who would be in the room, and I decided that I had to be there, too. The consulate general's PR lady, the intense, highly skilled, results-oriented Deborah Daoust, pooh-poohed the idea as an impossibility until she got the message that her new colleague didn't see throwing in the towel as a winning strategy. Deborah made a call to Governor Locke's office and got me invited.

Of the 200 people in the room, I had previously met only two, Congressman Jim McDermott and Senator Patty Murray. The first-term, "soccer mom" senator gave me a friendly wave from the dais where she and other congressional representatives were making the best of the delay in the VP's arrival. Her gesture prompted Congressman Norm Dicks to lean over and ask who I was and, probably, what I was doing in the room. Jim McDermott strolled down to shake my hand and kill some time. When he returned to the platform, Dicks whispered in his ear, and both congressmen headed my way. This was the jackpot! My office had been trying, without success, to arrange a session with Dicks. He and I agreed to meet at his Tacoma office the following day. That meeting would turn out to be much more than a courtesy call.

The bonus effect of the Murray, McDermott, and Dicks gestures was that nearby attendees began to introduce themselves to me. Why not? For all they knew, I could have been a candidate-in-waiting or a lobbyist with policy ideas and deep pockets. As the session broke up, I was approached by other Democratic fixers and office-holders. I came away with a pocketful of business cards, several lunch dates, two speech requests, and an invitation to go fishing.

SERVICE ABOVE SELF

When I first met Washington state's secretary of state, Ralph Munro, he recommended that I join Seattle Rotary 4, the world's largest Rotary Club and, as the name implies, the fourth-oldest after Chicago, San Francisco, and Oakland. He offered to sponsor me. After a few days mulling it over, I decided against it. The club's massive size, more than 700 members, suggested it could be nothing more than an impersonal, unwieldy circus and a waste of time, though I kept my thoughts to myself.

Some weeks later, Ralph reissued the invitation, and I gladly accepted. I was ready to admit how wrong my initial assessment had been, because by then I was beginning to appreciate Seattle 4's deep roots in the community, its pivotal role in the Boys and Girls Club, public television infrastructure, and a mind-boggling array of other contributions to quality-of-life initiatives. In time, I would also come to admire Seattle 4's international outreach, from polio vaccinations in Africa to education in China to food for North Korean children. I wanted to be part of the action.

With Ralph and the inimitable Anne Farrell as my sponsors, I joined Rotary. As I became active with committees and projects, insofar as my frenetic travel schedule allowed, I came to see the wisdom of Rotary membership from yet another perspective. It was a networking opportunity par excellence. Where else could I find in the one room every week many of the people I needed to know? Meetings with key players at Boeing, Starbucks, and other corporate giants no longer required painstaking legwork to find openings in their busy calendars. All that was needed was a brief face-to-face exchange at Rotary and my item of business was resolved or, at the very least, advanced. The secret was to arrive early at the lunch venue and leave late. More issues get resolved in Seattle 4 corridor chats than weeks of pre-scheduled meetings could ever hope to achieve.

Rotary's Seattle 4 enjoys another big plus. Its huge captive audience makes an invitation to address the club easy to accept. During my time, we heard from UN Secretary-General Kofi Annan, Nelson Mandela, Bishop Tutu, and several Clinton and George W. Bush cabinet members. Two of the speakers came at my initiative, the indefatigable Rick Hansen, Canada's paraplegic Man in Motion, and US war hero Lanier Phillips, whose remarkable story of redemption is recounted elsewhere in these pages.

A SALMON DEAL

The US and Canada signed the Pacific Salmon Treaty in 1985. An annex to the agreement stipulated annual catch quotas for each country until 1992. Since that time, a bilateral Pacific Salmon Commission had been trying, without much progress, to agree on quotas for succeeding years. By 1998, the talks had languished for six years. Prime Minister Chrétien had instructed me to pay attention to the commission's deliberations to see what options there may be to break the logjam.

I attended my first meeting of the commission at Portland, Oregon, in September 1998. Contrary to the seating protocol and for a reason, I positioned myself directly behind the two Alaska members of the panel. Within minutes, some body language that told me volumes caught my eye. I stored the information for future reference. A month or so later, the committee met again, this time in Vancouver, and, as at Portland, I took a seat just behind the two-man Alaska delegation. As Newfoundland fisherman and armchair expert Art Wicks used to say on a radio talk show, unwittingly recycling a Yogi Berra non sequitur, it was like déjà vu all over again!

The proactive Alaskan duo offered a small concession which the Canadian negotiator welcomed. Whereupon the guys from Alaska discreetly, yet noticeably, from my vantage point, exchanged elbow nudges, as they had done under similar circumstances during the Portland meeting. I could almost hear them say, "We sucked them in again!"

The Alaskans' game plan was clear. As long as the talks continued, their fishermen could fish away to their heart's delight since there was no agreement on interim quotas. The strategy was simple: Keep the Canadians at the table. Which is precisely what the Alaskans had done for the previous six years. That night, I called Fisheries Minister David Anderson at home to give him my assessment. The minister said, "I hear we made some progress today." "Yes," I responded, "we're making some progress."

The minister picked up on the "but" in my tone and asked what I had in mind. I told him we should now beat the Alaskans at their own game: Keep them at the table while we pursued another course of action. We had to enlist the White House. Its involvement would be a clear signal to the American negotiators that the president wanted the file off the table. Congressman Norm Dicks had regaled me with stories of his close friendship with Vice-President

Gore, who regularly called from *Air Force Two* to chat. Both men had been critical of the Alaskan position at the Seattle salmon forum in September.

Minister Anderson set the wheels in motion, and with pivotal interventions by Dicks and Gore, a White House interlocutor was assigned to the file. Lloyd Cutler, a no-nonsense troubleshooter who believed in setting deadlines and meeting them, quickly became the catalyst for a successful resolution to the prolonged salmon dispute. For that, we enlisted the help of Alaska's senior senator, the volcanic Ted Stevens, chair of the powerful Senate Appropriations Committee. No reasonable salmon quota would appease the Alaskan interests. Stevens knew that the solution lay elsewhere. Money would do the trick. With a decades-old reputation for delivering the bacon, Stevens came through with near-lightning speed. The State of Alaska was compensated to acquiesce on the quota matter. By June 1999, less than two months after the White House intervention, the negotiations were successfully concluded and salmon quotas for the ensuing twelve years were put in place.

TREADING WATER ON SOFTWOOD LUMBER

The Canada-US dynamic is complex. Troubleshooting, issue management, and crisis avoidance are the daily lot of public servants both in Ottawa and on the ground in dozens of American cities. Keeping current is a never-ending challenge for a head of mission and his/her team. It is crucial that the lines of communication to senior Ottawa bureaucrats and their political masters be open, massaged, and utilized.

A case in point during my time in Seattle was the festering softwood lumber dispute. Most of the softwood lumber produced in the United States comes from private land. In Canada, most comes from public lands, and producers pay stumpage fees set by the provincial government. It is these stumpage fees which are at the heart of the dispute or, more accurately, are the subterfuge used by US producers to protect their market share and restrict lumber imports from Canada. Private woodlot owners in the US charge that the stumpage fees are artificially low and thus constitute a subsidy to Canadian lumber interests.

I asked Ottawa for a handout which would rebut the subsidy allegation. The response was a torrent of statistics and verbiage lauding Canada's sustainable harvesting practices but not a solitary syllable to defang the subsidy charges. The powerful US lobby kept pushing the issue, so I decided the Consulate would produce and circulate its own handout. Our very able political officer, Patrick Higgins, packaged the Canadian position in an attractive brochure that included a *Seattle Times* op-ed authored by former president Jimmy Carter, a Georgia woodlot owner. The leaflet became a most effective tool in getting our message across, and several thousand brochures were distributed to vested interests, universities, and the inquiring public. The icing on the cake was a call from Ottawa: Would I mind if our pamphlet was made available to other consulates throughout the US?

Seattle, 2001. I was delighted to host the House of Commons all-party standing committee on fisheries, including several of my friends and former colleagues. L-R: Peter Stoffer (NDP, NS), Tom Wappel (L, ON), John Cummins (C, BC), Rodger Cuzner (L, NS), Suzanne Tremblay (BQ, QC), James Lunney (Ind, BC), me, Georges Farrah (L, QC), Chairman Wayne Easter (L, PE), Loyola Hearn (C, NL). (Author photo)

Becher Bay, BC, 2016. With former MP Roy Cullen, centre, and former federal minister of Fisheries and Oceans, David Anderson. Our annual salmon fishing trip is always a real blast. (Author photo)

BORDER ISSUES

It was another file that had me hustling from day one. Prior to my arrival in Seattle, the US Congress had enacted legislation (IIRIRA)[199], which drastically changed the country's immigration laws. Section 110 of the act required US border personnel to "collect a record of departure for every

199 The Illegal Immigration Reform and Immigrant Responsibility Act of 1996 (often abbreviated as "IIRIRA")

alien departing the US and match the record against the record of the alien's arrival."

Canada-US border experts warned that the new measures spelled disaster for the economies of both nations. US immigration attorney Greg Boos warned that Section 110 "will cause extreme delays at already congested land and sea ports of entry. With billions of dollars in goods crossing the border each day, this congestion would have a devastating impact on US [-Canada] trade, discourage incoming tourism, and in turn have a serious impact on US jobs, communities, and the economy as a whole."

Henry Chang, a Toronto immigration lawyer, mirrored that view, which was also widely shared by US legislators representing border states and by the Canadian government.

Canadian heads of mission throughout the United States, me included, buttonholed members of Congress at every turn and hammered home the Canadian message: Get rid of Section 110. Which is what eventually happened. But by then we were all struggling to keep our heads above water in the midst of an evil, monstrous catastrophe that, by comparison, made Section 110 seem like a bedtime story, namely the 9/11 attack and the myriad aftershocks it detonated.

A VULNERABLE FORTRESS

Jennifer and I sat side by side in the left front row of Alaska Airlines business class. We were part of a planeload of dignitaries on the airline's inaugural flight to Reagan Airport in the US capital. The late congresswoman Jennifer Dunn and I had become fast friends since my first visit to her Bellevue office two years earlier. She represented Washington state's eighth district in the US Congress from 1992 to 2005. She was truly a class act. She had a keen interest in Canada and was supportive of several bilateral issues I championed with her.

The five-hour flight to Washington neared its end. The aircraft banked hard left on its final runway approach. The massive Pentagon edifice directly below seemed almost perilously close to the plane's wing tip. I expressed surprise that a commercial aircraft was permitted such proximity to America's renowned military nerve centre: "Jennifer, it's a good thing we're a friendly aircraft!"

The date was September 4, 2001. Little did we suspect that a less amiable conjunction of an aircraft and the Pentagon would occur one week later, that a dastardly plot had been masterminded to shatter the calm before us. Jennifer phoned me the day after 9/11 and recalled what I had said to her just before touchdown the previous week.

A TRUSTED BOND

Just four months into his term, US President John F. Kennedy addressed a joint session of Parliament in Ottawa. He saluted the Canada-US relationship: "What unites us is far greater than what divides us. The issues and irritants that inevitably affect all neighbours are small indeed, in comparison with the issues that we face together."[200]

The enduring bond between the two countries is a long-standing collaboration based on shared values, Fox News notwithstanding, and stretching from economics to the environment to resource management. However, it is the defence relationship which best conveys the strength of the relationship. Canada and the US are signatories to more than 200 bilateral agreements on defence co-operation.

Seattle, 2003. Celebrating Canada Day on the lawn of the Consul General's official residence overlooking Lake Washington. L-R: Me, Congressman Rick Larson (D-WA), Congressman Dr. Jim McDermott (D-WA), Fort McMurray, AB, Mayor Doug Faulkner, Congresswoman Jennifer Dunn (R-WA). Mayor Faulkner is a native of my hometown, Bishop's Falls. (Author photo)

The North American Aerospace Defense Agreement (NORAD) provides aerospace warning, air sovereignty, and defence for the two countries. It has been operative since 1958. NORAD's command post is "inside the mountain" at Colorado Springs. I went there with other diplomats and politicians, about twenty in all, in February 2002. The horrors of 9/11 were still a raw memory. The Canadian officer who briefed us pointed to the control room, visible through a clear glass partition from where we sat. He told us that, as the tragic events of September 11, 2001, unfolded, the Canadian shift

200 Ibid

quotas at a stalemate, my long involvement with fisheries and related matters made me, Prime Minister Chrétien decided, a good fit for the Seattle posting.

Partisan politics can and does play a role in such appointments. There's no doubt that it did in my case. If I hadn't been a Liberal, Prime Minister Chrétien probably would not have named me to head the Seattle mission. Equally, though, if I had been deemed incompetent, I would not have been appointed. In the same vein, a Tory prime minister deployed Neil LeBlanc[203] to Boston in 2006 and Loyola Hearn[204] to Dublin in 2010. Both are high-profile Tories. As well, both were eminently well-qualified for their diplomatic assignments.

It was politics with a vengeance that led to the abrupt termination of Stan Keyes's consul generalship at Boston. That Keyes had received a meritorious service citation from the deputy minister of the Department of Foreign Affairs the previous day was of no consequence. What mattered was that Keyes had been a Liberal cabinet minister. A political score had to be settled. The new Tory prime minister, Stephen Harper, delivered.

Canada's ambassador to the UN's Food and Agricultural Organization (FAO) in Rome suffered a similar fate in 1984. One of Brian Mulroney's early actions as prime minister was to axe Eugene Whelan just three months after he had been named to the post by the previous Liberal government. Partisan callousness and venom were the reason, not Whelan's qualifications. He had been a farmer, an influential voice in national farm organizations, and, for ten years, minister of Agriculture. Whelan's friendship with his Soviet counterpart, Mikhail Gorbachev, helped set Russia on the road to democracy. But it was another credential that shortened Whelan's days at the FAO. His political party stripe was not the same as Mulroney's.

Jean Chrétien's treatment of appointees who had been named by his predecessor was less spiteful. Mulroney's choice for Clerk of the Privy Council, Glen Shortcliff, continued in that role for several months after Chrétien became PM. Former Tory cabinet minister Benoit Bouchard, named ambassador to France just months before Chrétien took office, served out his diplomatic term and was then appointed by the new PM as chair of the Transportation Safety Board of Canada. Perrin Beatty, who had served in Mulroney's cabinet, was handed the job of president of the CBC by Chrétien.

Politics with a twist certainly drove Chrétien's posting of Kim Campbell to Los Angeles. Eminently suited to promote Canada's interests in Hollywood and to show the flag in our biggest US market, the former Tory prime minister provided a golden opportunity for her successor to be magnanimous. I

203 Nova Scotia entrepreneur, politician, diplomat
204 Newfoundland and Labrador educator, politician, diplomat

believe the PM's decision was also driven by compassion for a fellow leader who had taken the fall for Mulroney's policies and who needed a fresh start.

VOICE OF AN ANGEL

At a memorial service for a close friend, I crossed paths with a remarkable woman. Pastor Patrinell Wright was the soloist, and what a voice! Her perfect pitch, her unbelievable range, her easy confidence left the audience spellbound.

I knew immediately I had to hear that gifted songstress again and again. If her singing was moving, even seductive, the few minutes I spent with her after the service were even more so. Her infectious humility, her inclusive demeanour, her passion—what was there not to like about this vibrant human being?

Pat and I became fast friends and remain so. At my invitation, she was the featured soloist at the annual Canada Gala. I can hear her now. Her renditions of "O Canada" and "The Star-Spangled Banner" evoked thunderous applause from 1,000 patriots. Then she would pause, lean into the mic, and, in a near whisper, tunefully sing, "Bless this house, O Lord we pray. Make it safe by night and day." Her invocation in song never failed to send shivers down countless spines and tears down many a cheek. Pat and I have since shared many stages, both in Washington state and in British Columbia.

Her Total Experience Gospel Choir, which she founded over forty years ago as part of her outreach to her beloved African-American community and which she continues to lead, is internationally renowned. Three of the choir members have been finalists on TV's *American Idol*. A former choir member, composer, and tenor-baritone, Ray Dalton, performs with Macklemore, a secular rap band.

Pastor Pat Wright just keeps on going. May it long be so!

A CLASSY GUY

Herb Bridge was a latter-day Peter Pan. A passionate Harley-Davidson aficionado and biker, his motorcycling forays are legendary. And yes, he did have a few adult achievement notches in his belt. His navy career spanned more than forty years; he rose to the rank of rear admiral. Co-owner of Ben Bridge Jewellers, named for his founding father, Herb and his brother grew the firm from one to more than seventy outlets stretching from Hawaii to Minnesota until its 2000 acquisition by Warren Buffett's Berkshire Hathaway. Herb was also a dynamic Seattle civic leader and philanthropist, earning the nickname "Mr. Downtown" and numerous local and national awards.

I met Admiral Bridge through Rotary. We quickly discovered we were kindred spirits. That great friendship, spawned two decades ago, flourished until his passing in April 2018 at ninety-three years of age. Soft-spoken and self-effacing, Herb had the common touch.

When I was winding down my Seattle sojourn, Herb and his late wife, Shirley, treated me to a lavish going-away dinner party at the exclusive Columbia Tower Club, perched atop the city's tallest skyscraper. Herb was a bona fide class act and one of the many enduring friends who helped make my stay in the US Pacific northwest such an invigorating and memorable chapter of my life.

DIFFERENT NATIONAL INTERESTS

Former Massachusetts governor Paul Cellucci became the US ambassador in Ottawa in April 2001 and quickly earned a reputation for cordiality and candour. During a Toronto speech on March 25, 2003, his blunt frankness was well on display as he berated Prime Minister Chrétien and the Canadian government for its decision not to join the US "coalition of the willing" in the invasion of Iraq.

The prime minister had told the House of Commons on March 17 that, in the absence of a UN Security Council resolution mandating military action against Iraq, Canada would not participate. As polls would soon show, Chrétien had made a hefty majority of Canadians pleased and relieved by his announcement. The Americans, and in particular the US administration, were less happy. Cellucci told his Toronto audience that the United States was "disappointed and upset that Canada is not fully supporting us."

I got to know Cellucci quite well. We shared a stage or otherwise participated in a half-dozen events in Whistler, Vancouver, Blaine, WA, Calgary, and Ottawa. In his memoirs, Cellucci noted, "I was accused of meddling in Canadian affairs."[205] He's dead on. He was meddling. A diplomat's credentials are not a licence to campaign against the duly-elected government of the host country. Even the meddler himself acknowledged that, "Public diplomacy is not about hectoring or lecturing or criticizing."[206] He must have come belatedly to that conclusion. He certainly did all three when he publicly thrashed Canada's Iraq stand. If Cellucci had a message to deliver, the appropriate venue was a bilateral meeting with Canadian government officials, not a chamber of commerce luncheon or a TV studio. He overstepped his role, abused his status.

Can you imagine what an uproar there would be if our ambassador to Washington went tripping around the US telling the Americans what their policy priorities should be? Indeed, there's no need to conjecture. Just recall President Johnson's tantrum after Lester Pearson had expressed his views on the Vietnam quagmire.

---

205 *Unquiet Diplomacy*, Paul Cellucci, Toronto: Key Porter Books, 2005, p. 118
206 Ibid, p. 219

MARCHING TO A DIFFERENT DRUMMER

Nine days after President Bush had actioned his Iraq plans, I was in Washington, DC, and decided to call a US Foreign Service friend at the National Security Council (NSC). He suggested we get together, and judging by the urgency in his voice, I surmised he had something more on his mind than a chat for old time's sake. I was right. As soon as we had settled in for lunch at the Bombay Club, a block from the White House, he started talking: "The [Canada-US] relationship has hit a bump. The White House is really ticked at Canada's position on the Iraq war. . . . Ambassador Cellucci was conveying a message from the top."

My NSC interlocutor cited recent anti-American swipes by Canadian public figures. The PM's director of communications, Francine Ducros, in an unguarded moment, had been overheard calling Bush a moron. Canada's Energy minister, Herb Dhaliwal, said the US president was "not being a statesman." And MP Carolyn Parrish publicly lambasted the Americans. My NSC friend disclosed that, "The White House expected swift discipline in all cases and interpreted the PM's handling of the incidents as condoning the message. In that context, Chrétien's 'unjustified war' comment was the straw that broke the camel's back. The White House was furious and decided to send a shot across the bow." My contact said he could foresee fallout. "While the administration won't be gunning for Canada, there will be adverse ripple effects."

He drew a distinction between the Canadian and the French positions. The reaction against the French was visceral among Americans. French wines were boycotted. French fries became revisionist freedom fries. "We'll buy our brie from Quebec, but not from France." The decision by France not to join the "coalition of the willing" spawned a raft of mean one-liners. Example: Why are there so many trees on the Champs Élysées? It's a good place for the French army to hide!

Soon after my NSC meeting, I met with our ambassador, Michael Kergin, in his Pennsylvania Avenue office, and briefed him on my illuminating session with my NSC friend.

SPEAKING TRUTH TO POWER

While on the US east coast, I fulfilled a long-standing invitation to address the law faculty at West Point, the famed US military academy. The earful I got from the NSC official had me praying for a natural disaster or some other airtight justification to rescue me from what would surely be a trial by fire at West Point, less than two weeks after Chrétien's announcement and four days after Cellucci's dressing-down. In the absence of a miraculous deliverance from my fate, I proceeded to West Point.

Military Professor Margaret Stock, a lawyer friend who hailed from Alaska, was my host. Over dinner with her husband and son, Margaret said that my audience would expect a rationale for Canada's decision against participation in the Iraq war. Next day, during my speech, I referenced Newfoundland's World War I situation when the then-independent country dispatched its regiment to the battlefields of Europe, three years before the US did. I told these American military officers that, on the very first day of the Battle of the Somme, the Newfoundland Regiment was decimated at Beaumont Hamel.

In 1999, I had participated in an event at Tacoma, Washington, marking the anniversary of D-Day, June 6, 1945. My stepdaughter Holly drew my attention to the inscription on a monument: WORLD WAR II, 1941–1945.

"Roger, they've got the dates wrong."

Eleven-year-old Holly, having been schooled in Canada, understood the war dates to be 1939–1945. I explained to her that 1941 was the year of America's entry as a World War II combatant and suggested that she note the inscription on an adjacent monument: WORLD WAR I, 1917–1918. Here also, of course, were the dates of US participation in the war, not its 1914–1918 duration. In my West Point speech, I recounted that incident, noting that, "The country[207] of my birth knows, first-hand, what it feels like to have its youth die in battle while a close neighbour sits on the sidelines.

"What have I just said? That your president and your military leadership were slackers not to enter those global conflicts until 1917 and 1941, respectively? No, I submit that in 1914 and 1939, the US opted against armed engagement because it was judged to be the decision which best served the US national interest at those times. The 1917 and 1941 entries into conflict by the US were done, I believe, for exactly the same reasons. Would you deny to another sovereign country, Canada, the prerogative to take military decisions which it deems to be in its national interests?"

The colonels and other assembled brass responded to my words with a standing ovation and rose a second time at the end of my speech. Their reception encouraged me to seek other military audiences. Subsequent speeches on Canada's Iraq position at a NORAD dinner in Anchorage and at a US Navy League event in Seattle also generated standing ovations. Nor do I think it was the brilliance of my oratory that brought these audiences to their feet. Rather, my listeners had finally heard a plausible rationale for what had been to them an inexplicable, even indefensible, act by Canada in sitting out the Iraq war.

Commander Arnie Lucsis of the US Navy attended the Seattle speech and critiqued it as follows in an email to colleagues:

207 Newfoundland was independent until it joined Canada in 1949.

> Consul General Simmons' comments about the recent diplomatic and geopolitical aspects of the American-Canadian relationship were a good reminder that friendship among close friends, allies and neighbours doesn't necessarily mean agreement on everything.
>
> As you recall, there were lots of senior active duty personnel present the other night including several freshly returned members of the Lincoln battlegroup. Simmons' point—though history, geography and circumstances have made us friends, we each must remember that we must do ultimately what is in our best interests as sovereign nations—was not lost on this crowd.
>
> No one seemed perturbed at his comments, and indeed, I think a lot of us found them a worthwhile and refreshing reminder of a different and valued perspective. His candor, knowledge and graciousness were much appreciated . . . not to mention the funny Newfoundland stories.

Soon after, the Seattle chapter of the US Navy League made me an honorary member and appointed me to its advisory board, the only non-American in that position.

As I was winding down my tour of duty at Seattle, my Rotary Club asked me to address the regular Wednesday lunch meeting. The audience that day had more than its share of small-government disciples, many of whom had long since bought into the stereotype of Canada as a socialist laboratory gone mad. So, for sheer fun, sprinkled with a healthy dose of mischief, I unloaded a one-liner:

"I relish the unmitigated joy of watching my Blue Jays beat your Mariners at Safeco Field, clear proof that unfettered free enterprise can sometimes triumph over massive government intervention!"

The roomful of free market zealots exploded in prolonged applause, acknowledging the blatant contradiction implicit in their economic dogma and taxpayer-funded sports palaces, a phenomenon that is standard practice throughout the US.

During my Seattle years, other speeches afforded me the opportunity to put the case for Canada. I gave a keynote address at Microsoft's annual Government Leaders' Conference, which brings together heads of government and senior ministers from around the world. The annual get-together of AILA, the American Immigration Lawyers' Association, which I addressed twice, in Chicago and Toronto, was a particularly receptive audience because of its many concerns over US immigration policy. Energy events in Anchorage, Houston, and Phoenix, a seminar on Canadian building technologies in Portland, OR, and a speech to the Daughters of the American Revolution in Lake City, WA, were all tailor-made occasions for getting out the Canadian message. In my five-year stint as consul general, I delivered over 600 speeches at service club lunch venues, university lecture theatres, and corporate and organizational AGMs.

A couple years after my return to Canada, I was once again in front of my favourite audience, my many friends at Seattle 4. I used my bully pulpit to salute the durability and strength of the Canada-US bond, but also to give voice to trade and border irritants and to lament President Bush's my-way-or-the-highway template. I told the audience of 600 corporate and civic leaders, "Sometimes, it appears the dismantling of the FDR-George Marshall mantra of multilateralism and compassion is in full gear."

A decade after I made that speech, along came the current White House occupant, a man who can hardly spell multilateralism or compassion, let alone appreciate or champion either. Donald Trump's withdrawal from the Paris climate accord and the Iran nuclear deal, his trashing of the Trans-Pacific Partnership, and his on-again-off-again disdain for NAFTA are not reassuring. His demonization of Mexicans as rapists and murderers, his stingy response to Puerto Rico after Hurricane Harvey, and his shameful DACA[208] rhetoric make me wonder whether he has all his marbles.

Fake reality, the quintessential oxymoron, is, sad to say, fast becoming the hallmark of the US presidency.

Vancouver, 2003. With the Honourable Lloyd Axworthy, former minister of Foreign Affairs, Canada, and Madeleine Albright, former US Secretary of State. (Author photo)

208 Deferred Action for Childhood Arrivals (DACA) is a Barack Obama US immigration program that allows some persons who arrived in America illegally as children to delay deportation and qualify for a work permit.

CHAPTER 21
SIDEKICK TO A MAN OF VALOUR

O for the touch of a vanish'd hand
And the sound of a voice that is still!
— ALFRED LORD TENNYSON

In addition to my intervention on behalf of Major Sarah Woodland, on only one other occasion have I been presumptuous enough to propose a candidate for an honorary degree. Memorial's president, Axel Meisen, came to my Seattle office in 2003. I suggested that he consider a man whose contribution to Newfoundland, to Canada-US relations, and to racial harmony was immeasurable, Lanier Phillips.

There is a certain symmetry in my two choices: a woman and a man; one Caucasian, the other African-American; one Canadian, the other American. However, singling out these two persons was not about political correctness or balance. Rather, it was their amazing impact on others.

Though Sarah Woodland and Lanier Phillips were contemporaries, they were nurtured in vastly different worlds. Yet both wielded influence in the same arena, Newfoundland, and heralded the same message of love, forgiveness, and transformation. Both triumphed in spades. We are the better because of the spiritual trails blazed by two illustrious honorary graduates of my great alma mater, Memorial University: Dr. (Major) Sarah Woodland and Dr. (Mess Attendant Third Class) Lanier Walter Phillips.

Lanier Phillips was a rare bird. Born in racist Georgia in 1923, he saw first-hand the terror of the Ku Klux Klan and was taught by his great-grandmother to fear white people: "Never look a white man in the eye. If you do, you'll get whipped or, maybe, lynched."

To escape the segregated south, Lanier joined the US Navy when America entered the Second World War in 1941 and was assigned to the USS *Truxtun*, a destroyer. Lanier was a mess attendant third class, the only aboard-ship position he was permitted to fill as an African-American. Washing dishes, polishing officers' boots, and doing other such menial tasks were his daily lot. He and the other four black men in the crew took their meals standing up since the dining mess was the exclusive domain of white men.

In mid-February 1942, the *Truxtun* and two other vessels, the *Wilkes*, also a destroyer, and the *Pollux*, a supply ship, sailed from Portland, Maine, destined for a US naval station at Argentia, Newfoundland. As they approached land in a severe storm, confusion and uncertainty reigned concerning the true locations of the three warships. Misinformation, wrong assumptions, indecision, and pigheadedness were among the causes. The consequences were catastrophic as all three vessels rammed the Newfoundland coast and two of them broke up in the heavy seas. Two hundred and three young Americans died in the icy North Atlantic that awful night, literally feet from safety. The good news is that 185 sailors did survive, saved by St. Lawrence miners and the men of Lawn, two small communities on Newfoundland's south coast.

WHEN HE SAW HIM, HE HAD COMPASSION ON HIM[209]

Lanier Phillips was the only black man to survive. The other four perished following what was literally a life-and-death decision. Thinking they had gone aground in Iceland and knowing that the US government had agreed that blacks would not be allowed ashore in that country, the five men contemplated a stark choice, whether to go ashore and risk being lynched or stay aboard and face almost certain death by exposure. Only Lanier opted to take his chances ashore.

As he landed on the narrow rock ledge underneath a forbidding cliff, fatigue and sub-zero weather were taking their toll, physically and mentally. Lanier recalled the moment: "I decided to die!" Other people had a better plan. As Lanier lay in a fetal position on the beach, he heard a voice above him. "Get that man up! He'll surely die there." Lanier caught a glimpse of the two men standing over him. Something truly staggering flashed across his mind.

A white man wants me to live!

With the help of the two strangers, Lanier made it up the precipice and was taken by horse-drawn sled to a nearby mining shack.

The women of St. Lawrence had come to the mine site to help with the

209 Luke 10:33, KJV

rescue operation. Many of the *Truxtun*'s survivors were coated in oil from the ship's ruptured tanks. The local ladies scrubbed them down as they arrived in the shack. Phillips, who had lapsed into unconsciousness, recalled waking up:

> "I was lying stark naked face up on a table. Two white women were hovering over me. Maybe, I thought, they belong to some pagan tribe and are preparing to sacrifice me. At that moment, I was more terrified than when I clung to the *Truxtun* wreck. One of the two ladies spoke. 'I can't get this one clean.' That's when I opened my mouth for the first time. 'Ma'am, that's the way I was born.'"

Violet Pike and Charlotte Kelly may have understood the words Lanier said. They certainly didn't comprehend the import of his utterance, having never before seen a black man. Without missing a beat, Mrs. Pike responded, "Don't worry, my son, we're going to get you clean, supposin' we're here all night."

OUTSTRETCHED HANDS

Today, a unique and moving memorial honours the memory of the lost, the courage of the survivors, and the selflessness of their saviours. Situated in the town square at St. Lawrence, it is the work of Newfoundland sculptor Luben Boykov, who ingeniously captures the moment of rescue. A steep marble incline represents the rock face that stood between the shipwrecked and safety. At the base of the incline, a prostrate figure in navy dress extends his right hand upwards. At the top, a man with a miner's light strapped to his forehead extends his hand toward the sailor. Their extended hands nearly touch, but not quite, symbolizing both the almost unfathomable gulf that separates them and the spiritual bond that unites them.

The striking memorial is a well-known Bible story in 3-D. All the elements are in play: two men from vastly different worlds, one with a desperate need, the other able and willing to meet that need. Boykov's masterpiece is aptly titled *Echoes of Valour*. I've always thought of it as the Good Samaritan sculpture.

TRANSFORMATION

Fifty years after the *Truxtun-Pollux* tragedy, I boarded the USS *Samuel Eliot Morison* at Montreal. St. Lawrence Mayor Fabian Aylward and I embarked on a two-day voyage to Chambers Cove, where the *Truxtun* had met its end and where Lanier Phillips had chosen an uncertain future ashore over almost certain death on the doomed ship. We paused over the deteriorating wreck, which can still be seen just below the surface. Our moment of reflection over, we headed into St. Lawrence harbour to participate in a reunion of many of the survivors, their families, and their rescuers. The town hosted a celebratory event, and Lanier Phillips was the after-dinner speaker. He spoke of that long-ago day when he had been touched by a white person for the very first time in his life. He recalled how astonished he had been to be treated evenly by white people: "I asked myself, did I die and go to Heaven?" Phillips's listeners were spellbound as he recalled that momentous morning half a century before:

> "Mrs. Pike took me into her home. She tucked me into bed, heated rocks in her stove to warm my feet, and spoon-fed me soup."

And then he spoke of the jolting, bitter aftermath:

> "A US navy ship arrived at St. Lawrence to pick up the white survivors. I was told I had to wait for a freight boat. . . . A few days later, now back in the southern US, I was hungry and tried to enter a military mess. As I reached for the doorknob, a white guard knocked me to the ground with his rifle butt."

The black sailor who had just survived a watery grave in the service of his country could only watch through the window as white men enjoyed a hearty meal. And not just any white men. The diners were German prisoners of war. In Lanier's absence from the south, and despite his transforming encounter with white people in Newfoundland, nothing had really changed. Except Lanier Phillips was a different man. At the St. Lawrence reunion, Lanier told his audience, "You people not only saved my life, you changed my life."

And changed he was. I was thoroughly captivated by his words and by the passion and sincerity with which he spoke them. Then and there, I told myself the whole world should hear his story and should hear it from him. Over the succeeding eighteen years, until I went to the Middle East in 2010, I organized events each year, with Lanier as the speaker, to coincide with the anniversary of the dramatic rescue. From San Diego, California, to Nanaimo, British Columbia, we took his message of racial equality to schools and colleges, to service clubs and editorial boards, to public meetings and broadcast audiences. We even participated in an online link between schools in Washington state and Newfoundland.

POIGNANT MOMENTS

Three memories stand out. In View Royal, near Victoria, BC, the 200 primary students who had assembled in the school library were the youngest audience Lanier had addressed, and he was concerned that he wouldn't be able to connect with them. He need not have worried. He asked rhetorically: "Should a black man have to serve a white man?"

Every five-year-old hand in the front rows shot up. I pointed to a cute little blonde girl who was bursting to respond to Lanier's question.

"Not unless he's hurt."

What is it the Book of Psalms says about "out of the mouths of babes"? The five-year-old had succinctly compressed the essence of Lanier's message into a single phrase. Human relationships ought to be catalyzed by need and compassion, not skin colour.

Montreal, 1992. The captain of the USS *Samuel Eliot Morison*, a US Navy frigate, greeted St. Lawrence Mayor Fabian Aylward, right, and me when we embarked on a memorable voyage to Chambers Cove, where Lanier Phillips was shipwrecked. (Author photo)

On Valentine's Day, 2003, Lanier addressed a public meeting at Seattle's Town Hall. As the crowd gathered, an elderly Caucasian gentleman approached Lanier and said, "I was on the *Pollux*!"

Edgar Brown, who also grew up in the US south, was an officer on the supply ship when it rammed the Newfoundland coast that fateful night sixty-one years earlier. Ensign Brown and Mess Attendant Third Class Phillips—two men, one white, one black—embraced. The years fell away, as did the bigotry of another time.

Seattle, 2002. At the annual Canada Gala. With Ensign Edgar Brown, left, USS *Pollux* survivor, and Mess Attendant Third Class Lanier Phillips, USS *Truxtun* survivor. (Author photo)

Pool's Cove, NL, 1993. L-R: Gordon Caines, Melvin Perham, Pius Fizzard, Bruce Savoury. (Author photo)

A never-to-be-forgotten moment happened in Santa Rosa, California. It was Sunday morning, and Lanier and I were standing with the pastor of a Baptist congregation in the entrance foyer of his church. Our sponsors for the California tour, Hugh and Connie Codding, were with us. As we awaited the arrival of parishioners, among the first to enter was an elderly African-American. Spotting Lanier, the man ran to him and, weeping uncontrollably, threw his arms around him and uttered words whose significance only Lanier could fully comprehend: "I was at Pearl Harbor." Decoded, the stranger's utterance had said, in effect, "I was a Mess Attendant Third Class in World War II, just like you. I know what you went through."

Lanier and I sat behind the pulpit with the pastor. A thousand people had come to church that morning. One person in particular had my attention. Sitting in the front row, that same elderly war veteran sobbed his way through the church service and Lanier's speech which followed. His name—and no, I'm not making this up—was Brother Love!

Lanier's presence had provided a measure of closure. Sixty years after Pearl Harbor, Brother Love had finally encountered someone who understood the humiliation and cruelty he had endured.

Hugh Codding. Now, there was a character! He served in World War II and was attached to a naval unit at Iwo Jima when the conflict ended. Rambunctious, larger-than-life, and savvy, he was a very wealthy business tycoon and owned a dozen shopping malls in Sonoma County, north of San Francisco.

Codding was in his mid-eighties when he and I met "down under" in a Trident nuclear submarine just off Bangor, Washington. I told him about Lanier and our annual speaking tours. Hugh invited us to come to Santa Rosa, and that's how we wound up in a southern Baptist church that memorable Sunday morning.

The previous week, Lanier and I had been in Burbank to meet with film industry people, after which we planned to take a commercial flight to San Francisco and a car to Santa Rosa. Hugh had a better idea. He sent his personal jet to Burbank, and we travelled direct to our destination in style. Yes, I sat up front with the pilot. This time, though, I had the good sense to keep my mouth zipped about my vaunted expertise at manoeuvring aircraft.

When we touched down in Santa Rosa, our pilot, CJ, drove us to the Codding mansion. Lanier and I spent the next couple of days salivating in the lap of luxury. Two old navy guys became buddies as they swapped war stories. I was impressed, awed, even, as Connie and Hugh, Caucasian both, showered affection and deference on Lanier, treating him like royalty, which he was.

BIGOTRY, ALIVE AND WELL

Lanier lived at the naval retirement facility in Gulfport, MS. It was home to hundreds of veterans. Only a handful were African-American. As Lanier and I walked the corridors, many of the white residents greeted him warmly; others shunned him. Some hugged the far wall as we passed. A white man boarded an elevator. Lanier and I followed. The white man abruptly left. My curiosity got the better of me. I exited the elevator on the next floor, raced down the stairs, and watched in disgust as the white guy boarded the elevator.

Lanier seemed never to be perturbed by such affronts. A lifetime of being on the receiving end of rank prejudice had long since taught him to bite his lip and move on. Occasionally, in response to my reactions of disbelief, he would calmly say, "They can't help it. That's the way they were reared. It's their problem, not mine!"

POWERFUL WORDS

By late 2007, no action had been taken by Memorial on my recommendation that it recognize Lanier Phillips's remarkable achievements. I decided to try one more time and mentioned my proposal to the university's chancellor, my old friend and sparring partner during the political wars, John Crosbie.

Lanier had moved to the Armed Forces Retirement Home (AFRH) in Washington, DC, after his former residence, the naval home in Mississippi, had become a casualty of Hurricane Katrina in 2005. In early 2008, on one of my frequent visits to Lanier's room, he excitedly showed me a letter from Memorial University. He would be awarded an honorary doctorate of laws and be the May convocation speaker. Crosbie had delivered yet again.

It was indeed a proud moment as I sat beside Lanier's daughter, Dr. Vonzia, his son, lawyer Terry, and daughter-in-law, Tamara, in the VIP box at the St. John's Arts and Culture Centre, the convocation venue. Lanier had been a bag of nerves in the days leading up to his convocation address. Though clear on the message he intended to deliver, he doubted whether he could measure up in front of so many academics.

Rising magnificently to the occasion, Lanier transported his listeners by his humility, humanity, and passion. He spoke for just thirteen minutes. As he finished, the 1,200-strong assemblage, faculty and dignitaries, graduands and their families, rose as one in thunderous applause, a tangible tribute to a legend whose powerful message and captivating storytelling style had electrified and inspired audiences all over North America.

FEISTY TO THE END

I had lunch with Lanier at his Washington retirement home the day after President Obama's 2009 inauguration. Age was taking its physical toll, though, with the aid of a four-point walker, Lanier was still mobile. Mentally, he was not diminished. He was the same engaged, inquisitive conversationalist I had first met nearly seventeen years earlier and, I believe, the same fighting spirit whose will to live landed him on a rocky shelf on a frigid wintry night fifty years before that. It was the last time I saw him, though we continued to connect by phone while I was on assignment in the Middle East.

Lanier spent his final years back in Gulfport, MS, at the rebuilt military retirement facility. Sadly, he passed away in March 2012, three days shy of his eighty-ninth birthday. He left us quite a legacy.

Many a sailor has been shipwrecked and lived to tell the tale. Few have been changed by the experience as thoroughly as Lanier was. Fewer still have catapulted their transformation into an irresistible plea for equality and compassion as effectively as the great-grandson of slaves, Dr. Lanier Phillips.

CHAPTER 22
BIONIC MARKETER

If you think it's expensive to hire a professional,
wait until you hire an amateur.
— Red Adair, American celebrity, 1915–2004

My Seattle posting was initially for four years. By early 2002, I was in wind-down mode. Already I had been offered the vice-presidency of a reputable BC firm and had received an overture from a western Canadian university to establish and head a centre for North American studies. And yes, my homing instinct had kicked in. Maybe, just maybe, I could find a new challenge and an income source back on the Rock. The time had come to make decisions for life after my all-too-brief interlude in the foreign service.

And then, John Manley's[210] cellphone rang. He and I had just come out of a meeting at the Olympia state capital with Governor Gary Locke and were headed back to Seattle by car. John handed me the phone: "It's the boss."

After the usual bantering, Prime Minister Chrétien popped the question: "How would you like to stay down there for another year?" "Down there" meant Seattle, of course. And I was delighted to say yes. It did require a little stickhandling in order to extricate myself from commitments predicated on my expected July departure. With that phone call and, later, a second extension, my tour of duty got stretched into more than five years.

In the spring of 2003, Foreign Minister Bill Graham summoned me to Vancouver for a chat. Would I consider staying at the Seattle post for yet another year? Flattered though I was, I had no choice but to turn thumbs down on the minister's request. I did so reluctantly.

The very special honour of representing Canada in the United States

210 MP, minister, deputy prime minister

proved to be an amazing experience, productive, immensely satisfying, and enjoyable. An additional year would have been the icing on the cake. But it wasn't to be. I had made personal and professional commitments that could not be easily unravelled.

I had spent considerable chunks of time as an entrepreneur. However, for most of my adult life I had been on the public payroll, as educator, politician, and diplomat. For the third time since my rags-to-riches undergraduate days, my main source of income would come from peddling my skills in the private sector. I dusted off the CV and rejigged it to put my best foot forward, all the while doing a bit of self-analysis: What is my marketable skill set? How do I get the attention of those who could use my services? Who would hire a recovering politician? Should I go back to consulting, as I had done with satisfying results twice before?

While pondering my potential options, the notion of a working relationship with a law firm never crossed my mind. Nonetheless, once the word got out that I would shortly be a free agent, I was approached by four Canadian law firms. Would I be interested in establishing/joining/expanding a government relations practice while doing US marketing? The two largest firms sent three-man teams to Seattle to take my measure, pitch me, and discuss terms.

They should have come a month earlier. I had just locked into a quite attractive arrangement as VP at WCG International, a Victoria, BC, enterprise. I would spearhead plans for expansion in the US and overseas. A consulting relationship was also established with one of Canada's law firms, Gowling Lafleur Henderson LLP, which took into account the WCG obligation.

HOW DULL . . . TO RUST UNBURNISHED . . .[211]

The WCG assignment was rewarding, yet frustrating. The US business plan was frequently revamped to accommodate emerging corporate realities. Other initiatives became part of my responsibilities, including pitches to the Canadian and UK governments with my good friend Roy Emperingham.

An amazing woman joined the WCG team when I did. Eloise Anderson is known internationally as a leader in public policy creation and implementation and has the distinction of having served as a cabinet member in two different US states, with Tommy Thompson in Wisconsin and Pete Wilson in California. As of January 2011, she's back at a cabinet table for a third time. Governor Scott Walker named her as secretary of Wisconsin's Department of Children and Families. An analytical type who can be passionate when

211 "Ulysses" by Alfred, Lord Tennyson, 1809–92

circumstances warrant and a conservative Republican, Eloise and I became and remain good friends. Whether at her party's convention in New York, cooling our heels at Nevada's Division of Welfare in Carson City, or having lunch in Victoria, she's always an absolute delight to be with.

Soon after we arrived at WCG, Eloise gave voice to a conundrum that had ensnared us both: "The boss is good at collecting trophies, not so good at polishing them!" Therein lay the frustration. Company management was ever on the lookout for talent to beef up its already impressive team and was successful at reeling in some of the very best. However, its focus on the next potential acquisition left little time or mind-share, it seemed, to effectively harness the skill sets of those already at the table.

As in any work environment, it's the people that make the difference, that make you float into the office in the morning or dread the thought of going there. I loved working with the folks at WCG. Their dedication, energy, and can-do attitude were invigorating. Humanity was their stock-in-trade, not a facade of pious posturing.

The tone was set from the top. Ian Ferguson is an astute businessman and a multi-tasker. He is, first and foremost, though, a man of compassion and integrity. His senior associates, including my good friend Dr. Jim Rae, brought to the team those same qualities and an impressive skill set.

Regrettably, today's WCG is but a shadow of its former self. The closely held company, Ferguson being the majority shareholder, was sold in 2008 to a Tucson firm. With the key decisions being made elsewhere, the company's fortunes took a nosedive, though it continues to fill a valuable niche in its area of service and expertise.

SETTING THE BAR HIGH

Gowlings[212] is a phenomenal organization. The firm got its start as Gowling & Henderson in 1887. In recent years, more than a dozen mergers have produced the vibrant full-service law firm we know today. I watched with admiration the successful morphing of the predecessor groups into a cohesive, productive, upbeat team. It takes a special person to spearhead an undertaking of such size and complexity. Scott Jolliffe was that special person. His leadership was key to the firm's transformation. His collegial approach, vision, and humanity helped ensure its continued pre-eminence.

In size, Gowlings is the largest or second-largest law firm in Canada, depending on the day, as professionals switch among organizations or estab-

212 Now Gowlings WLG, a sector-focused law firm with more than 1,400 legal professionals in eighteen cities around the world.

lish their own practices. But here again, it's the people, not its size or myriad areas of expertise, that make the firm such a dynamic and personable workplace. A more diverse, more high-powered team of legal trendsetters and support staff you will not find. I especially looked forward to the monthly telephone conferences of the government relations practice group, chaired by the no-nonsense, affable Henry Brown. My assignment at Gowlings took me to at least forty US cities a year, some more than once, especially the key markets, New York, Chicago, and Los Angeles.

The bonus prize during my time with Gowlings was the opportunity to get an insider view of the Canadian and US legal fraternity, to collaborate with many amazing people, and to cement several lasting friendships. James Freund is a retired New York attorney and prolific author. A day at an American Bar Association event was never quite complete until a bunch of us had gathered around the piano, drawn there by Freund's melodic mastery of the keyboard and his choice of feel-good oldies.

When Seattle's Karl Ege became chair of the ABA's Section of Business, he opted to hold its 2009 spring meeting in Vancouver. I was pleased to head up the host committee for the event, the first non-lawyer and non-American to hold that position. Twenty-five hundred lawyers from around the world attended.

My forays into the US are less frequent these days. Not to worry. CNN and MSNBC keep me up-to-the-minute on OJ sequels and United Airlines' customer service, while not neglecting the finer points of US Congressional stalemates and the latest manifestations of Donald Trump's panting egomania.

With six fabulous years at Gowlings under my belt, it was time to move on, time to tackle other endeavours, new challenges which would take me to Asia, Eastern Europe, and the Middle East. And maybe time to stir up a little more mischief!

But that's a story for another day.

ACKNOWLEDGEMENTS

Otto Tucker articulated the overall thrust of these pages. The acclaimed humour author Ed Smith flagged for me the tricks and pitfalls of being a published writer. I thank them both posthumously.

I am especially indebted to Salvation Army historian Gordon Moyles and his wife, Ada; *Seattle Times* columnist Joel Connelly; my work colleague in Baghdad, Nick le Du; former federal minister and senator Hon. David Smith; and my brother Dave, for their editorial guidance.

With thanks, I acknowledge the generous help of Bill Goulding of the federal Department of Fisheries; US immigration attorney Greg Boos; Andrea Hyde, Legislative Library, House of Assembly, St. John's; Loretta Barber, Library and Archives Canada, Ottawa; Catherine Parker, my former Ottawa PR press aide; and Joan (White) Upshall, my House of Assembly staffer; and her husband, Roy.

My sons, Paul and Mark, lent a hand wherever needed. Thanks, guys! As well, I offer my sincere thanks to the many other family members, friends, and strangers who have assisted me, as follows:

Alberta: Colin Alie, Rick Hoddinott, Sean Kealey, Doug Mitchell, Rose Poole, Cavell Simmonds, Bonnie Simmons, Jim Simmons, Robbie Simmons.

British Columbia: Sheila Cooper, Roy Emperingham, Jim Hart, Dr. Jim Rae, Don Simms, Darrel Stinson.

Manitoba: Hon. Dr. Lloyd Axworthy.

Newfoundland and Labrador: Thomasine Barry, Pat Brake, Maurice Budgell, Christina Caines, Wilson Calloway, Fran Chaytor, Glorina Drodge, Paul Drodge, Eleanor Grandy, Norm Harris, Rosemary Healey, Vera House, Don Huxter, Dean Ingram, Roger Jamieson, John and Fanny Kealey, Gwen Lomond, Bill O'Driscoll, Major Lindsay Oxford, Harold Piercey, Beatrice Pynn, Peggy Pardy, Violet Roberts, Cecil Roebothan,

Fred Rowe, Wade Rowsell, George Saunders, Roy and Jeanette Saunders, Ivan and Carol Seaward, Lloyd Seaward, Bernice Simmons, Dale and Marilyn Simmons, Valda Simmons, Scott Simmons, Gertie Short, Marion Smith, Lorne Thompson, Beaton Tulk, Joan and Roy Upshall, June Warr, Norm Whalen, Freeman White, Joe Ashley, Ken Ashley, Kim Ploughman.

Nova Scotia: Ed Tremblett.

Ontario: Stuart Barnable, Ethel Crews, Ron Marsland, Ken McKay, Herb Metcalf, Lieutenant Colonel John Murray, Lieutenant Colonel Shirley Rowsell.

Saskatchewan: Greg Ashley.

Alaska: Gail Phillips.

Georgia: Dr. Vonzia Phillips.

Idaho: Max Black, Dan and Cindi Mader.

Washington: Greg Boos, John Kucher, Ralph Munro.

Wisconsin: Eloise Anderson.

Haiti: Karen Huxter.

India: Bharti Tiwari.

Palestine: Jamal Abu Khadijeh.

As my attention turned to finding a publisher, I knew it had to be a Newfoundland company, being a strong believer in supporting the local economy. And it had to have a solid track record and an effective marketing strategy.

On all counts, Flanker Press was the easy choice. I am delighted that the firm's principals saw merit in my manuscript, and agreed to work with me. I extend a sincere thank you to the Cranfords, Garry, Margo, and Jerry. Their professionalism, thoroughness, and cordiality have made this an enjoyable interlude. Much appreciated!

Also, for their roles in the editing and the production of this book, I would like to thank Peter Hanes, Donna Morrissey, and Graham Blair.

BIBLIOGRAPHY

Birnbaum, Jeffrey. *The Lobbyists*. New York: Time Books, 1992.

Brown, Cassie. *The Caribou Disaster*. St. John's: Flanker Press, 1996.

Browne, William J. *Eighty-four Years a Newfoundlander*. St. John's: Dicks & Co., 1981.

Carter, Walter. *Never a Dull Moment*. St. John's: Creative Publishers, 1998.

Cellucci, Paul. *Unquiet Diplomacy*. Toronto: Key Porter Books, 2005.

Chandrasekaran, Rajiv. *Imperial Life in the Emerald City: Inside Iraq's Green Zone*. New York: Alfred A. Knopf, 2006.

Chrétien, Jean. *My Years as Prime Minister*. Toronto: Knopf Canada, 2007.

Clark, Joe. *A Nation Too Good to Lose*. Toronto: Key Porter Books, 1994.

Clarkson, Stephen & Christina McCall. *Trudeau & Our Times, Vol 1 & 2*. Toronto: McLelland & Stewart, 1990 & 1994.

Crosbie, John. *No Holds Barred: My Life in Politics*. Toronto: McLelland & Stewart, 1997.

DeFede, Jim. *The Day the World Came to Town*. Toronto: HarperCollins, 2002.

Eisler, Dale. *False Expectations*. Regina: University of Regina, 2006.

English, John. *Just Watch Me*. Toronto: Vintage Canada, 2009.

Forsey, Helen. *Eugene Forsey, Canada's Maverick Sage*. Toronto: Dundurn, 2012.

Goldenberg, Eddie. *The Way It Works*. Toronto: McLelland & Stewart, 2006.

Gwyn, Richard. *Smallwood, The Unlikely Revolutionary*. Toronto: McClelland & Stewart, 1968.

Heilemann, John & Mark Halerin. *Game Change*. New York: HarperCollins, 2010.

Hillier, Rick. *Leadership*. Toronto: HarperCollins, 2010.

Horwood, Harold. *Joey: The Life & Times of Joey Smallwood*. Stoddart, 1989.

Hoy, Claire. *Clyde Wells: A Political Biography*. Toronto: Stoddart, 1992.

Ingstad, Helge & Anne Stine Ingstad. *The Norse Discovery of America*. Oslo: Norwegian University Press, 1985.

Jamieson, Don. *No Place For Fools*. St. John's: Breakwater Books, 1989.

Jeffrey, Brook. *Divided Loyalties*. Toronto: University of Toronto Press, 2010.

Johnston, Donald. *Up the Hill*. Montreal: Optimum Publishing, 1986.

Martin, Lawrence. *Iron Man: The Defiant Regime of Jean Chrétien*. Toronto: Penguin, 2003.

McAllister, Anthony. *St. John's: The Greatest Gallantry*. DRC Publishing, 2011.

Murphy, Rex. *Canada & Other Matters of Opinion*. Toronto: Doubleday, 2009.

Neary, Steve. *The Enemy on our Doorstep*. St. John's: Jesperson Press, 1994.

Nicholson, G. W. L. *More Fighting Newfoundlanders*. St. John's: Government of Newfoundland and Labrador, 1969.

Nissen, Hans J. & Peter Heine. *From Mesopotamia to Iraq*. London: University of Chicago Press, 2009.

Noel, S. J. R. *Politics in Newfoundland*. Toronto: University of Toronto Press, 1971.

Rompkey, Bill. *St. John's and the Battle of the Atlantic*. St. John's: Flanker Press, 2009.

Rompkey, Ronald. *Grenfell of Labrador*. Toronto: University of Toronto Press, 1991.

Rossiter, Tom. *Faulkner: A Hockey History*. St. John's: Breakwater Books, 2011.

Saunders, George. *In the Centre of the Forest I Remain*. Grand Falls: Robinson-Blackmore Publishing, 1997.

Simpson, Jeffrey. *Discipline of Power*. Rexdale: John Wiley & Sons, 1980.

Smith, Ed. *From the Ashes of My Dreams*. St. John's: Flanker Press, 2002.

Soucoup, Don. *Failures and Fiascos: Atlantic Canada's Biggest Boondoggles*. Halifax: Nimbus Publishing, 2013.

Snir, Reuven. *Baghdad: The City in Verse*. Cambridge: Harvard University Press, 2013.

Tobin, Brian. *All in Good Time*. Toronto: Penguin, 2002.

Tucker, Otto. *That Nothing Be Lost*. St. John's: Harry Cuff Publications, 2003.

Wheare, K. C. *Federal Government*. London: Oxford University Press, 1963.

PHOTO BY PETER HANES

The Honourable Roger Cyril Simmons, PC, is a public policy consultant and former politician and diplomat in Canada. The son of Willis Simmons and Ida Williams, he was born in Lewisporte, Newfoundland. He studied at the Salvation Army College for Officers, Memorial University of Newfoundland, and Boston University and was a teacher/principal in Newfoundland's denominational school system. He subsequently became principal of Grant Collegiate, Springdale, and superintendent of the Green Bay Integrated School District.

Simmons became president of the Newfoundland Teachers' Association in 1968. During his second term, he resigned to manage the campaign of Justice Minister Alec Hickman, a candidate for the Liberal leadership.

In a 1973 by-election, he was elected to the Newfoundland and Labrador House of Assembly as the Liberal MHA for Hermitage. He was re-elected in 1975 and 1979 as MHA for Burgeo–Bay d'Espoir. Later in 1979, he successfully contested a federal by-election and became the Liberal Member of Parliament for Burin–St. George's, succeeding long-time federal cabinet minister and media icon Don Jamieson. He was re-elected in 1980 and appointed Parliamentary

Secretary to the Minister of the Environment and Minister of State for Science and Technology.

On August 12, 1983, he was named to the cabinet of Pierre Trudeau as Minister of State for Mines. He resigned ten days later after learning that he was being investigated by the Canada Revenue Agency for failing to file an income tax return. Simmons narrowly lost his seat in the 1984 election.

In April 1985, he returned to the Newfoundland House of Assembly as the provincial Liberal MHA for Fortune–Hermitage and served as Leader of the Opposition for a year. Simmons returned to the federal House of Commons in the 1988 federal election. He represented Canada at the Rio Summit in 1992. He was re-elected in the 1993 election and was defeated in the 1997 election.

In 1998, Roger Simmons was appointed Consul General for Canada in Seattle. He served in that position for five years and represented Canada at the World Trade Organization. Then, he was for six years a senior policy advisor with Gowlings, one of Canada's largest law firms, and later served as an advisor to the Iraqi parliament and an election observer in Ukraine.

INDEX